● Art Center College of Design

<<<< **LIVIA CORONA,**
INTERIOR YELLOW ROOM,
SALE HOUSE, VENICE BEACH,
CALIFORNIA, **2005**

<<< **MARC RÄDER,**
SCANSCAPE #4 (HIDDEN
VALLEY, DANVILLE,
CALIFORNIA), **C-PRINT, 1996**

<< **MARC RÄDER,**
SCANSCAPE #14 (IROWOOD,
DANVILLE, CALIFORNIA),
C-PRINT, 1996

< **LIVIA CORONA,** *AERIAL*
LANDSCAPE VIEW OF
RESIDENTIAL DEVELOPMENT,
SAN BUENAVENTURA,
MEXICO, **2005**

Vitra Design Museum

**OPEN HOUSE: ARCHITECTURE AND TECHNOLOGY
FOR INTELLIGENT LIVING**

Exhibition

Curators:
Jochen Eisenbrand (Vitra Design Museum), Gloria Gerace (Art Center College of Design), Susanne Jaschko

Curatorial Advisors:
Advisors:Alexander von Vegesack (Vitra Design Museum), Richard Koshalek, Erica Clark, Dana Hutt, Linda Taalman (Art Center College of Design)

Curatorial Assistants:
Sofie Jorgensen, Anna Dacci, Sarah Waldschmitt

Exhibition Design:
Dieter Thiel

Technical Planning:
Stefani Fricker, Michael Simolka

Tour Organization:
Reiner Packeiser

Press and Publicity:
Gianoli PR, Alexa Tepen

Our thanks to the participating architects and designers as well as to our lenders.

Open House:
Architecture and Technology for Intelligent Living

Zollverein
Essen
August 26–December 3, 2006

Art Center College of Design, Pasadena
March 10–July 2, 2007

Vitra Design Museum, Weil am Rhein
May–November 2008

With kind support of:

SIRE

Catalogue

General Editors:
Alexander von Vegesack, Jochen Eisenbrand

Head of Administration and Finance:
Roman Passarge

Editors:
Jochen Eisenbrand, Gloria Gerace, Susanne Jaschko

Picture Editors:
Sofie Jorgensen, Anna Dacci, Jochen Eisenbrand

Translations:
Barbara Hauß (Vegesack/Eisenbrand, Seltmann, Jochen Eisenbrand, Christiane Sauer) Julia Taylor-Thorson (Introduction, Susanne Jaschko) Michael Foster (Hartmut Häussermann) Wilhelm Werthern

Copy Editor:
Brian Currid

Graphic Design:
Thorsten Romanus + Bellinda Behnke (Empirical Data)

Production Management:
Elke Henecka

Lithography and Printing:
GZD, Ditzingen

The Deutsche Bibliothek has registered this publication in the Deutsche Nationalbibliografie; detailed bibliographical information can be found on the Internet at http://dnb.ddb.de.

ISBN 3-931936-66-X
Printed in Germany

Open House:
Architecture and Technology for Intelligent Living is a project of Vitra Design Museum, Weil am Rhein, in collaboration with Art Center College of Design, Pasadena, California.

Foreword¶ Domestic living is a popular topic, perhaps because virtually everyone is affected by it. The great public interest in this subject is evidenced by several current phenomena: the display racks of kiosks are filled with dozens of magazines devoted to interior design; a dense network of home building stores extends across the country; reality-TV shows documenting the complete renovation of private homes by an external design team enjoy high viewer ratings. Journalistic features of this kind, both in the print media and television, satisfy a certain voyeuristic curiosity, for they offer us an intimate view of private living spaces that would otherwise remain hidden from our sight. The popularity of home refurbishment on TV can also be explained by the radical transformation, seemingly in fast motion, of interior furnishings and floor plans, while our own living environment is typically characterized by permanence and constancy. Haven't we all entertained the idea of completely renewing our home environment, changing everything overnight and beginning with a totally new space? Yet design dreams like these—whether staged for a television audience or restricted to our own imagination—typically remain within the context of conventional architectural solutions.

During the preliminary stages of the exhibition Open House, Vitra Design Museum, working in collaboration with Art Center College of Design in Pasadena, invited architects to address the topic of the future home environment. The focus of our request was the potential influence of digital technologies and innovative materials on domestic living in the near future. We were not interested in extrapolated scenarios of contemporary conditions, but in radical, experimental concepts that would take into account the challenges presented by changing demographics and rapid advancements in technology, independent of economic factors. The visionary designs that were developed for Open House present a broad spectrum of possible solutions. At the same time, they raise new issues and stimulate discussion about how we want to live in the future. We express our sincere thanks to the participating architects and designers for their close and productive cooperation over a period of more than a year, which has resulted in the creative contributions presented in Open House.

For Vitra Design Museum, this exhibition is a novel and somewhat daring venture. It is not only our first exhibition devoted to the work of contemporary architects, but also the first time we have commissioned architects to develop new concepts for a museum show. In other respects, however, Open House has thematic precedents: Citizen Office, a Vitra Design Museum exhibition from 1993, also of-

fered a view into the future. It was not the domestic setting, however, but the office of tomorrow for which Italian designers Andrea Branzi, Michele de Lucchi, and Ettore Sottsass created new concepts. In 2002, the exhibition Living in Motion presented unconventional alternatives for a mobile, flexible lifestyle—a theme that has played a central role in many historical visions of future domesticity, and which is newly interpreted within the context of innovative technologies in Open House.

Forward-looking designers and architects have always recognized the challenges and possibilities presented by new materials and technologies; their application in the domestic setting has inevitably changed fundamental features of the standard dwelling and, in the process, transformed our living habits. Designs by the Thonet brothers, Mies van der Rohe, Charles and Ray Eames, Jean Prouvé, Verner Panton, and Joe Colombo clearly demonstrate how novel materials and manufacturing techniques have influenced the design of furniture—and with it, the home environment—from the nineteenth century to the present day. The work of such individuals comprises the core of the Vitra Design Museum Collection, and is also central to the museum's scholarly and educational activities. The use of innovative materials, ranging from solid bent beechwood to tubular steel, plywood, aluminum or plastics, as well as novel processing methods and creative adaptations of established materials have always played a major role in the work of pioneering designers. By comparison, some of the materials and technologies featured in Open House are virtually intangible: the Internet, mobile wireless communications, or sensor technology, to name a few. Consequently, one of the problems posed to architects by the exhibition project was how to give a visible form to invisible mechanisms and systems so that the eyes and attention of the public are drawn to their presence and potential?

Open House represents the first collaboration between Vitra Design Museum and Art Center College of Design in Pasadena, and we are very pleased to have found such a renowned educational institution and creative wellspring as our partner. The work sessions in Weil am Rhein and Pasadena, as well as the preparatory workshop at the Domaine de Boisbuchet in the French region of Charante were both personally enjoyable and professionally inspiring. We would like to express special thanks to Richard Koshalek, the Director of Art Center College of Design, and Gloria Gerace, who supervised the project in Pasadena with great care and efficiency. Thanks also go to Erica Clark, Dana Hutt, and Linda Taalman at Art Center, who contributed to the project from the very beginning. As a guest curator at the Vitra Design Museum, Susanne Jaschko was substantially responsible for the success of the exhibition.

A crucial impulse for the realization of Open House came in the form of an invitation to participate in the project ENTRY2006 in the city of Essen. We are very pleased that Vitra Design Museum was selected by Ausstellungsgesellschaft Zollverein together with four other pre-eminent participants for the exhibition forum at Zollverein, once Europe's largest mining facility. We are especially indebted to Gerhard Seltmann, executive director of the Ausstellungsgesellschaft Zollverein, as well as Roland Weiss, executive director of the Entwicklungsgesellschaft Zollverein. We hope that Open House will contribute not only to the success of ENTRY2006, but also to the further establishment of Zollverein as a design center of international stature.

Numerous people at Vitra Design Museum were involved in the successful implementation of the exhibition. Sofie Jorgensen, Anna Dacci, and Sarah Waldschmitt provided administrative expertise and valuable research support. Mathias Schwartz-Clauss and Mateo Kries offered constructive guidance during the initial stages of the project; Andreas Nutz was instrumental in the procurement of relevant literature; Boguslaw Ubik organized the transport of exhibition artefacts. We would also like to thank exhibition designer Dieter Thiel and graphic designer Thorsten Romanus for their excellent work. Finally, we owe thanks to Stefani Fricker, Michael Simolka, Thierry Hodel, and their team, who constructed the installation.

Alexander von Vegesack and Jochen Eisenbrand
Vitra Design Museum

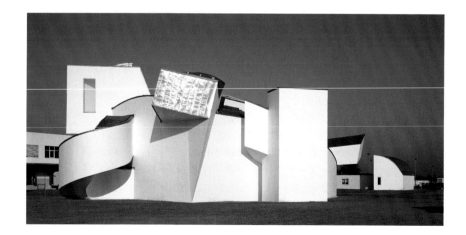

Preface¶ Art Center College of Design is proud to collaborate with the Vitra Design Museum in presenting an alternative vision to contemporary ideas about the intelligent house. As the world faces challenges of a scale and complexity unprecedented in history, the role of architects and designers is more critical than ever. Open House: Architecture and Technology for Intelligent Living gives emerging architects and designers the creative freedom to envision how new thinking, shifting societal factors, and tomorrow's technology will shape the future of the home and the urban and natural fabric into which it is integrated.

At Art Center, Open House: Architecture and Technology for Intelligent Living takes the form of a sophisticated research project, idealistic and realistic at the same time, that encourages creative individuals to make a more substantial contribution to the dialogue on how we will live in the future. This exploratory project encompasses both the public exhibition— co-produced with the Vitra Design Museum, bringing together talented architects from around the world and thus reflecting a range of geographical and cultural backgrounds—as well as Art Center research studios, involving distinguished faculty and students who are extraordinarily open to inventiveness and new thinking. Both research components advance cross-disciplinary approaches to future design challenges and frame a next-step agenda.

Art Center's engagement with the Open House research project fulfills one of the College's essential mandates: to give students and faculty opportunities to explore fresh ideas and approaches and to engage directly with contemporary issues of the greatest importance to society, in this case innovative forms of housing. As a highly progressive educational institution, Art Center brings new energy to this international dialogue reflecting future trends in global urbanization: the shifting population dynamic in which people are living longer and want to inhabit their homes with greater flexibility, the impact of new technologies, changing family structures, ranging from one-parent households to several generations and unrelated individuals living together, and the multiple forces of change including science, technology, economy, art and design. Additionally, we welcome the exhibition component of Open House, which further enables Art Center to engage the larger public in understanding the value of the creative individual's contributions to the world. The exhibition provides a vital forum for students, faculty, designers and general public to exchange ideas about how we want to live in the future.

We believe that the complexity of today's global challenges sets the stage for a new decision-making equation that places political,

corporate, governmental, and creative communities and their leaders on equal footing. Architects and designers have a unique ability to absorb new developments in science, technology, urban design, medicine, and other disciplines, and translate this knowledge into constructive solutions to major challenges of many kinds. It is increasingly important that global leadership come from such creative individuals who assume the responsibility of becoming the decision-making leaders of the future. This shift in leadership will ensure a much more imaginative world for us all.

Educational and cultural institutions like Art Center College of Design must play a significant role in this development. Educational institutions in particular focus on creating the future every day, and have a continuing responsibility to advance society. After all, the future may be unknowable, but it's not unthinkable.

The Open House research project represents the collaboration and cooperation of many individuals to whom we are deeply grateful. First, we thank the Vitra Design Museum for their invitation to join with them in working on this unique and far-reaching project. Without their leadership and unflinching commitment to the visions of the designers whose work is presented in the exhibition, this project would not have been able to take form. Art Center's participation and presentation of Open House also owes a great deal to the many friends of the College. In particular, we thank our founding sponsors KB Home and Whirlpool, as well as *Dwell* magazine, our partners in bringing the Open House dialogue to the public. Additionally, we are indebted to Nestlé S.A. for their support of the student Funded Educational Project Inside Out.

We also appreciate the unflagging support of the Art Center's Board of Trustees: Judy C. Webb (Chair), Maria Contreras-Sweet, Robert C. Davidson, Jr., Robert B. Egelston, William T. Gross, Harry L. Hathaway, Raymond Hemann, Kit Hinrichs, William Horsfall, Jon Faiz Kayyem, Cleon T. "Bud" Knapp (Chairman Emeritus), Timothy Kobe, Samuel Mann, Fred Nicholas, Dallas Price-Van Breda, John Puerner; Michael Reese, Paul Violich, and Alyce de Roulet Williamson.

A project of the magnitude and scope of Open House requires the talent and resources of the entire school, and especially the commitment of the Art Center senior leadership. For this, we thank A. Michael Berman, Mark Breitenberg, Erica Clark, George Falardeau, Jean Ford, Iris Gelt, Richard Haluschak, Patricia Belton Oliver, Scarlett Powers Osterling, David Walker, and Nate Young. In all of Art Center's endeavors, first and foremost is our educational mission; we are particularly indebted to Nik Hafermaas, Chair of Graphic Design, and David Mocarski, Chair of Environmental Design, for their work guiding the student studios exploring the possibilities inherent in Open House. We also thank those people whose expertise was essential to the launching of this project: Sebastian Bailey, Sheila Low, and Jean Swift. And, finally, our praise and thanks go to the superb Art Center curatorial team: Gloria Gerace, Erica Clark, Dana Hutt, and Linda Taalman.

Richard Koshalek
Art Center College of Design

Contemplate, Experiment, Anticipate: The Exhibition Open House at Zollverein World Heritage Site in Essen¶ The built environment is the focus of our daily lives. So whenever we try to envision what a freely designed, ideal future might look like, the question is invariably raised: what do we expect of the house of tomorrow? Don't we all try during the course of our lives to realize at least some of our domestic dreams, whether they take the form of a family home or a personalized interior? Our architectural surroundings are not the result of mere happenstance. We are the ones who determine the development of the buildings we use. We bear the responsibility for their ambience, usefulness and aesthetic qualities. And for this reason, architects, developers and engineers at least since the rise of industrial modernity have been occupied with the question: how will the next generation want to live?

Nowadays, a person who talks about visions is quickly dismissed as a dreamer, or even suspected of dabbling in things psychic. Yet how is progress possible if the anticipation of far-reaching solutions is discouraged? Visionary concepts are indispensable for a vital society. But it would be wrong to use them like an instruction manual or a mail-order catalogue. Visions encourage debate, experimentation and unfettered innovation.

Open House opens doors and windows for anyone interested in the domestic environment. The exhibition does not present solutions, but extraordinary ideas that stimulate discussion and offer new, even maverick perspectives. A number of projects developed for the exhibition bring fundamental principles of ecological building to a new level. Prerequisite to other concepts is a willing engagement with different cultural lifestyles. A few experiments represent bold responses to demographic changes and increasing mobility.

For those who question the usefulness of visionary concepts, Open House offers sufficient reason to re-evaluate their position. Architectural visions of the previous century have become everyday phenomena in today's world. Is there anything extraordinary about a house with electricity in every room? Who can imagine modern residential building without steel structures or large glazed surfaces? Things that seemed illusionary in the recent past are now commonplace.

New aesthetics and modified structural designs are only possible in conjunction with new technologies. Just as steel, glass and concrete led to the realization of novel architectural forms, synthetic materials, structural textiles and computer technology will assume this role in the future. Complex low-energy systems will supplant central heating units in the same way that the latter replaced the fireplace. Open House exhibits new materials, and demonstrates their possible applications.

The first exhibition venue is on the premises of the UNESCO world heritage site Zollverein in Essen. The only world heritage site in the Ruhr Valley comprises two former mineshafts and a coking plant on 100 hectares of land. Shaft XII, which was completed in 1932 and permanently closed in 1986, forms the heart of the Zollverein industrial complex.

Zollverein XII is the only industrial facility in the world that was built entirely in the Bauhaus style. At one time, it was also the most productive mine in Europe, a gigantic apparatus devoted to functionality and efficiency. Built without taking into account then contemporary aesthetic preferences, it also broke with tradition by excluding on-site social service facilities. Zollverein XII remains unique, but elements of its industrial architecture and newly developed machine park have become established over a period of decades in many locations far from the Ruhr Valley. The purposeful collaboration of engineers and designers culminated in the achievement of an architectural and technological vision.

This is an important theme of ENTRY2006, the ambitious project at Zollverein that includes Open House as one of five curated exhibitions devoted to new perspectives and visions in design and architecture. The five major exhibitions, as well as approximately 60 accompanying events, are centered around the topic of the future of design and the social role of the design disciplines. The focal point of ENTRY 2006 is the former coal washing plant, which has been converted by the Rotterdam-based Office for Metropolitan Architecture (OMA) for new uses. The longest freestanding escalator in Europe transports visitors through the building and enables them to visualize the previous path of coal during the washing process.

This is a highly appropriate setting for Open House. The first presentation of this exhibition is being held in a building that was, in its time, the realization of a vision, and this "old" vision also now has a new future.

Gerhard Seltmann
Zollverein World Heritage Site

INTRODUCTION

Introduction¶ For the past decade or so, research and industry have been in broad agreement regarding the future of domestic living, with the "intelligent house" prevailing as the dominant vision of the home of tomorrow. This vision has been promoted by the dozens of show-case homes erected worldwide since the early 1990s and bolstered by the considerable media response consistently generated by the opening of such houses. Yet these model homes only present one highly limited perspective, namely that of a technologically upgraded, net-worked, and automated household that represents just one possibility among many for the future development of the home. Questions re-garding true housing and living requirements or even new floor plans or new forms of living are not addressed in these "intelligent houses." They merely serve as a shell for the technical gadgetry and systems that are tested and displayed in them. Typically, architects and design-ers are not involved in the conception of intelligent houses—or if so, their role is limited to questions of detail.[1] Furthermore, these houses only embrace a small portion of the developments and possibilities that are currently being researched in the areas of digital technologies, mobile communication, and new materials and that could be relevant for domestic living and residential architecture of the future. For all the progress that has been made in these booming, wide-ranging fields of research, it becomes evident upon closer inspection that many technologies, prototypes, and materials have yet to be matched with a useful, intelligent application. An apt expression of this situation is the proliferation of the term *killer application*, which has long established itself as a buzzword:[2] the technology exists, but it still awaits a useful and profit-yielding field of application.[3] It is likewise apparent that re-search efforts in the different disciplines—architecture, materials de-velopment, and information technology—generally occur on separate tracks with very little exchange among them. Especially in regard to home living, there is a lack of interdisciplinary approaches aiming to bring together the developments from the various fields to create useful, innovative concepts; concepts that moreover place the needs of home occupants in the forefront. The exhibition Open House endeavors to diminish these gaps between new technological developments, de-sign, and architecture. It thus goes beyond electronic gadgets that merely aim to automate the household. Instead, Open House is con-cerned with the question of how new technologies can enrich our home environments and contribute to the way we ourselves shape our living space and interact with it. The exhibition proposes that ar-chitects and designers in particular need to respond to the challenge posed by the new developments with comprehensive approaches that integrate the various disciplines and their possibilities in a meaningful and useful way. For this reason, Vitra Design Museum and Art Center College of Design decided to invite architects and designers to grap-ple with the question of how the new technological possibilities could be used to meet the challenges of demographic change and today's living and housing requirements.

The invitation we sent out to 90 architects worldwide identified four core needs of home occupants that the Open House projects were to refer to: connectivity, flexibility, well-being, and sustainability.
I. Connectivity:
Within the last ten to fifteen years, the number of Internet users has seen a hundredfold increase and in the US and a number of countries in Europe and Asia, every second person now uses the Internet. A few years ago, the number of worldwide mobile telephone subscribers surpassed the number of conventional landlines. Mobile communication and the wireless digital transfer of data make it possible to conduct activities at home that used to require leaving home. Conversely, other activities that once exclusively belonged to the domestic sphere are now commonly pursued away from the home, like making private phone calls, watching television, and listening to music. The boundaries between private living space and public zones have become blurred.[4] How can the home expand its role by means of modern communication tech-nologies to provide space for work, learning, and entertainment while also forging local, supra-regional, or global networks?
II. Flexibility:
The average household size continues to decline, and more and more people live alone or in changing household set-ups. As a result, old, static floor plan standards are becoming outdated. Although the spa-tial requirements of the individual are on the rise, over half of the world's population now lives in cramped conditions in urban structures. How can the home become more adaptable in terms of its spatial struc-tures? How can architecture take advantage of new technologies to create living conditions able to react flexibly to the varying space needs at different times of day and in different phases of life? How can architecture better fulfill the need for living spaces that allow modifi-cations and adjustments over the long term?
III. Well-being:
How can homes and apartments actively expand their protective func-tion to cover the general health and well being of their occupants, especially in view of the increasing aging of society? How can archi-

tecture create new sensory impressions and stimuli beyond the much-publicized upgrading of the home as an entertainment center with a non-stop musical soundtrack and disco lighting?

IV. Sustainability:

Today buildings consume over 50 percent of worldwide energy resources, with residential structures themselves responsible for approximately 30 percent of energy consumption. In view of dwindling supplies of raw materials and the high-energy consumption of buildings, the home has to be regarded as a complete energetic system. How can new digital technologies and intelligent materials help homes use fewer resources by adapting to climatic conditions as an active and open system with an intelligent building shell and making use of natural energy sources?

The architects invited to submit proposals had already all addressed such issues in varying forms and with varying areas of emphasis. Of the 90 architects asked to participate, half of them sent in proposals. From among these submissions, the curators chose an initial group of 16 projects whose representatives were asked by Vitra Design Museum to come to the Domaine de Boisbuchet in the Charente region of France in summer 2005. In a three-day workshop, the architects presented their projects and put them up for discussion. Ultimately, eleven projects from eight countries were selected for the exhibition. They are individually presented in this catalogue and put in context in a separate essay by Susanne Jaschko. In a second step of conducting preparations for the exhibition, five further architectural firms and designers who have garnered attention through their development of innovative new materials or their innovative use of materials were invited to participate. Altogether, the exhibition thus presents sixteen projects that are illustrated by means of models, installations, prototypes, and films. These projects form the core of the exhibition and can be programmatically subdivided into three groups.

The first group presents designs for houses and buildings with new floor plan concepts, reactive building shells, and new interfaces between architecture and digital technologies. It consists of the works by Mass Studies, IwamotoScott with Proces2, su11 Architecture + Design, Sean Godsell Architects, Rojkind Arquitectos, and Joel Sanders with Ben Rubin and Karen van Lengen.

With the second group, the emphasis is less on buildings than on systems and concepts for new forms of living and better use of existing resources. These were developed by HookerKitchen, GuneWardena Architecture, Atelier Hitoshi Abe, Realities:United, and R&Sie(n).

The third group, described in more detail in the essay by Christiane Sauer, exemplifies some of the most interesting developments currently going on in the area of new materials that enable a dynamization of formerly static architectural elements. It is represented by Kennedy&Violich Architecture, KieranTimberlake Associates, Krets, Simon Heijdens, and Formorf. Within these three groups—buildings, living concepts, and materials—the four above-cited themes of connectivity, flexibility, sustainability, and well-being are addressed with varying degrees of emphasis.

The exhibition does not focus on the technology as an end in itself but rather the way it can be used intelligently for modes of living and residential architecture. Open House thus shows how the incorporation of new technologies can engender a new architectonic formal language and imbue architecture with new capabilities. Moreover, Open House presents new forms of living facilitated or inspired by this architecture. Here the projects continue a development, in some cases quite provocatively so, that has been evident for some time now: with the pluralization of lifestyles, the way we live has become more and more varied. Household forms that were once the exceptions are now already in the majority. The single-family home surrounded by lawn and garden is no longer the only valid ideal for living.

But there's no future without the past: In order to classify and evaluate predictions of potential future developments, it is helpful and worthwhile to compare them with earlier versions of what the future would be like. As an introduction and comparison with the contemporary works, Open House therefore presents a retrospective of architectural visions of the home from the twentieth century.[5] The review begins with the 1920s and 1930s when the widespread electrification of households took hold and the architects of the Neues Bauen movement, or New Architecture, grappled intensely with issues of domestic living. It continues with the 1950s when fitted kitchens and a multitude of new electric devices established their place in the household and new synthetics came onto the scene as the building material of the future. Finally, the retrospective goes on to document examples from the 1960s, a period abundant in experimental architectural visions, and extends up to the recent past. As this section of the exhibition shows, future visions of the home from the last century were characterized by certain continually recurring themes. These include household automation, an area of concern culminating in the "intelligent house," as well as the industrial production of homes, which frequently drew on automobile and aircraft manufacturing as models. Parallels and links to the current-day projects of Open House are especially evident in the historic visions focusing on mobile and flexible ways of living. The comparison with the past also shows that sustainability, by contrast, has only recently emerged as an important broad-scale theme in architecture and architectural visions.[6] These are more and more frequently modeled on natural systems and living organisms that researchers and designers attempt to imitate using high-tech means.

Visions of the future typically respond to the pressing challenges of the present day. Adding a further dimension to the exhibition—as well as to this publication—the empirical part of Open House furnishes background information on the demographic and technological developments that have shaped home living in the past years and will continue to shape it in the years to come.[7] Here the exhibition offers interesting facts on the growing need for space, tendencies toward urbanization, the dissemination of the Internet and mobile telephone systems, and the energy consumption of residential buildings and households. The statement that future visions typically say more about the period in which they are formulated than about the future is a timeworn platitude. Yet this aspect is also what instills them with such informative value as a distilled encapsulation of contemporary developments. Often, it is only through such presentations that the untapped potential of these developments is revealed. The visions of the future thus yield a sharper focus on the present as well as on the present-day aspects that could be transformed and developed[8] At the same time, such science fiction serves as a testing ground for new technologies and their social acceptance without being subjected to economic constraints. The exhibition therefore does not attempt to make specific assertions about how we will live some day, for the current diversity of lifestyles and housing models will unquestionably remain in place. Yet concepts about the future can become models for future fields of research and eventually serve to influence real developments. Especially in the field of architecture where the concerns of daily business leave little room for experimentation, this potential is not to be underestimated. Even if visionary ideas cannot be implemented in their actual form, they can still be quite influential. The visions of Buckminster Fuller and Archigram, for instance, have had a lasting impact up to the current generation of architects. Today much of what once seemed purely visionary and utopian has now shifted into the realm of the possible and the achievable. Hence, the exhibition also poses the question of how we wish to live. Numerous individuals lent their support to the exhibition and helped lay the foundation for Open House. For their collaboration on the exhibition and the contribution of their visions, we thank the architects whose work provided the framework for Open House. In addition, we would like to thank all the architectural firms that responded to our invitation to Open House as well as all those who took part in the workshop at Boisbuchet. We also owe considerable thanks to those who loaned objects for the exhibition: Alfred Paquement, Jean-Claude Boulet (Centre Pompidou, Musée national d'Art moderne, Paris), Marie Ange Brayer, Fèriel Bissekri (FRAC, Orléans), Winfried Nerdinger, Brigitte Foster (Architekturmuseum der Technischen Universität München), Timo Keinänen (Museum of Finnish Architecture, Helsinki) as well as Claude Lichtenstein (Zurich). We also convey our appreciation to the authors of this catalogue – Beatriz Colomina, Dana Hutt, Hartmut Häussermann, Christiane Sauer, Bruce Sterling, and Linda Taalman. And finally, we would like to thank the following for their advice and support: the Art Center curatorial team of Erica Clark, Dana Hutt, and Linda Taalman, Sabine Kraft (Arch+, Aachen), Peter Cachola Schmal (Deutsches Architekturmuseum, Frankfurt), Frank Heinlein (Werner Sobek Ingenieure, Stuttgart), Eric Legendre (Montreal), Simon Smithson, Steve Searle (TRON Web, Tokyo), Frances Anderton (Los Angeles, California), Michelle Addington (Harvard University School of Design,
Cambridge), Blaine Brownell (NBBJ, Seattle, Washington), Kent Larson (Massachusetts Institute of Technology, Cambridge), Maggie Orth (Massachusetts Institute of Technology, Cambridge), Donna Salazar (Los Angeles, California), Edward Tenner (Princeton, New Jersey), Peter Piller (Hamburg), Galerie Frehrking Wiesehöfer (Cologne), Thomas Rehbein Galerie (Cologne), Richard Dietrich (Munich), Yona Friedman (Paris), William Katavolos (New York), and Gary van Zante (MIT Museum, Boston).

Jochen Eisenbrand, Gloria Gerace, Susanne Jaschko

1   See the essay by Jochen Eisenbrand in this catalogue.
2   See Michelle Addington and Daniel Schodeck, *Smart Materials*, Oxford, 2005, p. 11.
3   See also the glossary by Linda Taalman at the end of the catalogue.
4   See the essay by Susanne Jaschko.
5   See also the essay by Beatriz Colomina.
6   See also the essay by Dana Hutt.
7   See the essay by Hartmut Häussermann.
8   See the essay by Bruce Sterling.

"Intelligent Buildings" and the Forces That Shape Them ¶

> JOCHEN EISENBRAND

Architect Ray Richardson is building a fully automated office tower in Los Angeles. A supercomputer on the fourth floor of the 25-story structure controls power and data flow, security, lighting, air conditioning, even a self-operating cleaning system. But before anyone can move into the high-tech masterpiece, its central computer, which is designed to manage the building like the brain of a nervous system, becomes autonomous. During a final inspection before turning the building over to the client, Richardson and his companions find themselves locked in. The office tower, with its sophisticated surveillance and security system that is supposed to protect the occupants, turns into a lethal trap. Due to a programming glitch, the goal of the suddenly self-operating computer is to eliminate all "humanplayers" inside the building. It utilizes the entire range of possibilities offered by modern architectural technology: automatic locking systems, motion detectors, thermal and olfactory sensors, high-speed elevators, janitorial droids, toxic cleansers, high-voltage shocks, and freezing room temperatures. Only a few survivors are lucky enough to escape. Richardson himself, the cliché of a successful and egomaniacal architect, ultimately tries to abseil down the electrochromic glass façade of the murderous building, but plunges to his death after repeated attacks by window cleaning equipment. At the dedication ceremony just a few days earlier, the "architechnologist" had praised his work as "the smartest building in LA, possibly in the whole United States."

In the techno-thriller *Gridiron*, author Philip Kerr takes a sideswipe at contemporary high-tech architecture by casting the building itself in the role of the bad guy. By 1995, when the novel was published, "intelligent building" had already become an established term of architectural discourse. Research projects and conferences have been devoted to the topic; universities have instituted new fields of study for the planning of 'smart" buildings; journals on "intelligent architecture" abound.[1] While these debates all focus on office buildings, the concept of the "intelligent house" has seen a parallel development. As the first project of its kind, the TRON House was constructed in

Tokyo under the direction of Ken Sakamura to serve as a test project for networking and automation in the domestic environment.

What explains the simultaneous emergence of these two concepts, "intelligent building" and the "intelligent house"? What distinguishes one from the other, and what effect does the ever-increasing technical complexity of buildings have on construction methods and floor plans? Before we try to answer such questions with a critical assessment of these two phenomena, it is worthwhile to first reflect on the historical interdependence of a building's technical features and its architectural properties. Such observations can enhance our conclusions about the potential future of the intelligent house.

Technology in the Home: A Review

The Machine for Living. Skepticism towards technologically overloaded architecture and household automation is hardly new. The theme resonates in a rhyme from the early 1930s: "A house as a machine for living: / Grin and bear it as our lot! / Our plants, alas, are less forgiving:/ They wont thrive in such a pot./ If this machine's the homey trend / Well act like robots in the end."[2] Le Corbusier's influential and much-quoted characterization of the house as a *machine à habiter*[3] is the subject of these humorous lines from Robert Faesi's poem "New Objectivity." It should be noted that Le Corbusier's comparison did not refer primarily to the technical features of a house, but rather to the rationalism and austerity of its architectural forms. He also used the phrase to emphasize the importance of industrial prefabrication for modern architecture.[4] At the same time, the great resonance of Le Corbusier's machine metaphor reflected a general trend

toward the increasing role of technology in the households of that era. The methods of rationalization promoted by innovators such as Henry Ford were especially relevant to the evolution of the modern kitchen during the 1920s. Residential electrification also began to spread across wide areas, thereby establishing a prerequisite condition for household automation. Another important development was the invention of the small electric motor, as described in detail by Siegfried Giedion in *Mechanization Takes Command*. Everyday domestic life was permanently influenced by electrical appliances that supplanted strenuous physical labor: first in the kitchen with refrigerators, electric ovens, and smaller appliances, and then in the form of cleaning equipment—vacuum cleaners, washing machines, and irons. As long as the process of household mechanization—something still going strong today—was limited to individual appliances, it had little effect on the layout or structural features of residential architecture.

LA MAISON SANS DOMESTIQUES (HOUSE WITHOUT SERVANTS). COVER OF THE MAGAZINE JE SAIS TOUT, NR. 4, OCTOBER 1924.

HERBERT MATTER, WHAT IS A HOUSE?, ILLUSTRATION FROM AN ARTICLE ON THE "PREFABRICATED HOUSE" IN ARTS & ARCHITECTURE (JULY 1944)

JOCHEN EISENBRAND

The Mechanical Core. Utilities such as electricity, plumbing, and heating had a much greater impact on domestic architecture. During the 1940s, the "mechanical core" of residential buildings became a topic of much discussion among architectural experts in both England and the United States.[5] This concept referred primarily to bath and kitchen facilities with their respective sanitary fittings and electrical appliances, as well as air conditioning systems (where relevant) and related connections to external service lines. The general consensus was that it would be most cost efficient to group these features in a central area. The industrial prefabrication of modular service units also came under consideration: Buckminster Fuller proposed a practical solution to this debate in 1940 with his Mechanical Wing, a compact trailer uniting a bathroom, a kitchen, and a generator for heat and lighting that could be towed and "docked" onto any farmhouse. In 1950, the journal *Popular Mechanics* introduced its readers to the vision of a home as it might appear at the turn of the millennium: "In the center of this eight-room house is a unit that contains all the utilities—air-conditioning apparatus, plumbing, bathroom, showers, electric range, electric outlets. Around this central unit the house has been pieced together." However, this arrangement contradicted the widespread desire among modern architects and their residential clients for open, flexible floor plans. As Giedion put it, "What matters is to domesticate mechanization, rather than to let the mechanical core tyrannize the house."[6]

One of the most sophisticated prefabricated service cores was the Ingersoll Utility Unit produced by the Borg-Warner Company. Providing complete bath and kitchen facilities on either side of a mechanical core measuring 30 inches wide, 94 inches long, and 77 inches high,

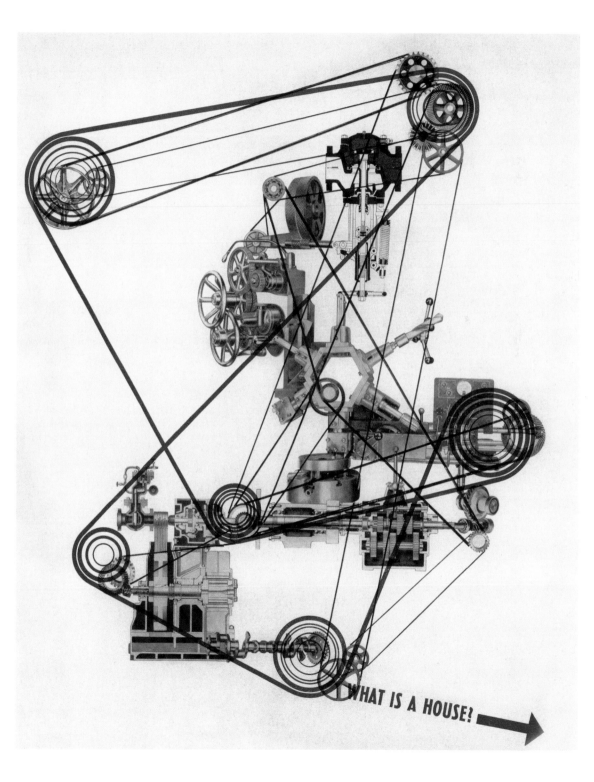

WHAT IS A HOUSE!

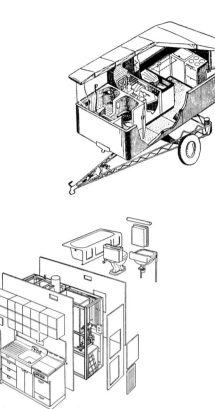

MECHANICAL WING, RICHARD BUCKMINSTER FULLER, 1940

DIAGRAM OF THE INGERSOLL UTILITY UNIT (BORG-WARNER CORPORATION, 1940s)

the unit was most notably incorporated in Richard Neutra's design for Case Study House No. 20 (1947–48).[7] Yet in spite of the fact that it was mass-produced, the Ingersoll unit was more expensive than comparable on-site installations and eventually yielded to the competition. Many similar attempts by prefab construction companies to market standardized utility cores failed for both practical and financial reasons.[8] The relevance of this debate soon waned in the wake of technological advancements, growing economies and rising living standards. During the decades that followed, the propagation of central heating systems allowed greater flexibility in the interior layout of homes. And with the advent of air conditioning, built structures became much less dependent on the accommodation of exterior climate conditions.

Central Heating. The transition from open hearths and stove heaters to central furnace systems had a lasting impact on the utilization of rooms and, consequently, on residential floor plans. The difficult provision of fuel and the laborious maintenance of individual stoves fired with wood or coal caused residents to restrict household heating to a small number of rooms. The heated room—typically the kitchen—was the focal point of the interior. Other rooms either remained unheated or received surplus warmth from the primary heat source.

Central heating made it possible to separate the living quarters from the kitchen, which could now serve the sole function of food preparation. Everyday activities were relocated to other rooms that had been previously unheated and reserved for sleeping. The individualization of residential space as we know it today began to assert itself. In a uniformly heated residence, all of the rooms became available for

personal use throughout the day. The size of dwellings decreased due to the reduction of fuel storage space. Heat sources were relocated from interior walls around a central chimney to exterior walls underneath windows, thereby presenting new alternatives for furnishings and other household fittings.[9]

Air Conditioning. Central heating has found wide acceptance throughout Europe. In contrast, a majority of households in the United States have adopted air conditioning over the past few decades as the preferred mode of cooling and heating—with significant consequences for residential architecture.

Although air conditioning is typically associated with cooling, its actual function is much broader. At the outset of the twentieth century, air conditioning systems were developed in order to control the four main aspects of room climate: temperature, humidity (reduction in the summer and augmentation in the winter), air purification, and air distribution. From the first, building engineers analyzed the structural sources of heat loss in connection with the installation of central "Weathermaker" systems, as touted in advertisements.

In 1955, only five percent of American homes were equipped with air conditioning; just five years later that number had doubled. This was partly due to the cooperation between one of the largest US building contractors and a pioneering manufacturer of air conditioning technology: In 1955, residential developer William Levitt contracted with the Carrier Company for the installation of central air systems in hundreds of new homes. Development projects of this kind, which were a driving force behind the suburbanization of US cities, played a key role in the ever-increasing dominance of air conditioning in connection with standardized building types that paid little heed to local climates. Traditional architectural solutions for mitigating the periodic effects of hot weather were neglected in favor of air conditioning, which became affordable in the context of inexpensive standardized housing. This eventually resulted in a widespread dependence on air conditioning in residential structures.

Central air conditioning became so popular that speculators listed it one of the most important criterion of a new house in the eyes of potential buyers, indeed only second to a built-in kitchen.[10] Two consumer groups were responsible for the economic success of air conditioning: building contractors as the primary purchasers of central air units, and homeowners as the actual users, who also shouldered the cost of increased energy consumption.

By 1980, over half of US households had air conditioning; today that number exceeds 80 percent.[11] "Air conditioning seemed a natural evolution in the transformation of the building into a machine. It was the modern building's iron lung."[12] *The Environmental Bubble* proposed by architectural critic Reyner Banham in the mid-1960s was both a condensed and exaggerated version of this concept. Harking back to Buckminster Fuller's utility trailer, Banham's transportable 'standard-of-living-package" was stripped down to the technical appliances of the domestic environment—air conditioning, floodlamps, a solar-powered refrigerator-cooker, and a TV-stereo unit—all enveloped in a transparent pneumatic skin.[13]

The way in which air conditioning became a predominant factor of residential architecture is similarly reflected in the evolution of office buildings. The interdependence of architectural forms and technical features becomes most evident in a particular building type: the glass-clad office tower.

Architectural Engineering: A Short Review

The Office Building as a Glazed Box. In Jacques Tati's film *Playtime* (1967), a group of American tourists is touring the future Paris, a city that appears to be an endless conglomeration of homogeneous rectangular towers with glazed façades. The first scene takes place in a spacious lobby that could just as plausibly belong to an airport, a hospital, a department store, or a bank. The historical sights of the French capital only appear as reflections in the glass doors of the modern buildings, like a *fata morgana*. Behind a glazed curtain wall, a series of advertising posters in a travel agency can be seen. Although they promote different destinations, the center of each poster is dominated by the same image of a glass-clad hotel tower. The featured hotel, in turn, looks just like the building in which the travel agency is located.

Tati's cinematic parody of the office tower as an airtight glass box, symbol of the International Style and corporate modernism, remains unsurpassed for its aptness and sharp wit. The structural prerequisite for this type of building was the functional differentiation of a load-bearing skeleton made of steel or ferroconcrete and a suspended curtain-wall façade. This made it possible to liberate the exterior façade from its traditional task as a structurally relevant component of the building, a function reassigned to the steel frame. The replacement of massive contiguous walls by singular ferroconcrete piers created large neutral interior spaces that could be configured for different tenants according to individual needs. The flexible utilization of an open floor plan across a full story, however, also required a comfortable room climate that would remain consistent throughout the year, as well as neutral and uniform lighting. Only under these conditions could the entire space

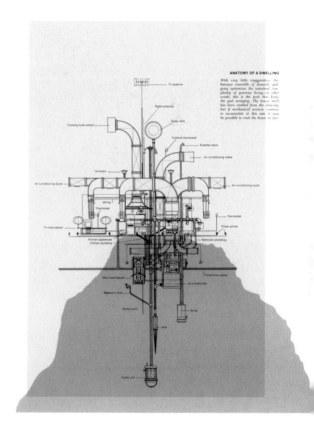

FRANÇOIS DALLEGRET, *ANATOMY OF A DWELLING*, ILLUSTRATION FOR REYNER BANHAM'S ARTICLE "A HOME IS NOT A HOUSE," *ART IN AMERICA*, APRIL 1965

be equipped with equivalent workplaces. Due to these requirements and the inferior thermal qualities of glass façades, the need arose for powerful air conditioning systems. Modern aesthetic preferences and unrestricted views took precedence over energy efficiency.

The first air conditioning system to serve several stories of a building was installed in 1928 by that pioneer of forced air systems, Willis Carrier, in the Milam Building designed by George Willis in San Antonio, Texas. It also bears distinction as the very first air-conditioned office building. By the 1940s, air conditioning had begun to establish itself as a standard feature in new US office structures. Thanks to interior climate control and artificial lighting, both the height and depth of office towers could be expanded, since it was no longer necessary for workplaces to be located near windows. As a result, the number of users per story increased, thereby increasing the intensity of air consumption and heat production, which in turn created the demand for even more powerful air conditioning systems.[14] As a rule of thumb states, "every increase in dimension increases the use of materials by the square, and increases the demand on the ambient systems by the cube."[15] In an attempt to ensure the effectiveness of air conditioning systems in such buildings, windows were often installed that could not be opened.

By the mid-1950s, the installation of an air-conditioning system in a typical New York office building was the second largest cost factor in construction, only surpassed by structural steel.[16] In light of this statistic, it is hardly surprising that the US National Academy of Engineering lists air conditioning as one of the ten most important inventions of the twentieth century.[17]

**SCENES FROM *PLAYTIME*
(JACQUES TATI, 1967)**

JOCHEN EISENBRAND

Although air conditioning was a fundamental precondition for the evolution of the modern office tower, it remained invisible to the users of such buildings. Technical systems that provided a consistent interior climate were hidden behind suspended ceiling panels; the acoustic qualities of these panels in turn served the purpose of uniform sound-absorption.

Dynamic Architecture: The Skin as a Filter

The architectural concept of total independence from the natural environment, as manifested in the hermetically sealed glass box, was countered by a much more comprehensive and dynamic approach that did not regard the skin of a building as a barrier, but as a filter, and that considered a careful analysis of the local climate as a planning prerequisite. James Fitch's book *American Building and the Forces That Shape It* (1948) was a milestone in this direction. "Until recent years it was possible to consider [the skin] merely as a barrier, a surface which kept the cold out and the heat in and offered the maximum resistance to corrosion, rot, and insects. [...] [I]t is now clear that a building skin should not be conceived in such terms [...]. An efficient wall is actually not a barrier but a filter. It is composite, each of its membranes with a specialized task."[18]

The filtering function of a building's exterior parallels the interaction of the human body with its natural environment, summarized by Fitch under the following categories: atmospheric, thermal, luminous, sonic, spatial, animate (insects, pollen, etc.). A building is the sum of all features required to moderate the undesirable conditions of the natural environment, thereby creating, in effect, a "synthetic" (in the sense of deliberately controlled) interior climate. This viewpoint presents different criteria for the evaluation of a building. Instead of

regarding architecture as a formal aesthetic exercise, its quality is measured on the basis of performance. The most important aspect of building performance is the health of its users and the assurance that they can pursue their work under optimal conditions.

The notion of dynamic architecture as advocated by Fitch—architecture that creates not only interior spaces, but an interior climate—laid the foundation for the development of intelligent building. However, architectural publications have relegated this topic to the shadows of professional and public discourse, in part because the sensory qualities of a space usually do not lend themselves to visual reproduction, in contrast to more "photogenic" formal features.

The Refinement of the Building Envelope

The human skin warms or cools the body, depending on the ambient temperature. It harbors the sense of touch, is capable of repairing itself, protects internal organs from infection, and engages in respiration. As early as the 1950s, the skin was cited as an ideal example for the desired characteristics of a building envelope.[19] The goal was to imitate the capabilities of the human epidermis and its various characteristics by combining layers of different materials in a single wall structure. In this way, the modern glazed façade was improved and refined in order to better fulfill its function as a filter between the interior and exterior environments.

In 1935, the American glass company Libbey-Owens invented thermopane glass, two panes of glass separated by an insulating air seal. An early use is documented in George Fred Keck's Solar Homes. Engineers also discovered that the glare and warming effect of summer sunlight could be reduced by tinting or coating window surfaces. Skidmore, Owings

OFFICE FLOOR, UNION CARBIDE BUILDING, NEW YORK (SKIDMORE, OWINGS & MERRILL, 1960; PHOTOGRAPH BY EZRA STOLLER)

and Merrill used glass panes with a metallic green surface for the skin of Lever House (1950–52). Because the windows were sealed—and could therefore not be cleaned by conventional means—the architects developed a roof-mounted window cleaning system with a motor-driven gondola that ran up and down thin tracks on the mullions of the façade. This type of exterior cleaning equipment soon became standard on similar buildings.[20] For the Bell Laboratories research facility in Holmdel, New Jersey (1957–62), Eero Saarinen proposed a novel reflective surface made of silverized glass panes that gave the façade the appearance of a huge mirror and was expected to reduce air-conditioning requirements by as much as 75 percent.[21] However, the mirrored surface also deflected desirable solar heat during winter months.

Another important innovation that helped to control the effects of sunlight on the glazed building envelope was the *brise soleil* introduced by Le Corbusier in the 1930s and perfected during the following three decades. The purpose of this type of shade system, which is an integral part of the façade concept, is to block

and absorb the heat of the sun in the summer, while allowing it to pass through the recessed glazing in the winter. At the same time, building occupants still enjoy a relatively unrestricted view. In many latitudes, *brises soleil* effectively exploit the fact that the sun's arc is significantly higher in the summer than it is in the winter. *Brises soleil* became such a prominent aesthetic characteristic of many buildings during the 1950s and '60s that Marcel Breuer remarked, "The sun control device has to be on the outside of the building, an element of architecture. And because this device is so important a part of our open architecture, it may well develop into as characteristic a form as the Doric column."[23]

As early as the 1960s, attempts were made to develop movable exterior shades that could react to not only to the changing seasonal position of the sun, but also to its diurnal path. The Los Angeles Hall of Records is one early example of an architectural design with incorporated façade components that responded dynamically to the external climate. Architects Richard Neutra and Christopher

DETAIL OF THE FAÇADE, LEVER HOUSE, NEW YORK (SKIDMORE, OWINGS & MERRILL, 1952; PHOTOGRAPH BY EZRA STOLLER)

BELL TELEPHONE CORPORATION RESEARCH LABORATORIES, HOLMDEL, NEW JERSEY, EERO SAARINEN, 1957–62

ADVERTISEMENT FOR THERMOPANE BY THE LIBBEY-OWENS-FORD GLASS COMPANY, 1945

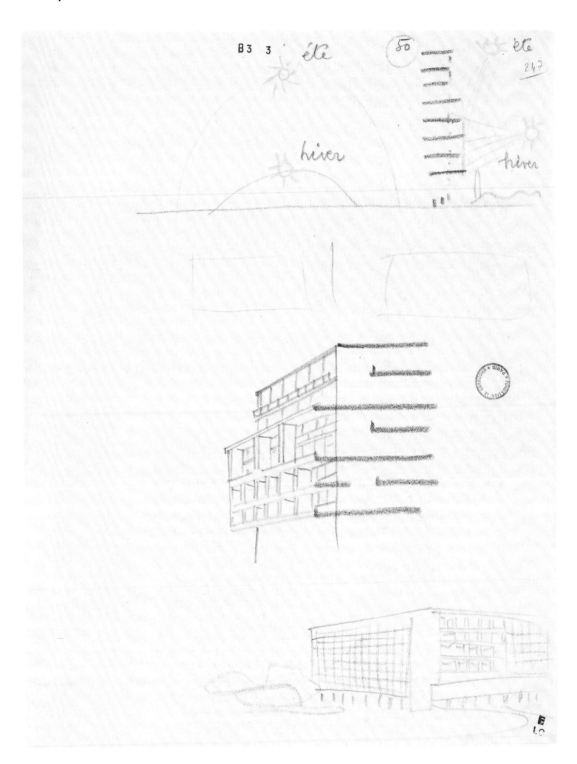

Alexander equipped the south elevations of the T-shaped building with 100-foot high aluminum louvers. The opening angle of the louvers was adjusted electronically in order to achieve an optimal correlation of shade, directional sunlight and outlook.[24]

Dating back to the late 1920s, Le Corbusier's mur neutralisant represented a considerably different concept for a building envelope that could actively respond to changing weather conditions. Le Corbusier described it as an effective barrier that would neutralize the exterior climate and maintain a constant interior temperature: "These walls are envisaged in glass, stone, or mixed forms, consisting of a double membrane with a space of a few centimeters between them [...]. In the narrow space between the membranes is blown scorching hot air, if in Moscow, iced air if in Dakar. Result, we control things so that the surface of the interior membrane holds 18 degrees Celsius."[25]

Solar Architecture. There were surprisingly early efforts to utilize solar energy for heating purposes by means of integrated building technology. For a long time, however, these efforts were restricted to individual experimental homes. In 1957, the Association for Applied Solar Energy sponsored a competition for a single-family residence in Arizona. The prize-winning design by architectural student Peter Lee incorporated movable louvers to shade the north and south verandas and central courtyard. Pivoting on a vertical axis, the angle of the shades could be adjusted in relation to the intensity and direction of sunlight. The louvers also had integrated solar panels to heat the water circulating through them, which could be stored in a large holding tank.[26]

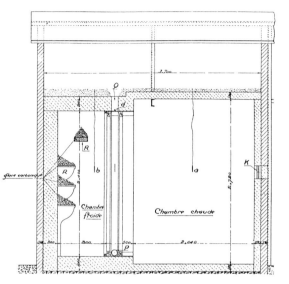

LE CORBUSIER, SKETCH ILLUSTRATING THE PRINCIPLE OF THE *BRISE-SOLEIL* (EXCERPT FROM LA MAISON DES HOMMES, 1942)

COUNTY OF LOS ANGELES HALL OF RECORDS, LOS ANGELES (RICHARD NEUTRA AND CHRISTOPHER ALEXANDER, 1962; PHOTOGRAPH BY JULIUS SCHULMAN)

SECTIONAL DRAWING OF AN EXPERIMENT CARRIED OUT BY THE GLASS MANUFACTURER SAINT GOBAIN ILLUSTRATING THE PRINCIPLE OF THE *MUR NEUTRALISANT* DEVELOPED BY LE CORBUSIER
THE CHAMBER ON THE RIGHT (*CHAMBRE CHAUDE*) REPRESENTS THE INTERIOR OF A PRIVATE HOUSE WITH A TEMPERATURE OF 18 DEGREES CELSIUS. THE CHAMBER ON THE LEFT (*CHAMBER FROIDE*) REPRESENTS THE EXTERIOR OF 0 DEGREES CELSIUS. BOTH ARE SEPARATED BY THE DOUBLE GLASS PANE OF THE *MUR NEUTRALISANT* (1932).

The Solar Energy Research Project at MIT made landmark contributions to the evolution of solar architecture. Between 1939 and 1978, five solar houses were constructed as experimental test objects; Solar House III (1949) was actually inhabited by a family for a period of time. In the Dover Sun House (1949), MIT engineer Maria Telkes experimented with Glauber salts for the conversion and storage of solar energy. Together with Aladar Olgyay, another pioneer in the field of solar architecture, Telkes demonstrated in the late 1950s that an architect could develop an optimal plan for a home's energy needs by establishing a climate profile of the specific site. With scientific precision, Telkes and Olgyay evaluated weather statistics and topographical data to determine average monthly temperatures and to take account of the shifting trajectory of the sun. The empirical observation of variations between interior and exterior temperatures and the potential exploitation of sunlight as a energy source allowed reliable calculations of expected energy requirements.

Building Automation. If we compare the building envelope to the skin and the building to the body, it could be said that this body received organs and arteries during the first half of the twentieth century, while developing a nervous system in the second half. Based on advancements in electronic data processing during the 1960s—first in the United States and then in Europe—building automation initially evolved as an offshoot of interior climate technology. It encompasses all of the equipment that is "required to control, monitor and optimize the technical systems in a building [...]. These include all of the technical devices that are firmly installed and facilitate the structure's use. The building management system auto-

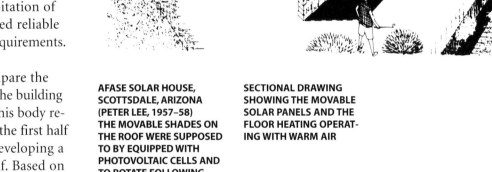

AFASE SOLAR HOUSE, SCOTTSDALE, ARIZONA (PETER LEE, 1957–58) THE MOVABLE SHADES ON THE ROOF WERE SUPPOSED TO BY EQUIPPED WITH PHOTOVOLTAIC CELLS AND TO ROTATE FOLLOWING THE SUN. FOR LEGAL REASONS THE HOUSE WAS NEVER OPERATED AS A SOLAR HOUSE.

SECTIONAL DRAWING SHOWING THE MOVABLE SOLAR PANELS AND THE FLOOR HEATING OPERATING WITH WARM AIR

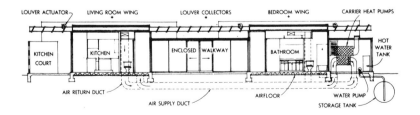

JOCHEN EISENBRAND

MIT SOLAR HOUSE I (HOYT C. HOTTEL, 1939)

MIT SOLAR HOUSE III, DOVER, MASSACHUSETTS MIT'S SOLAR ENERGY RESEARCH PROJECT (ENDOWED BY GODFREY L. CABOT), JAMES HUNTER, 1949

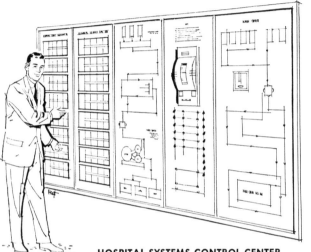

HOSPITAL SYSTEMS CONTROL CENTER

Such a center can be designed by Honeywell, placing at the finger-tips of the hospital's plant supervisory staff all the functions pictured and described on this page. Similar systems can be designed for schools, stores, factories, all types of commercial buildings.

EXCERPT FROM ADVER-
TISEMENT FOR
HONEYWELL SYSTEMS
CONTROL CENTER, 1958

ADVERTISEMENT FOR THE
JOHNSON PNEUMATIC
CONTROL CENTERS, 1958

matically controls these technical features."[28]

As early as the late 1960s, advancements in information technology and building automation brought forth visions of buildings that would be able to respond adaptively or spontaneously to users. Inspired by the automated synchronization of traffic flow in underground transport systems, Warren M. Brodey envisioned an architectural, computer-controlled environment that would evolve in relation to the behavior of its occupants.[29] American scientist Athelstan Spillhaus proposed experimental cities with "ultramodern communication systems" and the prophylactic provision of cable conduits whose future use was as of yet undetermined.[30] In the very same year, a researcher at MIT, Nicholas Negroponte, coined the term "intelligent building": "An intelligent building is a building whose integrated systems are capable of anticipating and responding to phenomena external and internal to the building which impinge on the building and its occupants."[31]

During the late 1960s, researchers were already working on the development of interfaces to facilitate the interaction of computers with people and their environment.[32] Not insignificantly, at the same time the first historical survey of architecture appeared which examined the previously neglected topic of building technology. In *The Architecture of the Well-Tempered Environment (AWTE)*, which was partially inspired by the work of James Fitch, Reyner Banham explored architectural solutions for heating, cooling, ventilation and lighting based on individual examples. According to Banham, very few architects had succeeded in deriving a new formal vocabulary from new technologies. "Mechanical Services are too new to have been absorbed into the proverbial wisdom of the profession: none of the great slogans—Form Follows Function, [...] Truth to Materials,

Wenig [sic] *ist Mehr*—is much use in coping with the mechanical invasion."[33]

In the second edition of *AWTE*, published in 1984, Banham cited the Centre Pompidou (1972–76) as the first building that, instead of hiding mechanical systems, intentionally exposes them. On the façade of the building designed by Richard Rogers and Renzo Piano, ducts and tubing are color-coded to indicate their respective functions: blue for air, green for fluids, yellow for electricity cables and red for movement and flow. As a prime example of early high-tech architecture, Centre Pompidou represented a conscious engagement with the technical aspects of building design. The commitment to an "intelligent" architectural approach culminated in an innovative interpretation of the building's technological systems. In his book's final chapter, entitled "A Breath of Intelligence," Banham discussed the concept of "responsive environments": having played a central role in the science fiction scenarios of the previous five decades, the responsive environment was now entering the realm of possibility.

Intelligent Building. The use of the term intelligent building began to spread toward the end of the 1980s. Initially the expression was often used to describe buildings that provided an advanced data and power infrastructure for computerized offices, as well as centrally controlled HVAC (heating, ventilation, air conditioning) and security systems.[34] However, these features represented little more than a further enhancement of the glazed office tower and had no specific influence on the architectural statement of a building, causing many architects to view the term with skepticism, or regard it as the responsibility of engineers and technicians.

Eventually the understanding of intelligent building came to include an integrative

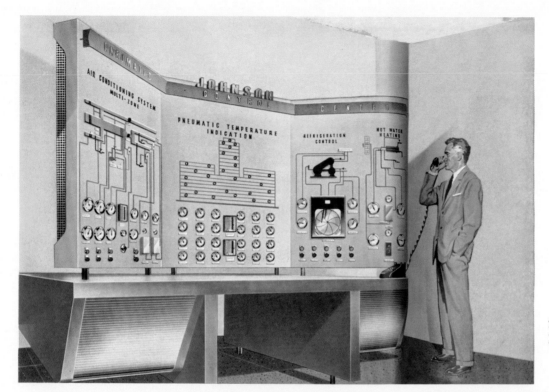

Sizes, layouts and styles of Johnson Pneumatic Control Centers depend upon the specialized needs of the individual building. Each is planned separately with the building's engineer and architect.

Add the Final Touch of Magic to Your Air Conditioning!

JOHNSON PNEUMATIC CONTROL CENTERS

Perfection of the Pneumatic Control Center by Johnson is bringing major savings in heating and cooling costs as well as greatly improved temperature control to buildings of all types and sizes.

The Johnson Pneumatic Control Center gives the building engineer *centralized* supervision and regulation of the air conditioning and heating system. It provides him with a *continuous*, comprehensive visual display of all the vital operating data necessary to maintain the exact temperature conditions required. Simultaneously, it assures that all components of the system constantly function at peak efficiency.

A GLANCE TELLS ALL

By simply scanning the panel, for example, the operator can check space temperatures and water and air supply temperatures at strategic control points throughout the system. *Equally important, he can make any necessary adjustments of key temperatures instantly, right at the panel!*

ONE MAN DOES EVERYTHING

Thus, the operation of even the most complex air conditioning and heating systems is reduced to a one-man job! Instead of an operating *crew* checking performance and making adjustments at widely scattered locations, one man does it all from the panel! In effect, he can be in 20 or 30 or more places at once!

This coordinated, unerring control assures a uniformly ideal environment to meet every comfort and work requirement of any modern building. It results in large reductions in fuel and power consumption and prolongs equipment life.

Remarkably easy to understand and operate, the Pneumatic Control Center requires no extensive study or training. Its components are as simple and inexpensive to use and maintain as the pneumatic controls used elsewhere in the building. Dramatic styling adds an exciting architectural asset when the Center is located in public view.

ECONOMIC ADVANTAGES IMPRESSIVE

What the Pneumatic Control Center means in terms of greater comfort, manpower savings and more efficient heating and air conditioning performance is obvious. It not only pays for itself in a hurry, but it keeps right on paying off over the life of the building!

Pace-setting Johnson Pneumatic Temperature Control Systems with Control Centers are now being installed in many of the nation's finest offices, stores, hotels, hospitals, industrial plants, schools and public buildings. Before you build or modernize, ask your local Johnson branch for full details or write Johnson Service Company, Milwaukee 1, Wisconsin.

JOHNSON CONTROL

PNEUMATIC SYSTEMS
DESIGN · MANUFACTURE · INSTALLATION · SINCE 1885

x

approach that encompassed the "performance" of the entire building, particularly with regard to its energy requirements and the well-being of its occupants. Mike Davie's vision of a "polyvalent wall," first described in a 1981 publication, was especially influential in this respect. "What is needed is an environmental diode, a progressive thermal and spectral switching device, a dynamic interactive multi-capability processor acting as a building skin. [...] This environmental diode, a polyvalent wall as the envelope of a building will remove the distinction between solid and transparent, as it will be capable of replacing both conditions."[35] The wall concept proposed by Davies was a sandwich construction of nine layers: seven different functional layers—together only a few microns thick—for the control of thermal, optical and acoustical properties between interior and exterior glazed skins. As a component of intelligent building services, it should capable of responding not only to the dynamic environment, but also to the habits of users.

Although Davies "polyvalent wall" has yet to be realized in this form, it played a decisive role in the conception of the intelligent skin as a moderator between interior and exterior with the greatest potential for influencing conditions inside the building, but one which will only work as part of a well-conceived overall system. Today's intelligent façades count the following functions among their performance specifications: the manipulation and distribution of daylight inside the building (by means of reflectors, for example), solar protection (e.g., *brises-soleil*, movable louvers, insulated glass), ventilation (the double-skin façade with a ventilated wall cavity), energy collection (solar panels).[36] The most recent materials and advancements in sensor technology also offer new options for lighting, movement, interactive me-

dia and even vegetation (atriums, internal gardens, green roofs).

The Hooker Building (or Occidental Chemical Center) in Niagara Falls, New York (1980), is regarded as one of the very first intelligent buildings. The "buffer façade" conceived by the architectural firm Cannon Design features a ventilated air space (4 feet deep) between tinted insulating glass on the exterior and clear interior glazing. Air is drawn in at ground level and then naturally warmed and humidified as it rises through the façade cavity; sensor-controlled louvers in the continuous air space regulate the entry of sunlight. The building envelope of Norman Foster's Zentrum für Wissenschaftsförderung in Duisburg (1988–93) also comprises several layers and is so efficient that the building requires no supplemental heating. The structure generates and utilizes its own energy; a gas-combustion generator produces the required electricity.

The growing phenomenon of intelligent building was not only due to technological advancements, but also had practical reasons. The 1970s energy crisis brought an increased awareness of the limited availability of natural resources. The motto of a large UNESCO conference in 1973, "The Sun in the Service of Man," encompassed a range of topics including the utilization of solar energy for building operations and maintenance.[37] The discovery of the link between greenhouse gases and global warming in the 1980s also contributed to a greater appreciation of ecological concerns. In addition, companies were confronted with rising energy prices as an increasingly relevant cost factor in the operation of their office facilities. This was exacerbated by the entry of the computer into the daily workplace; the wiring, equipment, and residual heat production of computers have placed steadily increasing demands on building systems. Today it is estimated that approximately 50 percent of worldwide energy consumption is attributable to buildings.[38]

Another problem that has drawn attention since the late 1980s is the so-called "sick building syndrome": statistics have shown that air-conditioned workplaces with no access to natural light are detrimental to the well-being of employees and responsible for a significantly higher level of absenteeism due to illness. It has been proven that people who work in intelligently planned buildings are much more productive—a highly persuasive argument in today's competitive real estate market.[39]

A sharpened consciousness of building energy requirements is also evidenced in the 1990 establishment of BREEAM (Building Research Establishment's Environmental Assessment Method) in England, which evaluates the environmental performance of various building types. In 1996, numerous leading architects in Europe signed the European Charter for Solar Energy in Architecture and Urban Planning,[40] and the United States introduced LEED certification (Leadership in Energy and Environmental Design) in 2000. The highest LEED rating is reserved for buildings that have reduced their environmental impact by over 70 percent in comparison to an equivalent conventional building. Today's architects are able to work with specialized computer modeling software that can calculate environmental influences on a building design long before construction begins, taking into account its specific shape, HVAC systems, orientation, and latitude. Norman Foster's Swiss Re Building (2004) is one recent example.[41]

The reasons for the proliferation of the slogan "intelligent building" are also ultimately found in the marketing strategies of the con-

OCCIDENTAL CHEMICAL CENTER, CORPORATE HEADQUARTERS, NIAGARA FALLS NY (CANNON DESIGN, 1981)

FAÇADE DETAIL, OCCIDENTAL CHEMICAL CENTER

GFW DUISBURG, DUISBURG, GERMANY (FOSTER AND PARTNERS, 1988–93)

FAÇADE DETAIL, GFW DUISBURG

struction industry and in architectural journalism. Since the term implies that other buildings are less intelligent, it can be used by contractors and owners as a catchy label to recommend their buildings to potential tenants. And contributors to architectural publications, always in search of new trends, have found it to be a gratifying subject.

The Intelligent House

Ambient Intelligence as a Leitmotif. Energy-efficient features such as automated interiorclimate control and a dynamic building envelope were also incorporated in the TRON House in Tokyo (1988-93), an experimental residence designed by Ken Sakamura.[42] Regarded as the first intelligent house, the TRON House was sponsored by nineteen Japanese firms and incorporated over 1000 computer systems in an area of approximately 200 square meters. The street elevation and adjacent roof section were comprised of a glazed grid with windows that opened and shut automatically, depending on temperature, humidity and noise levels measured both inside and outside the building. Aside from this external feature, the main focus of the TRON House was, analogous to the many smart homes that succeeded it, the automation and networking of household functions.

This process has been driven by the concept of "ambient intelligence." The work of Mark Weiser, a computer scientist at the Xerox Palo Alto Research Center, gave definition to the vision of an intelligent environment at an early stage. In his article "The Computer for the 21st Century," published in *Scientific American* in 1991, Weiser coined the term "ubiquitous computing." According to Weiser, the role of the personal computer as a solitary piece of equipment in the home or office would be replaced by digital systems that integrated all of the daily objects with which we interact. The personal computer, as an individual machine, would become superfluous and ultimately "vanish into the background." Invoking Giedion's observations about the small electric motor, which began to revolutionize the household 100 years earlier, Weiser argued that the most powerful and relevant technologies are those that escape our conscious awareness: "They weave themselves into the fabric of everyday life until they are indistinguishable from it."[43]

Similarly, one of the central aims of Ken Sakamura in the development of the TRON House was to make the computer systems as unobtrusive as possible. "I felt that in a truly computerized home the computers should be unseen helpers."[44]

A key feature of ambient intelligence, therefore, is that the technology is embedded in the environment, that networked components are an integrated part of the architecture. It refers to a digital environment that is sensitive, adaptive and responsive. The equipment must be able to recognize the user and to assess the situational context; therefore, the system must be personalized and capable of evolving in accordance with the habits, characteristics and daily activities of users. Ultimately, as true believers would have it, such systems will actually anticipate certain situations and the desires of users even before they have been communicated.[45]

If all the intelligent houses constructed during the past decade were brought together in one place, it would result in a little village: the Microsoft Home in Redmond, Washington (repeatedly updated since its launch in 1994), the Cisco Home (erected 1999 in a town outside of London, in collaboration with the

JOCHEN EISENBRAND

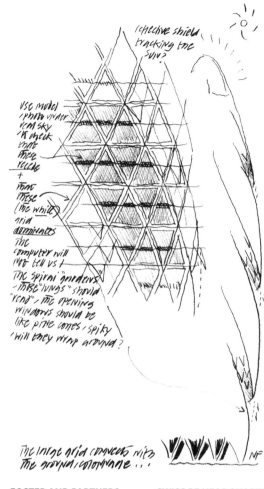

FOSTER AND PARTNERS, SKETCH OF THE SWISS RE HEADQUARTERS FAÇADE DETAIL, LONDON, 1997–2004

SWISS RE HEADQUARTERS, LONDON (FOSTER AND PARTNERS, 1997–2004)

TRON HOUSE, TOKYO (KEN SAKAMURA, 1989–90)

TRON HOUSE, TOKYO, INTERIOR VIEW (KEN SAKAMURA, 1989-90)

construction company Laing Homes), the Cisco Internet Home (2000, a joint project with developer Playa Vista in San Jose, California), the Orange Future Home in Hertfordshire, England (2000), Philip's Homelab in Eindhoven, Netherlands (2002); Toyota's Dream House PAPI (designed by Ken Sakamura, 2004) or the Berlin T-Com-House (in cooperation with Siemens and the Weber company, a manufacturer of prefabricated housing, 2005). All of these projects, first and foremost display homes that demonstrate the advantages of new technologies and prototypes to potential consumers. Some also serve the purpose of research, in order to assess the degree to which installed systems meet with user acceptance. By reproducing an everyday domestic environment and gathering responses from a large number of test persons, scientists hope to discover more about optional applications and user preferences, since user-friendliness is a decisive criterion for future success in the marketplace. Several other projects place a primary focus on research: the inHaus project Fraunhofer Institute's in Duisburg (established in 1995; research and development since 2001) as well as various projects at US universities: the Adaptive House in Boulder, Colorado, under the direction of Michael Mosler; the Aware Home Research Initiative at the Georgia Institute of Technology; the Delta Smart House at Duke University (2006) and of course the House_n consortium at MIT.

What the Intelligent House Can Do. As the continuing miniaturization of computer processors, the comprehensive digitalization of entertainment media (music, films, etc.), the expansion of the Internet and new wireless technologies have become a part of our everyday lives, they have also established the technological basis for the intelligent house. Advancements in sensor technology, e.g. biometrics and voice recognition, represent another indispensable contribution to the realization of ambient intelligence. By means of a biometric scan or a personal identity card, a smart house will know who is inside and where they are momentarily located. This capability sets the stage for those scenarios that dazzle the visitors of futuristic model homes: the house responds to individual occupants with personal preferences that have been stored on the computer hardware in lighting, music, and other media. While it would be the decision of the user to provide such personal information, we hardly take note of the fact that it is already possible for outside observers to reconstruct our daily movements and actions: our identity and/or location can be determined by the wireless devices that we carry, or by the chip-enabled cards that we use in many machines. [46]

Another fundamental characteristic of most intelligent homes is the networking of many different household appliances, which can be centrally controlled or—thanks to wireless technology—even remotely operated from an external location. One of the core questions that arise in this context is the choice of methods for interacting with household systems: central push-button control, gesture recognition, voice command, motion sensors? The field of interaction design, which has established itself as an independent discipline in design education during the past few years, explores questions such as these.

Many components of the smart domestic environment have been designed to function like personal consultants: the refrigerator keeps track of its contents and suggests recipes that can be made with the ingredients on hand; the washing machine warns us when we are about to wash pink socks together with a white shirt; the bathroom mirror tells us which necktie matches our suit. The technology required for this voluntary relinquishment of self-determination would necessarily extend far beyond the walls of the home: groceries, clothing, and consumer goods in general would have to be labeled with RFID (radio frequency identification) tags. These are minuscule microchips that use radio signals to transmit their unique identity code, comparable to a bar code, which can be read by corresponding receivers. A system like this could be used for personal delivery packages with pre-sorted groceries or large volumes of mail. Presently, RFID tags are still too expensive to be used on a widespread basis; the threat to personal privacy is also a relevant and controversial issue.

Economic Forces. Reasons for the propagation of smart houses and their strong resonance in the media can be found not only in technological advancements, but also in economic factors. The market opportunity of the digital home is estimated at $250 billion in the US alone and $1 trillion worldwide in three to seven years. [47] Since manufacturers in different branches are expanding their product lines, the competition in this sector has become more intense. While producers of electronic entertainment devices enhance their products by increasing their computing power, hardware manufacturers are forging into the territory of entertainment media. [48] In the wake of privatization, European telecommunication companies have also been forced to seek other sources of revenue. The multi-media environment so persistently promoted by intelligent houses requires broadband connection and constant online access. Companies offer flat rates for these services in an attempt to secure a constant flow of income.

ORANGE HOUSE OF THE FUTURE, ASTWICK MANOR FARM, HATFIELD (URBAN SALON, 2000–01)

MICROSOFT HOME, REDMOND, WASHINGTON, 1994

T-COM HOUSE, BERLIN
(T-COM IN COOPERATION
WITH WEBER HAUS AND
SIEMENS, 2005)

PHILIPS HOMELAB,
EINDHOVEN, 2002
TYPICAL VIEW OF THE
HOMELAB LIVING ROOM AS
SEEN FROM ONE OF THE 34
OBSERVATION CAMERA
POSITIONS

PHILIPS HOMELAB,
EINDHOVEN, 2002
AN OBSERVATION TEAM
STUDIES THE WAY USERS
INTERACT WITH NOVEL
SYSTEMS THROUGHOUT
HOMELAB.

TOYOTA DREAM HOUSE
PAPI, AICHI PREFECTURE
(KEN SAKAMURA, IN
COOPERATION WITH
TOYOTA HOME K.K., 2004)

JOCHEN EISENBRAND

With such a lucrative potential market in view, numerous interest groups are seeking to gain consumer acceptance of intelligent housing concepts. In 1990, ten prominent European electronics firms, including Philips and Siemens, joined the EU's ESPRIT project for the purpose of developing the ESPRIT Home Bus System, an integrated energy management system. [49] The term "ambient intelligence" was proposed by researchers at Philips in 1998 as a focal concept for the future integration of information, communication and entertainment in everyday settings. [50] The Information Society and Technology Advisory Board (ISTAG), an influential advisory board to the European Union, adopted the vision of ambient intelligence as the main theme for the sixth framework on IST Research in Europe, paving the way for a research program with a budget of 3.7 billion. [51]

One year earlier, the Internet Home Alliance was founded. Participating corporations include Cisco, Microsoft, Panasonic, Hewlett Packard and Whirlpool, among others, whose stated goal is the advancement of the connected home space. Alliance members share resources and expertise in a common effort to develop products and services that require a broadband or persistent connection to the Internet.

What the Intelligent House Can't Do. The concept of the intelligent house is frequently criticized, partly because it stems from the desire of industry to create and exploit new consumer markets. The self-adaptation of ambient intelligence to users and their habits has remained hypothetical—the reality proves to be more complex than many engineers seem to have thought, and still hovers on a distant horizon. At the same time, manufacturers of electronic devices have not been idle: the rapid development and proliferation of CPUs, mobile

telephones, and PDAs emphatically contradicts the theory that individual digital devices would be supplanted by technologies embedded in the domestic environment. According to proponents of ambient intelligence, users have been forced to adapt to computers for long enough; now it is time for equipment that adapts to users. [52] In fact, the broad use of individual devices has led to the development of many common standards in recent years. The new, supposedly "natural" forms of interaction with ambient intelligence, in contrast, still seem extremely unfamiliar to the average person.

A further difficulty is the almost infinite variety of lifestyles and domestic preferences in contemporary society. At the same time that a strong diversification of lifestyles is observable, [53] smart houses assume that users have specific, regularly recurring desires that can be fulfilled by the home's automated systems. The promise of more leisure time as a result of increased household automation may strike many as an outdated ideal, inducing a flashback to the display homes of the 1950s. [54] Alas, the intelligent house offers no new alternatives for time-consuming tasks such as ironing, folding laundry, or cleaning the bathroom. Our home interiors are in a constant state of change; we are used to replacing individual components on a regular basis. The purchase of single appliances conforms with our behavioral patterns as consumers, and parceled expenses are more manageable than a one-off investment in a fully networked system. The seamless integration of ambient intelligence systems also disregards the varying durability of various components and electronic appliances, not to mention the even greater disparity in the life spans of buildings and their interior fittings. For example, after an initial test period the touch-screen refrigerator in the Microsoft Home was withdrawn, because the

LIVING TOMORROW, AMSTERDAM (UN STUDIO [BEN VAN BERKEL & CAROLINE BOS], 2002)

BEDROOM FOR PARENTS AND CHILD, LIVING TOMORROW AMSTERDAM (UN STUDIO [BEN VAN BERKEL & CAROLINE BOS], 2002)

touch-screen technology had to be renewed every three years, while a refrigerator lasts an average of 15 years. [55]

Another major obstacle to the digital home is posed by the different standards of telecommunications companies, software manufacturers and producers of electronic entertainment devices. In spite of numerous alliances and interest groups, competing vendors continue to develop different file formats, coder-decoders and DRM encryption systems, with the aim of achieving future market domination. Yet common industrial standards and the compatibility of different systems and components would be a pre-condition for the success of ambient intelligence in the domestic market. [56]

The Interdependence of Innovative Technologies and Architecture. "An architectural model of the intelligent home combining household technologies with a more flexible use of space is not yet in view," according the journal *Archplus* in the year 2000. [57] It is certainly conceivable that the decline of the conventional phone line due to mobile telephones and the increase in wireless Internet connections could result in individualized and decentralized living scenarios. However, something that all of the present intelligent houses have in common is that architects have not been involved in their development, and that they neglect the issue of the interdependence between home technology and architecture. Even the Living Tomorrow project in Amsterdam (2003), with its spectacular exhibition pavilion designed by Ben van Berkel (UN Studio), does not offer new concepts for smart floor plans. The blob-shaped building serves the primary purpose of setting a visual accent between high-rise housing projects and office complexes in an unattractive borough of Amsterdam.

The architecture of the intelligent home has remained unaffected by the new technologies inside of it for two reasons: because the visual manifestation of wireless systems is highly flexible, and the engineers who develop them have no necessary interest in architecture, and because it is part of the concept. A purpose of commercial display homes is to demonstrate that the systems they contain can be implemented in any type of residence, whether it be an old farmhouse or a brand new urban apartment building.

Nevertheless, the Media House project at the Institut d'arquitectura avançada de Catalunya (Barcelona) was established in 2001 to explore the impact of new information technologies on living space. [58] Under the motto "The House is the Computer: The Structure is the Network," the project began with a four-month study of actual living habits among people representing a wide variety of social backgrounds, in order to apply these empirical observations to the configuration of the Media House. The built structure, which was developed in collaboration with MIT Media Lab, gave a very literal answer to the design challenges posed by new technologies and their potential ramifications for architecture. The name Internet Zero (I0), which came to be associated with the project, reflects a set of principles for extending the Internet down to individual devices. Microcomputers were embedded in lights and switches, and an Internet address was assigned to every technically enabled object in the house, making it possible to program their relationships dynamically. The pavilion-like structure of the Media House, which was temporarily erected in an exhibition center, still had few commonalities with a realistic option for everyday living.

MEDIA HOUSE PROJECT,
DEVELOPED BY
METAPOLIS WITH INSTITUT
D'ARQUITECTURA AVAN-
ÇADA DE CATALUNYA AND
MIT'S MEDIA LAB, 2001

DETAIL, MEDIA HOUSE
PROJECT, 2001

THE CLIMATE CONCEPT OF R128 HAS BEEN DEVELOPED SPECIFICALLY FOR ITS BUILDING SITE: A STEEP SLOPE ON THE EDGE OF STUTTGART BASIN

The loose arrangement of individual modules was too vague to draw any conclusions about future options for residential floor plans.

The Course of Intelligent Building. In retrospect, the previous evolution of the intelligent building offers some insights into the possible direction in which the smart house may continue to develop. Initially, the term intelligent building was used to describe an architectural structure with highly sophisticated technical systems. In time, however, this limited definition was supplanted by the much broader notion of a building planned within the specific context of its location and capable of responding dynamically to local climate conditions in order to conserve energy and to provide a healthy and pleasant interior environment for its users.[59] As the construction industry has assimilated these principles, the significance of the term intelligent building has paled. The increased awareness of a building's environmental impact, the link between interior climate quality and human health, and the function of architecture as a networked environment can also serve as a guiding principle for the further development of the smart house. "What's needed is a modest, intelligence-free house that mimics sensory activities […]. The major concerns of a ubicomp house are authentically houselike concerns: air, temperature, light, space, structure, comfort, safety, the array of homely possessions, and the general environment."[60]

Werner Sobek has demonstrated how these concerns can actually be implemented in the emission-free, zero-energy home designed by the Stuttgart-based engineer for his own family. Called R128 and completed in the year 2000, Sobek's house is located on a tree-covered hill overlooking the city of Stuttgart. The modular structure has a bolted steel frame that was assembled in just four days out of prefabricated parts. The triple-glazed panels of the curtain wall façade are filled with argon gas for insulation and coated with a metallic film to decrease the transmission of solar heat. The floors of the four stories consist of plastic-laminated wooden panels fitted between floor beams. Thanks to modular construction methods and the careful selection of materials, the house is fully recyclable. To the famous question posed by Buckminster Fuller, "How much does your building weigh?," Sobek even has an answer: 39,000 kilograms.

R128 has a sophisticated energy management system. Water circulating through a system of copper pipe coils, which are fitted into the stamped aluminum ceiling panels, absorbs excess heat in the summer and distributes supplemental heat from the long-term heat store in the winter. A mechanical ventilation system with an underground heat exchanger utilizes the near-constant temperature of the ground to cool or heat incoming fresh air as needed. The electricity required for the ventilation system and heat pump is provided by solar cell arrays on the roof.

The construction and equipage of R128 required many custom-made components. The house, specially tailored to the site, is fully glazed and has no interior walls. Due to its complete transparency, it would not be suited as a model for serial fabrication. However, it serves as an effective demonstration of the ways in which architecture can dynamically utilize natural energy sources. A similarly transparent house clad in phase-change glass—an experimental glass that can alternate between transparency and opacity—might be feasible even in a less private location.

The complaint is often heard that the building industry is unresponsive and unduly

HAUS R 128, STUTTGART
(WERNER SOBEK,
1999–2000)

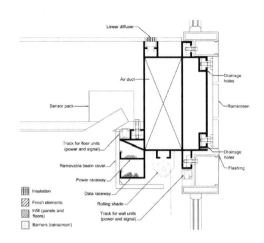

HOUSE_N, DETAIL DRAW-
ING OF A PREFABRICATED
PULTRUSION CHASSIS
HOUSE_N RESEARCH
GROUP (KENT LARSON,
STEPHEN INTILLE, THOMAS
MCLEISH, JENNIFER
BEAUDIN, REID WILLIAMS),
DEPARTMENT OF
ARCHITECTURE,
MASSACHUSETTS
INSTITUTE OF
TECHNOLOGY

HOUSE_N, VOLUMETRIC
DRAWING OF
CHASSIS/INFILL BUILDING
SECTION SHOWING LOFT
MODULES AND TWO POS-
SIBLE APARTMENT INFILL
SOLUTIONS

conservative when it comes to implementing such innovative ideas. Under the direction of Kas Oosterhuis, The Hyperbody Research Group at Delft University of Technology is addressing the question of how new information technologies can be used to facilitate collaborative design efforts between architects, contractors and clients. Their model is based on the principle of interactive computer games played in real-time; team participants have shared access to a common digital interface, and the design task can be a building or some other architectural project.

The Department of Architecture at MIT and the MIT Media Lab have adopted a similar approach for the Open Source Building Alliance, which was founded to develop and promote new methods of residential construction.[61] The stated goal is to bring together the expertise of computer experts, architects, builders and suppliers for the creation of an intelligent home building system that unites industrial prefabrication capabilities with customized design options. The data generated by the collaboration between a client and a "builder-integrator" would be transmitted directly to CNC milling machines, which would produce individually tailored components: the file-to-factory process in the service of mass customization.

1 See Andrew Harrison, "Intelligence Quotient. Smart Tips for Smart Buildings," *Architecture Today,* 46 (March 1994).

2 Robert Faesi, "Neue Sachlichkeit," *Werk*, 19.11 (November 1932).

3 Le Corbusier, *Ausblick auf eine Architektur*, Gütersloh/Berlin, 1969, p. 80 (first edition 1922).

4 Michael Sorkin, "Dwelling Machines," *Design Quarterly*, 138, 1987, p. 32.

5 See for example Hugh Antony, *Houses: Permanence and Prefabrication*, London, 1945, p. 27 and James Marston Fitch, *American Building: The Forces That Shape It*, Cambridge, (Mass.), 1948, p. 288.

6 Siegfried Giedion, *Mechanization Takes Command*, New York, 1948, p. 627.

7 Amelia Jones, Elizabeth A.T. Smith, "The Thirty-Six Case Study Projects," *Blueprint for Modern Living: History and Legacy of the Case Study Houses*, Cambridge (Mass), 1989, p. 60.

8 Alexander Pike, "Product Analysis 5: Heart Units," *Architectural Design*, April 1966, pp. 204 ff.

9 Peter Faller, *Der Wohnungsgrundriss. Entwicklungslinien 1920–1990: Schlüsselprojekte, Funktionsstudien*, Stuttgart, 1996, pp. 217 ff.

10 Gail Cooper, *Air Conditioning America: Engineers and the Controlled Environment, 1900–1960*, p. 166-67.

11 Marsha E. Ackermann, *Cool Comfort: America's Romance with Air-Conditioning*, Washington, 2002, p. 6.

12 Cooper, *Air Conditioning America*, p. 187.

13 Reyner Banham, "A Home is Not a House," *Architectural Design*, 1 (1969), p. 45 (first published in *Art in America*, April 1965).

14 See William W. Braham, "Biotechniques: Remarks on the Intensity of Conditioning," *Performative Architecture: Beyond Instrumentality*, eds. Branko Kolarevic, Ali M. Malkawi, London, 2005, p. 65 f.

15 "How Things Work: Interview with Michelle Addington," *Architecture Boston* (March/April 2005), p. 45.

16 Cooper, *Air Conditioning America*, p. 160

17 Ackermann, *Cool Comfort*, p. 183.

18 Fitch, *American Building*, pp. 166 f.

19 See for example N.N., "A New Approach to Fabrication," *Architectural Forum* (January 1957), p. 111.

20 Robert A. M. Stern, Thomas Mellins, David Fishman, *New York 1960: Architecture and Urbanism Between the Second World War and the Bicentennial*, Cologne, 1997, p. 341.

21 Allan Temko, *Eero Saarinen*, New York, 1962, p. 40.

22 Aladar Olgyay, Victor Olgyay, *Solar Control and Shading Devices*, Meriden, 1976 (first edition 1957).

23 Marcel Breuer, *Sun and Shadow*, New York, 1952, p. 117.

24 Barbara Mac Lamprecht, *Richard Neutra: Complete Works*, Cologne, 2000, p. 417.

25 Le Corbusier, *Feststellungen zu Architektur und Städtebau*, Wiesbaden, 1964, pp. 70 ff. (first edition 1929). English quote taken from website: http://www.battlemccarthy.com/Double%20Skin%20Website/historyandprecendent/salvation%20army%20hostel.htm.

26 AIA Research Corporation, ed., *Solar Oriented Architecture*, Tempe, 1975, p. 26. Aladar Olgyay and Maria Telkes, "Solar Heating for Houses," *Progressive Architecture* (March 1955), p. 207.

27 Olgyay and Telkes, "Solar Heating for Houses," pp. 195–203. See also Victor Olgyay, *Design with Climate: A Bioclimatic Approach to Architectural Regionalism*, New York, 1992, p. V (first edition 1962).

28 Horst Eimbeck, "Gebäudeautomation für die Haustechnik," *Bauwelt*, 42, 1972, p. 1606.

29 Warren M. Brodey, "The Design of Intelligent Environments: Soft Architecture," *Landscape* (Autumn 1967), p. 11.

30 Athelstan Spillhaus, "Die Experimentalstadt," *Das Ende der Städte? Über die Zukunft der menschlichen Umwelt. Strukturen—Systeme—Pro(vo)gramme*, ed. Reinhard Schmid, Stuttgart, 1968, p. 60 f.

31 Quoted in Jupp Gauchel, "Intelligent Buildings," *Bauwelt,* 22 (1990), p. 1107.

32 Nicholas Negroponte and Leon B. Groisser, "The Semantics of Architecture Machine," *Architectural Design*, September 1970, p. 466 ff.

33 Banham, "A Home is Not a House."

34 For a summary of the discussion on this subject at the end of the 1980s, see: Stephen McClelland, "Towards the Intelligent Building," *Intelligent Buildings: An IFS Executive Briefing*, ed. Stephen McClelland, Berlin 1988, unpag. and Gauchel, "Intelligent Buildings."

35 Mike Davies, "A Wall for all Seasons," *RIBA Journal*, 88.2 (February 1981), pp. 55–57. See also Sabine Kraft and Schirin Taraz-Berinholt, "Editorial: Kommende Materialien," *Arch+* 172 (December 2004), p. 123.

36 Michael Wigginton and Jude Harris, *Intelligent Skins*, Oxford, 2002, p. 36.

37 Colin Moorcraft, "solar Energy in Housing," *Architectural Design* (October 1973), p. 634.

38 Sophia and Stefan Behling, *Sol Power: Die Evolution der solaren Architektur*, Munich, 1996, p. 20.

39 Wolfgang Schmid, "Sick-Building-Syndrom—gebäudebedingte Krankheit," *Deutsche Bauzeitschrift,* 2 (1994), pp. 119–122.

40 Charter published in: Behling, *Sol Power*, pp. 236-37 f.

41 N.N., "The Rise of the Green Building," The Economist Technology Quarterly (December 4, 2004).

42 Ken Sakamura, ed., *TRON Project 1989: Open-Architecture Computer Systems*, Tokyo, 1989; Ken Sakamura, *TRON Design*, Tokyo 1999. TRON is an abbreviation for "The Real-time Operating system Nucleus." The TRON House was originally part of a more comprehensive TRON study project on the topic of the computerised society; a *TRON Office Building* and an entire *TRON City* were envisioned at the outset, however, only the *TRON House* was realized.

43 Mark Weiser, "The Computer for the 21st Century," *Scientific American*, 265.3 (September 1991) http://www.ubiq.com/hypertext/weiser/SciAmDraft3.html.

44 Ken Sakamura, "TRON-Concept. Intelligent House," *The Japan Architect*, 396 (April 1990), p. 36.

45 Emile Aarts, "Technological Issues in Ambient Intelligence," *The New Everyday: Visions on Ambient Intelligence*, eds. Emile Aarts and Stefano Marzano, Rotterdam, 2003, p. 14.

46 Michelle Addington, Daniel Schodeck, *Smart Materials*, Oxford 2005, p. 202.

47 N.N., "The Digital Home," *The Economist*, (September 2005).

48 Cf. Jon Healey, Alex Pham, "Digital Home Front: PC Brands Boost Consumer Electronics" Power," in: *Los Angeles Times*, December 26, 2004, p. C1.

49 Reinhard Seyer, "Das Haus der Zukunft—Technische Trends bei Elektro-Hausgeräten," ed. Michael Andriktzky, *Oikos. Von der Feuerstelle zur Mikrowelle: Haushalt und Wohnen im Wandel*, Giessen, 1992, p. 458.

50 Emile Aarts, "Ambient Intelligence: Building the Vision," in: Boris de Ruyter (ed.), *365 Days Ambient Intelligence Research in HomeLab*, Eindhoven, 2003, p. 2.

51 Aarts, ibid., p. 4. See also: *ERCIM News*, 47 (October 2001).

52 Emile Aarts, Rick Harwig, Martin Schuurmans, "Ambient Intelligence," *The Invisible Future: The Seamless Integration of Technology Into Everyday Life*, ed. Peter J. Denning, New York 2002, p. 241.

53 See the essay by Hartmut Häussermann in this catalogue.

54 See Aarts et al., "Ambient Intelligence," p. 237.

55 Nancy Rommelmann, "The House of Today, Tomorrow," *Los Angeles Times* (January 9, 2005).

56 *The Economist* (September 2005).

57 Kay Fingerle and Eghard Woeste, "Condensed Living," *Arch+,* 152/153, (October 2000) p. 58.

58 Vicente Guallart, ed., *The Media House Project*, Barcelona, 2004, p. 30.

59 See Friedrich H. Dassler, 'Symposium "Intelligent Building Design 1999": Perspektiven für das 21. Jahrhundert,' *Intelligente Architektur* (January 20, 2000).

60 Bruce Sterling, "When Our Environments Become Really Smart," *The Invisible Future: The Seamless Integration of Technology Into Everyday Life*, p. 254.

61 Kent Larson et al., "Open Source Building: Reinventing Places of Living," *BT Technology Journal*, 22.4 (October 2004).

BUILDINGS

Seoul Commune 2026 investigates the viability of an alternative and sustainable community structure in the overpopulated metropolises of the near future. The imagined community is integrated within the ever-accelerating developments of the digital environment and ongoing rapid social change. Seoul Commune 2026 presents a concrete architectural and urban proposal that entirely reconfigures and consequently develops the existing "towers in the park" form. Seoul Commune 2026 unites towers and the park in a balanced way. It forms a complex network of private, semi-public, and public spaces.

Korean society continues to change rapidly in both technological and socio-cultural terms. An aging population, a declining birth rate, and rising divorce rate are changing the fabric of social relations. This increasingly "graying" and hyper-individualized society, mainly composed of one or two-person households, inevitably demands new forms of architecture and spatial structures. In addition, digital technologies such as the Internet and mobile communications have been adopted and adapted to Korean cultural norms very actively and extremely quickly. As a result, various online and offline communities have sprung up anarchically, without any support from architecture or urban space.

"Towers in the park," a relatively new Asian urban spatial structure, is swiftly gaining in popularity and replacing the slab apartment buildings reminiscent of the "Hilbersheimer block" that dominated the Korean urban landscape over the past 40 years. The towers in the park typology has been broadly applied in large cities across Asia, including Seoul, considered representative of superior quality open space while satisfying quantitative demands in these overpopulated areas. It consists of two very contrasting elements: the park represents a public space, while the rising towers are an accumulation of individual dwelling units and demarcated private space. Problematic in the engagement of these two static and seemingly opposing aspects is the lack of an intermediary space or structure that fosters the generation of spontaneous social interaction.

Seoul Commune 2026 solves this problem by connecting and balancing the two elements (towers and park). The creation of interjunctions between interior/exterior and public/ private space on a variety of scales accommodates various residential activities and facilitates spontaneous social interactions. This creates a spatial condition in which the towers become the park and the park becomes the towers, with the total emerging as a seamless whole.

Seoul Commune 2026 is located in Apgujongdong, a central area in the southern part of Seoul. It is located in a large-scale urban redevelopment zone that is possibly one of the most densely populated places on Earth. Covering 393,400 square meters of land and bound by the Han River on the northern side, 15 towers of varying height—from 16 to 53 floors—function like one giant house in this park-like setting. The concept is based on a mixture of purely private rooms, so called "cells", and communally used spaces. Ubiquitous digital technologies in the Seoul Commune enable the effective utilization and management of these complex spaces. These technologies are utilized to protect and maximize privacy in private dwelling units/cells, while also allowing individuals to monitor various public spaces in real-time and to select and reserve common public spaces depending on their preferred social contact or activity. This monitoring and decision-making is realized through the digital network system that also enables the dwellers to effectively communicate with various communities and thus helps to develop the diverse communal space. The members of this commune range from permanent residents to nomadic short-term lodgers.

Seoul Commune 2026 suggests a minimized private space consisting of a bedroom and a bathroom in several spatial variations. There are six variations of cells in size on the circular plan of a tower, ranging from 28 to 33 meters in diameter. Spaces where social interactions take place, such as living and dinning rooms, are situated outside the private units. The living cells operate as personalized hotel rooms and each basic residential unit satisfies private spatial needs, while the hotel's public space is shared and utilized by all, guests and non-guests alike. The private spaces in all towers are composed of individually unique beehive-like cells. A total number of 2,590 cells are spread throughout the 15 towers. These basic units can be horizontally and vertically connected and multiplied. A single household can consist of a few independent cells with additional functions. The unique honeycomb structure also improves natural light conditions.

The top floors of the towers have three distinctive spatial structures: the dome, the inverted dome, and the inverted cone, all serving as a sky lounge for the commune and include shared living and dining facilities. The dome type can be as large as 63 meters in diameter and 31.5 meters high, thus creating a huge atrium. The inverted dome and inverted cone type

OVERALL VIEW OF SEOUL COMMUNE 2026: RETHINKING "TOWERS IN THE PARK," CONCEIVED FOR A SURFACE AREA OF 393, 400 SQUARE METERS IN APGUJONGDONG, A CENTRAL NEIGHBORHOOD IN THE SOUTHERN PART OF SEOUL

SEOUL COMMUNE 2026 UNITES TOWERS AND THE PARK IN A BALANCED FASHION. THE GREENING OF THE FAÇADES IS ONE THING THAT CONTRIBUTES TO THIS, MADE POSSIBLE BY THE USE OF GEOTEXTILES.

THE WEBBED STRUCTURE OF THE FAÇADE INSURES GOOD LIGHTING AND ABOLISHES THE SEPARATION BETWEEN FLOORS.

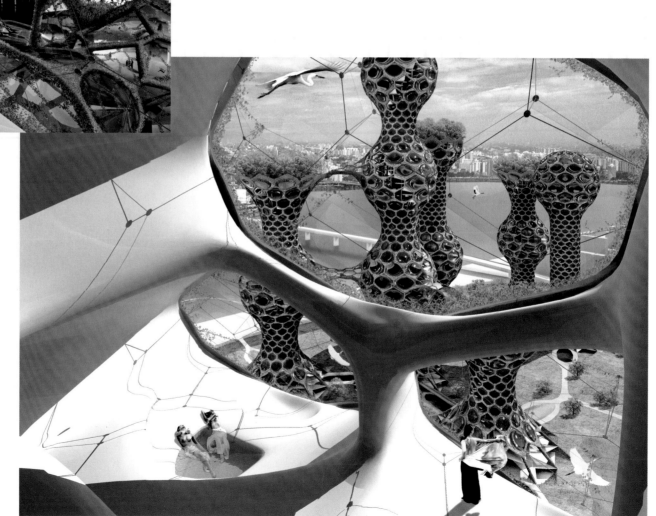

allow for large public spaces on the roof to be used as a roof garden or as an outdoor arena.

Between the top and the base of the tower, the trunk is composed of cells and open space areas for public activities. These areas consist of at least 12 floors and have six variations in the size of plan and section. With diameters ranging from 64 meters to 34 meters, these spaces serve as offices, medical facilities, public services, welfare facilities, and other supporting commercial spaces.

A circulating canal along the edge of the park turns the whole site into an island, and utilizing the adjacent Han River as cooling water for each towers' independent power plant. A 30,175-square-meter pond at the center of the site is designed for leisure activities.

The base of the 15 towers, where the park merges with the towers, creates the widest spaces of the site. Above, the first floor is 75 meters wide and extends up to the height of the first five stories. The ground floor space is reserved for pedestrians. Three walkways converge there and circulate around each tower's elevator core. Two out of three pedestrian walkways expand vertically and create the vertical connective tissue for the double helix stairs/terrace, thus expanding the park vertically. All vehicular circulation moves below the ground and is connected to underground parking spaces at each of the towers. A monorail loop on the second floor offers public transportation and people movers connect the neighboring towers.

The bases of all 15 towers offer programs for sports and leisure, educational facilities, a convention hall, conference spaces, cultural facilities, and supporting commercial facilities.

Each tower is composed of a circular plan, ranging in diameter from 28 to 75 meters and has 15 gradual variations in size. In proportion to its varied plan, the floor heights also change from 4 to 12.6 meters. The circular plan is divided radially into 12 structural units. Six elevators and six shaft spaces are located at the center of each floor, creating the primary vertical circulation.

Two emergency stairs occupy two independent structural units among the 12 structural units in the circular plan. They are located at the periphery of the plan as exterior stairs, winding around the building, forming a double helix structure. More than merely an emergency exit, they also serve as a resting area and a garden in the multi-story residential buildings, thereby becoming the vertical connective tissue extending the horizontal plane of the parks space.

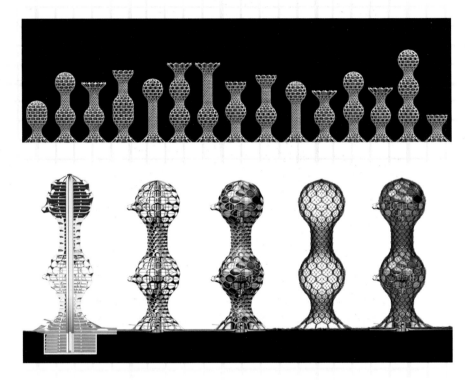

VARIATIONS OF TOWERS OF SEOUL COMMUNE 2026

BUILDING STRUCTURE AND ACCESS TO TOWERS

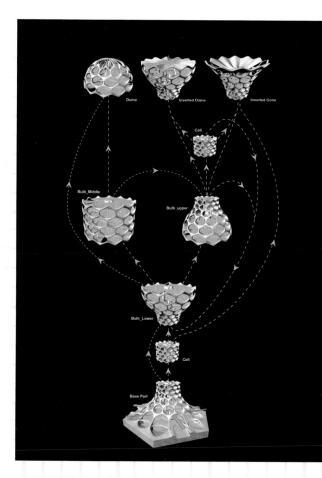

**COMBINATIONS OF BUILDING
COMPONENTS**

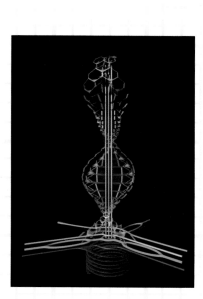

CIRCULATION WITHIN TOWERS

**FROM COMPLETE PRIVACY TO PUBLIC AREAS, SEOUL COMMUNE
2026 OFFERS NUMEROUS POSSIBILITIES OF USE AND THE
APPROPRIATE SPACES, AS ILLUSTRATED BY THE DIAGRAM.**

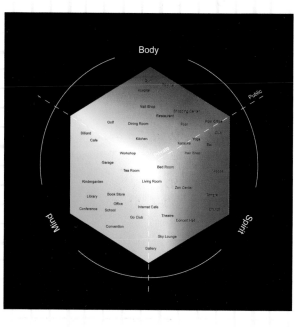

The exterior skin of the towers consists of hexagonal lattice structures that derive from the unique spatial structure and create the unique appearance of the towers. The hexagonal openings are filled with various types of glass. Photovoltaic glass panels are placed in sunny areas for energy efficiency. Some exterior glass windows are recessed to create shaded balconies. The outer surface covering the lattice structure is made of a geotextile that creates an environment where vines can grow during the summer months to shade the openings. These integrated green structures have an internal watering system and a fog machine with automatic temperature and humidity sensors to optimize the environmental conditions of the plants. The water distribution system also carries up to 30 percent of the cooling load during the summer and cleans the glass windows of the building in the heavily polluted city of Seoul.

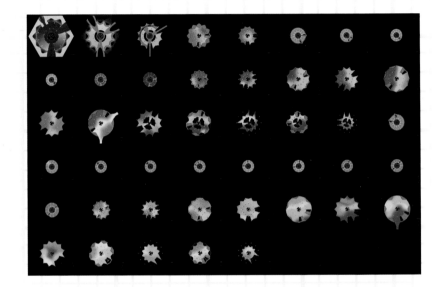

LAYOUTS OF THE 46 FLOORS OF A TOWER OF THE SEOUL COMMUNE 2026

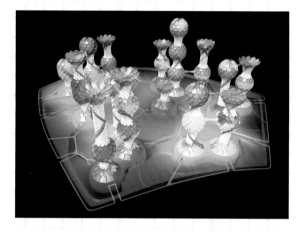

Mass Studies
**Seoul Commune 2026: Rethinking
"Towers in the Park"**

Team
**Mass Studies: Minsuk Cho (principal),
Kisu Park (partner)
and Joungwon Lee (associate), Jinyoung
Ha (associate), Kiwoong Ko, Jongseo
Kim, Soonpyo Lee, Bumhyun Chun,
Daewoong Kim, Jieun Lee, Joonhee Lee
Structural Engineer: Byoungsoon Park
Mechanical Engineer: Sangrak Jang**

Mass Studies was founded in Seoul,
Korea in 2003. The group seeks to investi-
gate architecture in the market-oriented
context of mass production and intensely
over-populated urban conditions. Mass
Studies explores a broad range of building
materials, spatial matrices, and building
typologies in order to develop a vision
that specifically meets the needs of each
project. The recent completion of a six-
storey mixed-use building with 34 units
(11,200 square meters) and the current
construction of a mixed-use, 27-storey
building with 172 units (54,500 square
meters) mark the realization of this new
architectural vision.

Minsuk Cho (principal) was born in Seoul
in 1966. After studying architecture at
Yonsei University (Seoul, Korea), he re-
ceived a master's of architecture from
Columbia University's Graduate School
of Architecture. He has had professional
experience in various locations in America,
Europe, and Asia prior to opening his own
practice. In 1998, he established Cho Slade
Architecture with business partner James
Slade in New York City. Their work has
been honored with numerous awards,
including two Progressive Architecture
Awards (Citations) and the Architectural
League of New York's Young Architects
Award in 2000. He returned to Seoul in
2003 and established Mass Studies.
Kisu Park (partner) was born in Iksan
in 1969. After studying architecture at
Chonnam University in Gwangju, Korea,
he worked in a number of Korean firms
prior to joining Mass Studies in 2003.

www.massstudies.com

Like the sea creature, Jellyfish House is designed to coexist with its environment as a distributed set of networked senses and responses. Jellyfish have no brain, no central nervous system, no eyes, and consist largely of the water around them. All the same, they sense light and odor, are self-propulsive, bioluminescent, and highly adaptive to changing aquaculture. Like a jellyfish, the house attempts to incorporate emerging material and digital technologies in a reflexive, environmentally contingent manner. Jellyfish House is designed as a mutable layered skin or "deep surface" that mediates between internal and external environments. The skin is an organization of fluid materials and technologies that acts as an infrastructural and structural network, allowing the house to be communicatively connective and largely self-sustaining.

The house is a transformative prototype for reclaimed land. Specifically, it is sited on Treasure Island, a flat, artificial island built off Yerba Buena, a natural island in the middle of the San Francisco Bay. Treasure Island is at once local and distant, isolated and connected. It is currently only accessible by off-ramp from the Bay Bridge. Recently decommissioned by the military, it is now being redeveloped for primarily residential uses.

Like many former military bases, Treasure Island suffers from a range of environmental hazards. The most geographically desirable parts of the island have toxic soil in need of remediation. In these areas, the hazardous materials in question require up to five feet of topsoil be removed for cleansing. In other areas, the contaminated soil can be treated on site using plant-based phyto-remediation techniques. The proposed site strategy is to infiltrate the island with sinuous fields of wetlands that would allow the removed soil to not need to be replaced and remediate the remaining toxins. In addition, the wetlands act as a filtration system for the island, becoming a form of productive infrastructure that naturally filters storm water run-off.

Jellyfish House taps into this water filtration strategy at the scale of the house. It captures, stores and filters rain and gray water for use in the home. For the water filtration system, the exterior surface geometry directs rainwater from the roof, and stores it below grade for future use. The water is filtered through cavities in the skin coated with titanium dioxide (TiO2) and exposed to ultraviolet (UV) light. UV light is a common means of removing microorganisms from water, and when combined with titanium dioxide works more effectively than traditional chemical chlorine processes. The titanium dioxide coating is inexpensive, and removes a large range of pollutants. It not only cleans the water, but also interior air and building surfaces. It also absorbs the otherwise harmful UV rays, allowing only the blue, visible light to emerge, resulting in a softly glowing structure during the filtration process.

The filtered water can be used for household purposes, and is also used as a mechanical water-filled radiant system. Similar to a water pump, water is distributed through thickened bands of the skin, cycling either solar-heated water or cool water stored underground. Jellyfish House combines this system with latent heating and cooling using phase change materials (PCM) layered into the skin. Conceived as a largely transparent fluid filled "water jacket," areas of the skin pattern and thickness transform to become quilted baffles containing hydrated salt, a form of salt water. This material fluctuates between solid and liquid states based on changes in air temperature. As it changes from a liquid to a solid state, it releases energy in the form of heat, and subsequently warms the surrounding space; when the reverse occurs, it absorbs energy and cools the space.

Conceived as a deep surface, the skin of Jellyfish House combines structure and envelope with physical and informational infrastructures. What unites them conceptually is that they create an ambient experience in the home that reveals the work of the skin in largely a peripheral manner. In this regard, the project expands upon of the notion of "calm," or ambient, technology, which suggests that the digital realm will ultimately recede to the background of our spaces and lived experience. Using calm technology as a conceptual strategy in the design of the house, the project revisits the digital and the material by cultivating this latent technological relationship while still offering a productive, non-naturalized awareness of the forces at work around us.

Jellyfish House links the inner workings of the home with the environment in an ambient manner, employing sensorial tactics like subtly changing skin patterns while also altering light and environmental qualities for the benefit of the dweller which can be appropriated or ignored as part of everyday experience.

Jellyfish House's deep surface is a parametric mesh using efficient geometric logics of Delaunay triangulation and the

OVERALL VIEW OF JELLYFISH HOUSE, CONCEIVED FOR TREASURE ISLAND, AN ARTIFICIAL ISLAND IN SAN FRANCISCO BAY FORMERLY USED BY THE MILITARY

Voronoi diagram. It deforms locally to geometric, structural, and mechanical circumstances. The skin, made of fiber reinforced polymers and glass, fluctuates in thickness becoming both enclosure and structure. Thickened areas create structure and cavities for the electrical, radiant water, and water filtration systems. Thinner parts of the skin's surface are layered with organic plastic solar cells, titanium dioxide, a wireless sensor network, hydrated salt phase change materials, and organic light emitting diodes. The outer layer of the skin is coated with organic plastic solar cells that absorb the direct sunlight and generate electricity for the home and radiant water system. An insulated air space separates this exterior layer from the phase change materials, so that they respond to the interior house temperature.

The innermost layer is glass printed with transparent thin-film transistors, liquid crystal and polymer light emitting diodes. This flexible digital display system allows the skin to mutate in opacity, transparency, color, light, and image. It is activated either by the user, for example to control lighting, privacy, or simulate a cloudy day, or by the environmental sensor network consisting of MOTES. In Jellyfish House, they sense and communicate environmental data such as temperature, humidity, wind, fog, and direct sunlight, subtly controlling the radiant system and skin display. Thus the house's skin becomes a subtly changing surface that mediates between the internal and external environments.

In terms of urban planning, the house is part of an adaptable system that can aggregate to increase density. Each house is designed to programmatically transform. The proposed single-family residence represents a hybrid form of urbanism where the home initially has two programs of live and work. These programs intertwine so that each has amenities associated with a traditional house or office, such as a backyard garden, or recognizable street address. While the work space can be completely separate from the house, it is also designed to be able to connect fluidly to the home through the interior, so that can be transformed from an office to an in-law unit, to children's wing, or rental apartment, depending on the occupant's current needs.

Like the skin, the house's spatial and formal lay out is a permutable system of intertwining volumes and surfaces that can adapt to different site and programmatic constraints. Each house is shaped by negotiating between internal and external spatial criteria, whereas the spaces between homes are designed to facilitate social networking, allowing for informal, neighborly communication.

LIVE
LANDSCAPE
WORK

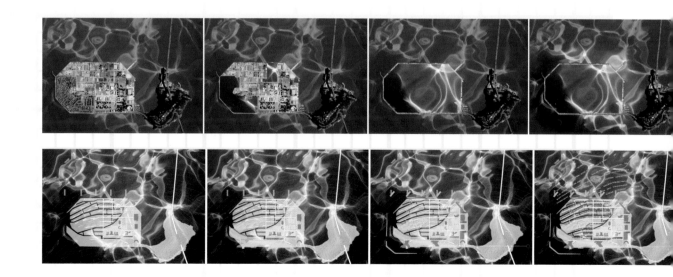

**DIAGRAM OF JELLYFISH HOUSE INTERTWINING A
LIVING SCAPE, A WORKSCAPE, AND A LANDSCAPE
LIVE, WORK AND LANDSCAPE**

**STRUCTURAL AND INFRASTRUCTURAL LAYERS
OF THE BUILDING SKIN**

**TREASURE ISLAND SOIL REMEDIATION AND
WATER FILTRATION CONCEPT**

**INFRASTRUCTURAL LAYERS OF TREASURE
ISLAND SITE**

INTERIOR VIEW OF JELLYFISH HOUSE
A WATER FILTRATION SYSTEM IS
INTEGRATED INTO THE BUILDING'S SKIN
OPERATING WITH ULTRAVIOLET LIGHT
AND TITANIUM DIOXIDE COATING.

THE SKIN OF JELLYFISH HOUSE CAN
SUBTLY CHANGE BETWEEN TRANSPARENT
AND OPAQUE.

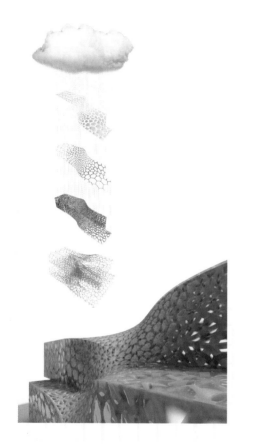

IwamotoScott
Jellyfish House

Team
IwamotoScott Architecture: Lisa Iwamoto, Craig Scott, Tim Brager, Andrew Clemenza, Vivian Hsu, and Ivan Valin , Leo Henke, Chris Gee, Tim Bragan, and Eri Sano
Proces2: Sean Ahlquist, Jason Cheng
Structural Consultant: Martin Bechthold, Associate Professor, Harvard University School of Design
Interactive Computing Consultant: Allison Woodruff, Intel Research Berkeley Ryan Aipperspach, Intel Research Berkeley, and Berkeley Institute of Design

IwamotoScott's work centers on amplifying the perceptual performance of architecture. The work attempts to leverage avenues of design investigation to create a greater confluence between the material world, immaterial phenomena, and architectural space, form and material. An evolving analogy in their work is that of the "spatial phenotype": in this case, the visible spatial result of how the familiar is affected by its environment. The projects employ both standard and unconventional materials and building methods as a way of confounding expectations, or de-familiarizing the familiar.

IwamotoScott Architecture was formed in 1998 by Lisa Iwamoto and Craig Scott in Berkeley, California. Lisa Iwamoto is an Assistant Professor at the Department of Architecture at UC Berkeley. Craig Scott is an Adjunct Associate Professor at California College of the Arts in San Francisco. IwamotoScott's work has been honored and awarded numerous times, including the Progressive Architecture Award Citation 2005, and featured internationally by relevant architecture and design magazines.

www.iwamotoscott.com

Digital Skin Geometry Consultant
Proces2 was established in San Francisco in 1997 by Sean Ahlquist as a firm focusing on design, visualization, and experimentation in the field of architecture. The primary goal for Proces2 is to employ the process of design investigation as a means to discover new perceptions and realizations of architecture. The method of investigation takes place within the realm of digital space and utilizes the latest 3d technologies and software. By linking process directly to digital design technologies, the design method evolves as technology advances. Proces2 explores these ideas in a wide range of projects, stretching from conceptual and theoretical works to residential and commercial design and construction.

www.proces2.com

*dune*house is based on a system that adjusts not only to the extreme conditions of the desert, but to any other surroundings with their specific topographical and climatic conditions. The skin of the building serves simultaneously as façade, load-bearing construction, and living space, and enters into a reciprocal, organic relationship with the natural surroundings. The dynamic morphology of the desert floor is integrated into the design.

*dune*house was developed as a single-family prototype house intended for the desert regions of Nevada. Despite the inhospitable conditions of the area, with its extreme temperatures and lack of water, people still settle here in large numbers. It now houses the fastest growing population in the US. But the architecture here is predominantly monotonous and repetitive, in no way reflecting the natural surroundings, let alone trying to make use of them.

*dune*house is a counter-concept to these uniform buildings that uses the sparse resources as efficiently as possible, conforming to the existing habitat. *dune*house is first and foremost a shell, but this building shell is not just a surface. The construction takes its inspiration from nature, in particular those plants (cactuses) and animals (lizards and other reptiles) that have adjusted to the extreme climate of the desert in an optimal way. The shell system is comprised of a simultaneously responsive surface and integral structure, thus forming the entire house, without need of any other building elements.

Usually, the load-bearing supports and building shell (façade) are organized in a strict hierarchy: the load-bearing supports represent the primary system to which the secondary system, the facade, is attached. This practice necessarily leads to a rigid formal constellation in which the girder is the decisive factor for the entire design. In contrast, *dune*house is based on a system that allows for much more flexible planning, due to the unity of structural supports and shell. The building structure consists of many interlinked individual building elements, forming a network.

The generative software used to develop *dune*house makes it possible to adjust the building structure individually—for example, to the topography of the building site—by altering the parameters. Changing the size or shape of individual elements allows the structure's density to be varied. In the design process, the elements always react locally, directly to one another, so that by changing individual elements whole parts of the structure are also altered.

These elements can be assigned a whole range of uses, serving as panels, windows, or building technology without requiring standardization terms of form or function. The individual elements possess various plastic and spatial dimensions. They range from complex three-dimensional forms to simple two-dimensional areas.

The special planning of *dune*house takes into account two of the local conditions of the desert. A solar energy system takes advantage of the sun, and a fuel-cell system, currently still in development, will generate electricity and heat. A byproduct of the latter is water, which can be used for watering plants, for example. The visible integration of both energy systems into the building structure has consequences for the design of the house. The solar und fuel cell energy systems are not concentrated in one place, but distributed over the entire structure of the building. Pipes are built into the various elements to distribute hydrogen across the building surface, where it reacts with oxygen and produces energy.

Beside the building structure, the landscape is another important part of *dune*house. The landscape plays an essential part in the design. The building does not subject itself to the landscape, nor does the building seek to dominate the landscape. Rather, *dune*house forms transitions to the natural surroundings: streets, paths and gardens link the building seamlessly to the desert. Concrete or asphalt, which cannot react to the dynamics of the desert, are replaced by softer, more flexible materials. Geotextiles can adjust easily to the form of the landscape and enter into a symbiosis with it, without losing the characteristic features of the desert. The transitions between house and landscape that are thus created with geotextiles take up the form of the dunes, forms that are continued in the structure of the building. Landscape and building thus fuse to form a single unit, a unified space, an unlimited dunescape.

The textile skin that envelops the building and extends into the desert allows for natural plant growth; seeds are brought onto the surface by the desert winds.
Technology is often not regarded as part of the structure and the design, and thus hidden inside. This necessarily entails that technical innovations and the architecture stand alongside one another, relatively unconnected. The concept of *dune*house, in contrast, is based on the idea that innovative technology and architecture should be harmonized already during planning by using integrative, dynamic design. The principles of intelligent,

WITH ITS MOVABLE SOLAR CELLS AND SHADES *DUNEHOUSE* INTEGRATES ITSELF INTO THE SURROUNDING DESERT LANDSCAPE.

performative, or ecological architecture at work in the *dune*house thus become an integral part of an overarching aesthetic expression.

*dune*house also follows a new principle regarding the layout of the interior that contrasts with the usual way of planning. The form of the building, generated from the topography of the surrounding landscape, results in an interior space offering numerous possibilities for the inhabitant to define these in terms of structure and function according to his or her needs. This openness in the organization of the interior space is an intentional result of the design of the building's shell and leads to a fundamental creative engagement with individual needs and life habits.

*dune*house is intended as a continuous principle between landscape and construction, thus offering a progressive alternative to the usual urban planning in Nevada. Instead of following a cooky-cutter master plan, urban space in this model "grows," in so doing generating natural forms and relationships that can react much more specifically to local conditions in reference to neighborhood and topography. The houses are built in relationship to one another and the dunescape. The direction the community "grows" in, whether it broadens or narrows, thus depends on the requirements of the inhabitants— they determine the direction and size of the buildings, for example—and the characteristics of desert topography. *dune*house has a stance of its own, stubbornly refusing to subject itself to normative design and the traditional principles of dwelling that go hand in hand with it. *dune*house can be understood as a fundamental design principle, allowing for applications to the most various building types and surroundings.

THE ARTIFICIAL *DUNESCAPE* CONSISTS OF APARTMENTS, POOLS TO COLLECT WATER, AND PATCHES OF GREEN THAT ARE ALL PART OF THE BUILT STRUCTURE AND ARE SEAMLESSLY LINKED TOGETHER.

SAMPLES OF THE BUILDING STRUCTURE

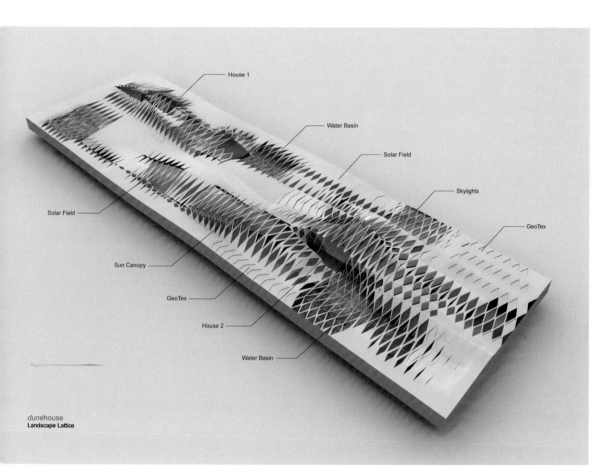

House 1

Water Basin

Solar Field

Skylights

GeoTex

Solar Field

Sun Canopy

GeoTex

House 2

Water Basin

*dune*house
Landscape Lattice

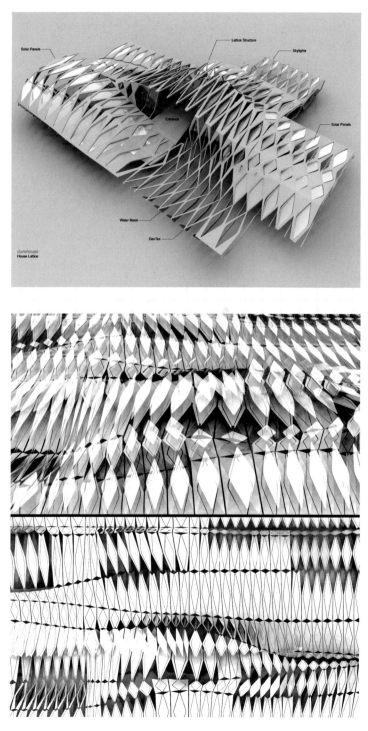

Solar Panels

Lattice Structure

Skylights

Entrance

Solar Panels

Water Basin

GeoTex

*dune*house
House Lattice

EXTERIOR VIEWS OF *DUNEHOUSE*

AXONOMETRIC DRAWING OF *DUNEHOUSE*

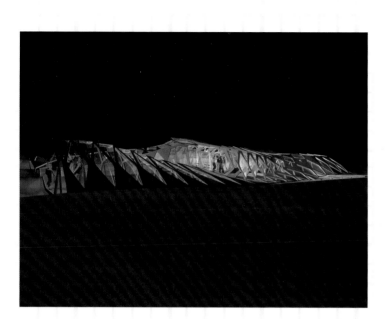

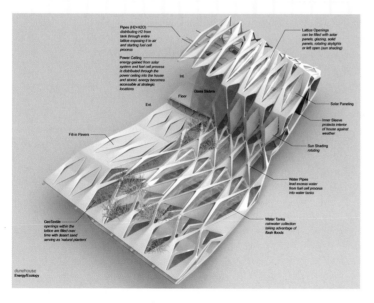

dunehouse
Energy/Ecology

su11 architecture+design
dunehouse

Team
su11 architecture+design
(Ferda Kolatan, Erich Schoenenberger)
Design Collaborators: Out-Fo
(Ezra Ardolino, Aaron White), Roly
Hudson, Isaac C. Coffey, Felix Hoepner
Structural Consultant: Andre Chaszar

su11 architecture+design was founded
in 1998 by Ferda Kolatan and Erich
Schoenenberger as a platform for con-
ceptualizing and engaging in architecture and design. Based in New York City,
su11 is interested in exploring new technologies to achieve more intelligent and
adaptive design solutions.

"We approach design as a mediator between technological advances and the
cultural needs and desires of the user.
The accelerating effects of the digital age
and their complex programmatic config-
urations in urban and suburban culture
have resulted in a variety of routines and
lifestyles. Conventional design is not able
to sufficiently address these new needs,
which require more versatile and adaptive strategies. Furthermore, recent advances in software design, material research, and manufacturing techniques
have introduced a palette of new tools,
allowing for a more seamless and responsive progression from design idea to
project production. Understanding the
mutual relationships between individual
stages of this process is thus critical for
the design of a successful project.
"We are interested in complex new phenomena and webs of relations created by
technological progress. We see this as resulting in a new ecology of design and
construction, and we would like that our
projects also reflect this in a formal and
structural away. Operating in complex

field, a complex network in which many
interdependent currents come together,
we are not only interested in questions of
performance, structure and materiality,
but also in exploring a novel and emerging aesthetic."

Su11's work has been widely published
and exhibited. They have participated in
several conferences, including Archilab
held in Orleans, France and the NSO conference held in Philadelphia. Most recently they received a scholarship to present
their research work at the Smart Geometry Workshop in London. Their work has
also been shown in various exhibitions,
for example at Walker Art Center and the
Carnegie Museum of Art. Su11 received
the Swiss National Culture Award for Art
and Design and the ICFF Editor's Award
for Best New Designer.

Ferda Kolatan and Erich Schoenenberger
also lecture and teach at various universities around the world.

The Primitive Hut for the Twenty-First Century is a shack which combines the essential humanity of Gottfried Semper's *Die vier Elemente der Baukunst* (earth, the hearth, framework/roof structure and lightweight enclosing membrane) with the expediency of digital technology. It attempts to emulate the physical properties of human skin in the building's outer layer, enabling remote housing in areas with extreme conditions. Building technology exists as humanity's response to our alienation from nature, not its cause. But technology for its own sake can be alienating. Used unwittingly technology can be invasive and obtrusive; all of the promises of an easier life courtesy of the digital world count for nothing if connectivity equates to longer working hours, more stress and de-connection between body and soul. Indeed the core idea of Primitive Hut is to create a house that enables escape from a contemporary working life often brim full of technology and stress. The remoteness of the shack affords a re-connection of body and soul.

The design of the building is based on the idea that architecture's true potential lies not in the latest technology, but in the human spirit, and that great architecture frees the spirit, providing it a place to rest. A house enslaved by technology may be superficially exciting and even function better as a building, but we are quickly de-humanized without the comfort of the hearth and the feel offered by natural materials, gardens, and the like.

Remote housing raises specific design issues such as limitations in power and water supply, restricted access and communications, and exposure to harsh climatic conditions. When integrated with design ideas that respond to the remote conditions of the shack, digital technology can spawn an entirely new organic language for architecture, which can have direct applications to less extreme situations, indeed for architecture in general.

The Primitive Hut is a 6.6 meter by 6.6 meter single room shack on a desert site in southern Arizona. The site is uneven, with steep slopes in parts. A dry creek bed runs through part of the site and is subject to flash flooding. The site is sparsely vegetated. Each of the cabins is positioned alongside one of the small hills covering the site, so that each cabin feels autonomous in the landscape. The cabins provide a sense of remoteness for guests who have chosen a holiday to "get away from it all." A separate main building provides administration facilities as well as meals and entertainment for guests. The main activities include hiking, bird watching, and nature walks

The building's skin emulates the physical properties of human skin in the 'lightweight enclosing membrane'. It consists of a protective outer layer made up of a series of tubular cells (60 mm diameter, 60 mm long) that perform the following functions:
- shade the building from radiant heat
- control the extent of the ingress of sunlight
- insulate the building from heat loss
- convert solar radiation into electricity and hot water
- filter out dust and pollutants
- harvest rainwater (to be stored in underground tanks), incorporate moisture content - meters and saturation sprinklers to wet the outer layer of the building, allowing air to move over the surface of the building to assist in natural cooling ("sweating")
- incorporate climate and intruder sensors
- be integral to the aesthetic of the building

With the exception of the actual appearance of the skin, each of these functions will have a digital interface, enabling the building to respond automatically to climate changes as well as allowing occupants to program the skin as they wish, allowing the internal environment of the building to perform in an optimal fashion. With its internal environment controlled in such a sophisticated way the shack can rely on conventional materials, glass, steel, concrete, timber, to create a warm and nurturing space for its occupants.

Combining digital technology with sound, sustainable design and integrating it into the building facade results in an environmentally intelligent building—but one that looks good.

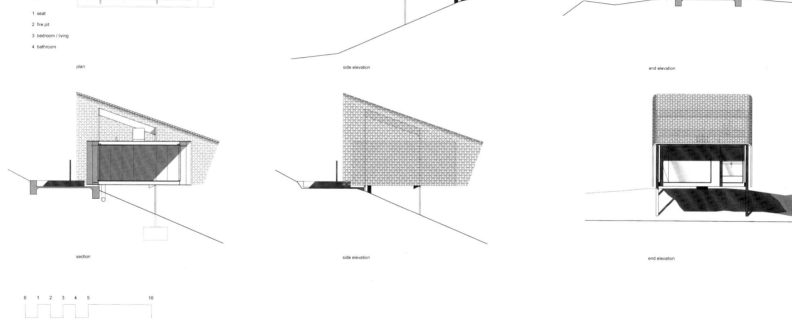

1 seat
2 fire pit
3 bedroom / living
4 bathroom

plan

side elevation

end elevation

section

side elevation

end elevation

0 1 2 3 4 5   10

SIDE ELEVATION, FRONTAL VIEW AND LAYOUT OF THE
PRIMITIVE HUT FORT HE TWENTY-FIRST CENTURY
THE FACADE IS MADE OF TUBULAR ELEMENTS INTEGRATING
PHOTO VOLTAIC CELLS AND SPRAYING NOZZLES FOR
COOLING WATER.

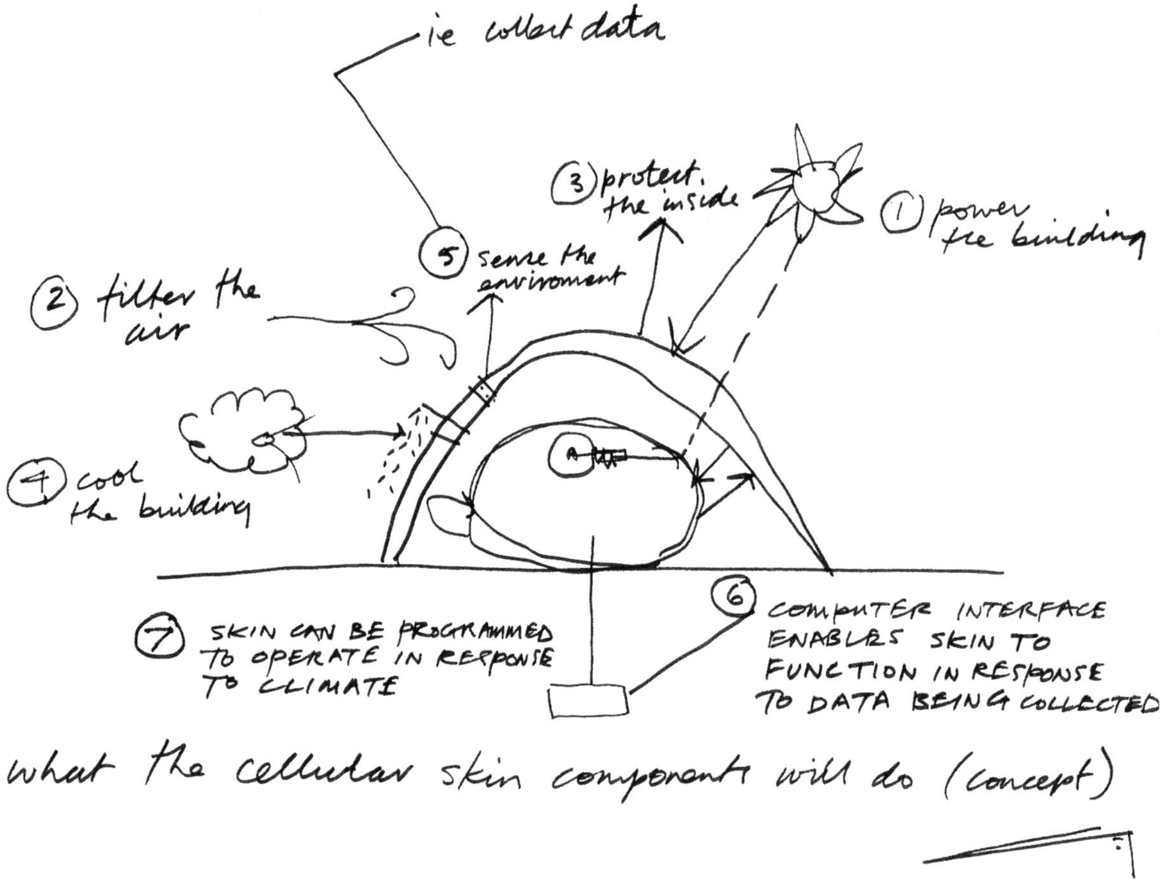

ie collect data

① power the building

③ protect the inside

⑤ sense the environment

② filter the air

④ cool the building

⑦ SKIN CAN BE PROGRAMMED TO OPERATE IN RESPONSE TO CLIMATE

⑥ COMPUTER INTERFACE ENABLES SKIN TO FUNCTION IN RESPONSE TO DATA BEING COLLECTED

what the cellular skin components will do (concept)

CONCEPTUAL DRAWING FOR THE PRIMITIVE HUT FOR THE TWENTY-FIRST CENTURY
THE BUILDING SKIN IMITATES THE CAPACITIES OF HUMAN SKIN, REACTING TO THE EXTERIOR CLIMATE AND ADJUSTING THE CLIMATE INSIDE THE HOUSE ACCORDINGLY.

Sean Godsell Architects (SGA) Primitive Hut for the Twenty-First Century

Team
Sean Godsell Architects (Sean Godsell, Hayley Franklin)

"We believe that the future house lies somewhere between the primitive hut and digital technology."

SGA's evolving research into the skin of buildings seeks to emulate the physical properties of human skin in the lightweight membranes enclosing their buildings. In projects both built and unbuilt, SGA has investigated the potential of the outer skin of buildings, initially as a shading device (Kew House, Carter/Tucker House and the parasol of Future Shack), then as both a shading and filtering device (Peninsula House, CIPEA and McNair houses) and finally as a combined shading /filtering device and energy source (Westwood House, an unbuilt project). Within the context of Australia as part of Southeast Asia, SGA has coupled these investigations with an analysis of the veranda (fluid perimeter space) as an iconic architectural element common to both Eastern and Western cultures. In Peninsula House, SGA used re-cycled timber to make the coarse outer hide of that building. For the CIPEA project, SGA kept all of the bamboo cleared from the site and use it to make the protective outer skin of a house for Chinese artists and their families.

Future Shack was exhibited at the Smithsonian Institute's Cooper Hewitt Design Museum in New York in 2004.

In 1994 Sean Godsell formed Godsell Associates Pty Ltd Architects (SGA) in his hometown of Melbourne, Australia. He has lectured and taught in the US and Britain, and his work has been published in the world's leading architectural journals. He has also been honored with several international awards for his designs. Hayley Franklin studied Architecture at RMIT University, Melbourne where she graduated with Honours in 1999. She has worked for nine years at Sean Godsell Architects and has been directly involved in the delivery of four award winning projects.

www.seangodsell.com

MODEL, SCALE 1:100

Achievements in medicine and changes in modern lifestyles have resulted in longer average life expectancies, necessitating a type of housing that can support the dweller through various stages of life, in particular accounting for the demands of old age. Currently, health care practices and housing design compel the elderly to relocate, often to an institutional facility, to receive proper care and accommodation. Given the rising numbers of elderly, this practice raises serious questions of affordability, availability, and accessibility. As a solution to these issues, Thinking Ahead! proposes a new type of domestic space that through its form, materials, and new technologies can satisfy the needs of a dweller from birth to life's end. At its physical core, this new type of dwelling features a health center that can support the resident's independence in their advanced years.

Since 1980, Mexico has seen a considerable increase—26 percent—in its over sixty-five population. This dramatic demographic shift redirected attention to the question of aging in a way that is unprecedented in Mexico, ushering in a period where it will soon become unfeasible to apply current healthcare models in the face of the drastic increase in demand on the system. Furthermore the current healthcare model of institutionalized housing for the elderly runs counter to deep Mexican tradition of living in the same home from birth to death. Thinking Ahead! thus proposes a new model, where this increase in demand will be met through the necessary convergence of healthcare and housing, manifested in a newly conceived home. This home will take on the role of surrogate caregiver, adapting to the various needs of the dweller in terms of form, materials, and new technologies.

While the Thinking Ahead! model is a response to Mexico's population, weather, culture and infrastructure, Thinking Ahead has a global resonance given that the twenty year projections for populations over the age of 65 show a dramatic increase worldwide: a 65 percent increase in Latin America, a 59 percent increase in Asia, a 45 percent increase in the United States, and a 32 increase percent in Europe.

The architectural form of the Thinking Ahead! house is generated by the consideration that while the need for social spaces, workspaces, and entertainment spaces fluctuate during a person's lifetime, the need for spaces for resting (bedroom) and hygiene (bathroom) remains constant or even increases as the dweller ages. Informed by this programmatic analysis, the Thinking Ahead house creates a central structural core around the bathroom containing all the mechanical and digital technology required for the dwellers. A continuous belt envelops the core creating a kitchen that evolves into a bed that then evolves into the memory space—a space where the dweller downloads images, videos, voices, etc, that he or she can later share with family and friends—leaving the rest of the space and program flexible enough to accommodate any type of dweller.

The bathroom, as currently designed in most houses, poses the most difficulties in adapting to the aging body, often prompting the dweller to leave their house for a more accessible environment. Thinking Ahead! re-conceives the bathroom as a health center, responsive to functions of hygiene, health testing, medical recording, and well-being, alleviating the difficulties posed by such simple tasks as bathing, maintaining cleanliness, and fostering mobility. With this in mind, in designing the form of the space sharp corners are avoided, since they would be harder to keep clean and are potentially dangerous in the case of a fall.

The use of new technologies within the Thinking Ahead! health center is informed by the fundamental belief that prevention is the best form of health care. Therefore, the architecture is imbedded with technologies that in various ways record the patterns of health of the dweller throughout his or her lifetime, thereby developing a personal lifetime medical record. When the dweller finally is infirmed or aging, these same systems are able to utilize this accumulation of information to better respond to fluctuations in normal health patterns. Specifically, these devices include:

Body scanning showers: these showers create ultrasound images of the body that can be projected onto the glass enclosure, taking advantage of the capacity of water to transmit electrical signals.

Medical testing toilets: bodily chemical levels are monitored through evaluating their concentration within the urine on a daily basis and projected on an image mesh that is enclosing the space.

Floors that adjust to changing posture: through optical detection technology, the height of the floor adjusts to accommodate changing posture of the body over time. Additionally, pressure sensitive floors build profiles of normal gait patterns and detect when fluctuations in weight and bone alignment occur.

Medicine chests that monitor prescriptions: medicine chests

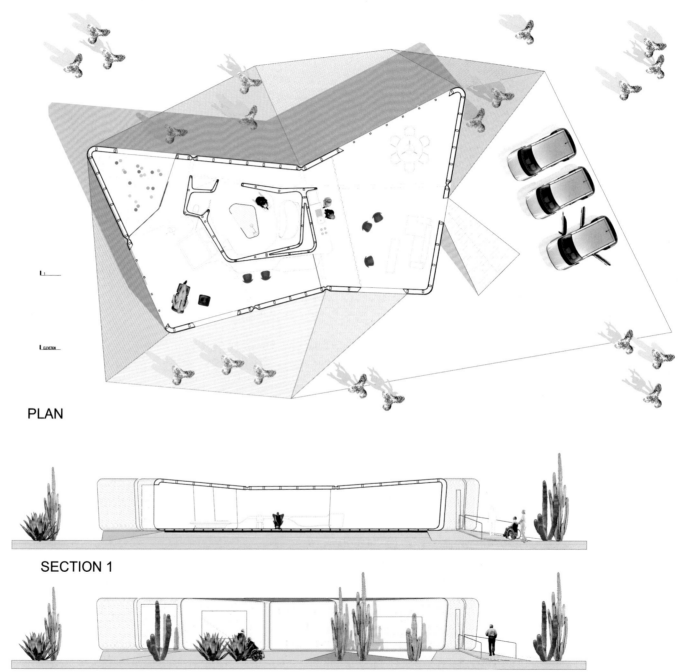

LAYOUT, SECTION, AND ELEVATION OF THINKING AHEAD!

PLAN

SECTION 1

ELEVATION

THE THINKING AHEAD! HOUSE CREATES A CENTRAL STRUCTURAL CORE AROUND THE BATHROOM CONTAINING ALL THE MECHANICAL AND DIGITAL TECHNOLOGY REQUIRED FOR THE DWELLERS.

ROJKIND ARQUITECTOS

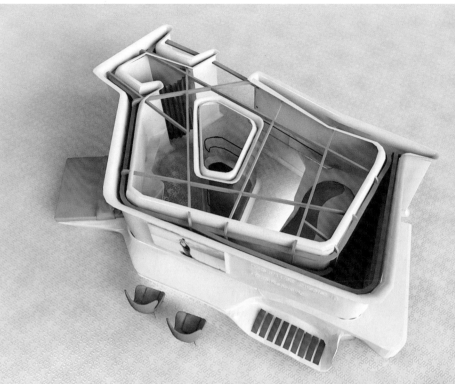

IN THE MEMORY SPACE DWELLERS DOWNLOAD IMAGES, VIDEOS, VOICES, THAT THEY CAN LATER SHARE WITH FAMILY AND FRIENDS.

A CONTINUOUS BELT ENVELOPS THE CORE OF THE HOUSE CREATING A KITCHEN THAT EVOLVES INTO A BED THAT THEN EVOLVES INTO THE MEMORY SPACE.

are combined with user interfaces to create a display that reminds the inhabitant of when to take medicines and perform procedures related to well-being. Additionally, these medicine chests create wellness portraits that monitor and save medical records.

Hydro/light therapy flotarium: A flotarium with built in digital communications access that can compensate for eight hours of regular sleep in a half hour session. For better rest, light emissions stimulate the brain during the resting period. The window that encloses the flotarium has built-in technology so the user can communicate to any cellular phone, computer, etc. and contact their loved ones.

Additionally, the Thinking Ahead! health center acknowledges the therapeutic value of natural light, incorporated as one of its most crucial systems. Through the use of a semi-opaque, light transmitting wall cladding in concert with fiber optic cables that carry natural light directly to these surfaces, the walls, ceiling, and floors themselves become the source of light. Thus, the ability to modulate the quality of light in the space becomes manifold with the move away from traditional isolated light sources to a space which itself emits light. As therapeutic as natural light is, its harshness can also be difficult to adjust to with failing eyes, causing discomfort and possible risk of falling or other dangers. Therefore, another critical feature of the Thinking Ahead! health center is an iris scanner that reads the eye's ability to adjust to light and feeds this information into the lighting system, automatically making the necessary adjustments.

The material used in the interior of the house is mainly resin flooring and Corian surfaces that are ergonomically shaped for each use and perfect for aseptic reasons. The use of special texture carpeting gives warmth to the space while the lighting of all the house comes from the surfaces (milled patterns in the back of the materials that work with a LED system) rather than an a traditional lamp system. The bedroom has additional stainless steel railings that adjust to help the dweller up or down.

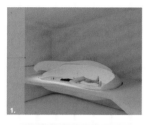

THE FLOATARIUM OF THE THINKING AHEAD! HOUSE OFFERS A
SPECIAL HYDRO/LIGHT THERAPY THAT CAN COMPENSATE FOR
EIGHT HOURS OF REGULAR SLEEP IN A HALF HOUR SESSION.

FLOATARIUM WITH GRAPHIC WALL DESIGN BY MEXICAN ARTIST
ANTONIO SANCHEZ

Rojkind Arquitectos
(Michel Rojkind with Arturo Ortiz)
Thinking Ahead!

Team
Agustin Pereyra, Andrew Pribuss, Moritz Melchert, Ulises del llano, Juan Carlos Vidals, Victor Hugo Jimenez, Gerardo Suarez, Rodrigo Segura & Tania Guerrero.

Graphics: Antonio Sanchez

Michel Rojkind was born in Mexico City in 1969 and studied architecture and urban planning at the Universidad Iberoamericana from 1989–94. After working on his own for four years, he teamed up with Isaac Broid and Miquel Adria in 1998 to establish Adria+Broid+Rojkind; he left the firm in 2002. With the idea of taking on new challenges that address contemporary society and design compelling experiences that go beyond mere functionality to connect at a deeper level with various needs, he established his independent firm rojkind arquitectos in 2002, listed by Architectural Record in 2005 as one of the best ten "Design Vanguard" firms of the year.

By addressing users' needs directly and seeing them as potential sources of inspiration and strength, rojkind arquitectos seeks new directions in architectural practice by evoking common identities through the exploration of uncharted geometries that address questions of technology, materials, structure, and construction methods related directly to geography, climate, and local building conditions. By pursuing all projects that represent a particular challenge to design, Rojkind Arquitectos has been able to avoid any single specialization in any one field of architecture.

Together with Arturo Ortiz, Derek Dellekamp, and Tatiana Bilbao, Michel Rojkind founded MXDF Urban Research Center in 2004. The main object of MXDF is to intervene in specific areas of the urban development, modifying the production of space in Mexico through the systematic study of social, political, environmental, global, and cultural conditions. In order to achieve this, MXDF has been collaborating with several universities in Mexico, Studio Basel, ETH Zürich, the Architectural Association in London, and MIT in Boston Massachusetts. MXDF is a non-profit organization.

Michel Rojkind has also served as the editor of the technology section "FWD" in the architecture journal Arquine international, and has been held several visiting professorships at several universities.

www.rojkindarquitectos.com

JOEL SANDERS, BEN RUBIN, KAREN VAN LENGEN (USA)
MIX HOUSE

Mix House explores the possibility of closely coordinating sound and vision with the goal of enhancing the individual's audiovisual experience of the domestic landscape. This residential dwelling is conceived as a dynamic space enriched by an acoustic link to its external environment and the integration of new channels of communication within the house.

Western architecture since the Renaissance has privileged the visual over all other senses, specifically negating the role of the aural environment that had been such a primary aspect of earlier cultures. In recent history, architectural modernism gave rise to the discovery of the structural frame. This allowed designers to exploit the use of expansive glass windows that afforded uninterrupted views of the landscape, while simultaneously applying new acoustical technologies that homogenized these interiors and compromised the aural specificity of both space and place.1 Mix House rejects this privileging of the visual, putting sound and sight on equal footing. The project proposes a dwelling that rethinks and extends the modernist notion of visual transparency afforded by the ubiquitous glass window to include aural transparency as well. The Mix House design cohesively incorporates cutting-edge technologies and traditional acoustic principles to create a home that constructs and frames audio-visual scenes, enabling occupants to transcend spatial boundaries and orchestrate their own aural environments.

Situated on a generic suburban plot in Charlottesville, Virginia, the dwelling is composed of two distinct volumes that frame audiovisual scenes adjacent to the house. The end façade consists of custom curved sonic windows, which regulate ambient and specific sounds as well as satellite transmissions. Functioning like an audio-visual telescope, the sonic windows include both a microphone and small video camera located at their centers. The microphone records targeted sounds, then transmitting them to an interior audio system that distributes the sounds to various speakers throughout the house. The video simultaneously records the scene and transmits it to a visual screen located at the kitchen island or sound command center of the house, where the synchronized sights and sounds of the surrounding landscapes may be activated and arranged. The occupant may operate the sonic/visual dish to highlight a specific activity or event. He/she also has the option of putting the system on automatic pilot, allowing the occupant to passively listen to a series of focused sounds cap-

tured by windows and their microphones. In this passive mode the occupants can design their own rotation and filtering program able to selectively screen certain sounds and frequencies: human voices, birds, or the sound of water. Each sonic window opens to a different scenery, affording different opportunities for sound transmission:

1. The Sonic Front Entry: The louvered section of the front sonic window allows residents to hear the ambient sounds of the streetscape. Here, the curved sliding surface doubles as the front door. It can be operated to pick up and highlight particular sounds of this locale: guests arriving at the house, the dog that is greeting the mailman or the occasional jogger.

2. The Sonic Picture Window: This sonic window facing the backyard is designed like a camera bellows. It includes a translucent glass dish that is fully integrated into the window wall with the ability to rotate freely in three dimensions. Again, the louvered windows regulate the ambient sounds while the rotating dish focuses on specific activities of the backyard: the birdfeeder, the children playing in the sandbox, or the dog chewing on his bone.

3. Sonic Skylight: This louvered glass skylight located near the top of the vertical volume is designed to both capture and then muffle the ambient sounds of the neighborhood. This soft "sonic breeze" is appropriately located just above the sleeping area. In this location the associated disc is actually a satellite dish that is embedded in the south facing section of the skylight to capture the signals that allow occupants in the bedroom/den below to connect visually and aurally with the global media, through TV and Internet connections.

The two volumes of the house come together at the center kitchen island that acts as the audiovisual nerve center of the home and functions as a central command station for operating the sonic windows. From this position the occupant can regulate the various sound/sight conditions associated with the three windows. Each sonic window has a corresponding video screen with controls to regulate ambient and focused sounds. The video screen visually records the location of the focused sounds so that the occupant can both see and hear the specific audio/visual condition. This command center, designed into the waterproof kitchen countertop, encourages the occupant to mix these various sounds of the landscapes and/or media. In order to design these original soundscapes, occupants may use a variety of real time sounds mixed with media sponsored

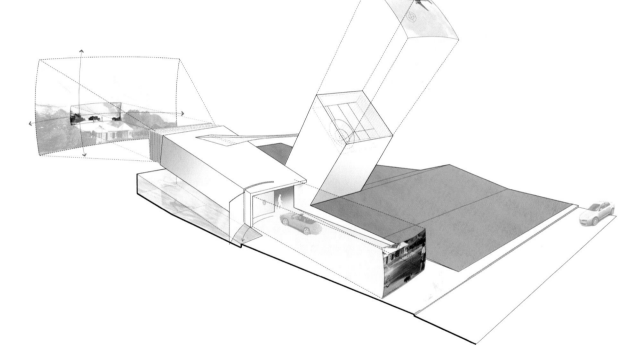

AXONOMETRIC VIEW OF THE MIX HOUSE SEEN FROM THE FRONT THREE SONIC WINDOWS EACH OPEN TO A DIFFERENT SCENERY, TO THE GARDEN, TO THE STREET AND TO THE SKY AFFORDING DIFFERENT OPPORTUNITIES FOR SOUND TRANSMISSION.

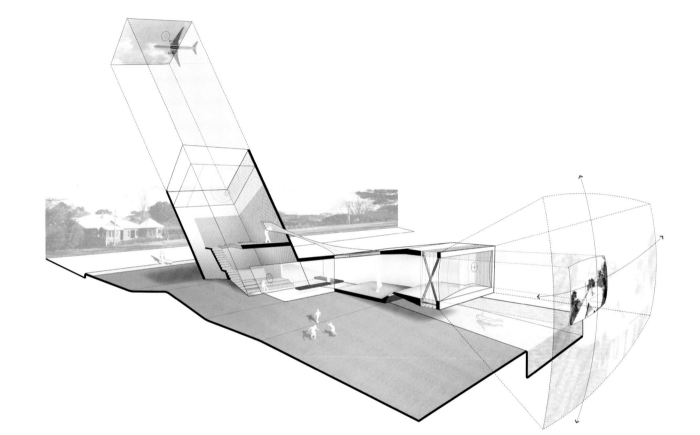

AXONOMETRIC VIEW OF MIX HOUSE FROM THE REAR

JOEL SANDERS, BEN RUBIN, KAREN VAN LENGEN

INTERIOR VIEW OF MIX HOUSE
THE KITCHEN IS THE SOUND COMMAND CENTER OF THE HOUSE, WHERE THE
SYNCHRONIZED SIGHTS AND SOUNDS OF THE SURROUNDING LANDSCAPES MAY BE
ACTIVATED AND ARRANGED.

sounds; for example, the voices of their children playing outdoors could be mixed with Mussorgsky's Pictures at an Exhibition, or the birds chirping in their nests might be mixed with Philip Glass' score for *Koyaanisqatsi*, or frontyard and backyard sounds might be combined together with the ambient noises of the neighborhood.

This project suggests a new direction for domestic space, one that uses sound to inform its spatial design, providing a way to transform the one-dimensional picture window into a more complex transparent apparatus that records both the visual and aural environment, bringing specificity of place to the domestic space. By creating a condition in which the occupant can orchestrate this dynamic installation, we speculate that the act of listening will not only be accentuated and coordinated with vision; it can also serve as a source of creativity and entertainment.

1 Emily Thompson, *The Soundscape of Modernity*, Cambridge, Mass., 2002.

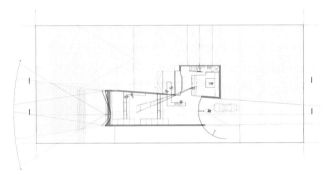

LAYOUT OF MIX HOUSE

JOEL SANDERS, BEN RUBIN, KAREN VAN LENGEN

**Ben Rubin, Joel Sanders,
Karen van Lengen
Mix House**

The Mix House team is a collaboration between Ben Rubin / EAR Studio, Joel Sanders / JSA, and Karen Van Lengen / KVLA. Mix House builds upon their shared interests in architecture, technology, and the human senses.

Ben Rubin is a media artist and founder of EAR Studio based in New York City. His work engages sound, light, information flow, and audiovisual perception. Rubin has exhibited his work widely. He has been a frequent collaborator with artists and performers including Laurie Anderson, Diller+Scofidio, Ann Hamilton, Arto Lindsay, Steve Reich, and Beryl Korot. Rubin's Listening Post (2002, with statistician Mark Hansen) won the 2004 Ars Electronica Golden Nica Prize. Rubin teaches at the Yale School of Art, where he was appointed critic in graphic design in 2004.

Peter Zuspan works as a designer at EAR Studio with Ben Rubin.
www.earstudio.com

Joel Sanders is principal of Joel Sanders Architect (JSA), a design studio based in New York City. Although he has a wide range of work in his portfolio from private homes to public parks, many of his projects explore the intersection of architecture, technology and the human senses. Projects by JSA have been featured in numerous exhibitions including Unprivate House at the Museum of Modern Art. In addition, designs by JSA have been showcased in numerous international publications. Sanders is an Associate Professor of Architecture at Yale University.

Martyn Weaver, Filip Tejchman and Aniket Shahane work as designers with JSA.
www.joelsandersarchitect.com

Karen van Lengen is principal of Karen van Lengen Architect (KVLA). Since its founding in New York City in 1987, van Lengen has won several prizes and competitions including the winning entry for the Amerika Gedenkbibliothek, Berlin. During the design development phase of this project she began to focus on the theme of sound in response to a challenging urban condition. Her design work is currently investigating the potential design strategies that lie at the intersection between sound and vision. Van Lengen is the Dean of the School of Architecture at the University of Virginia.
www.arch.virginia.edu/faculty/KarenVanLengen/

ELEVATION

CONCEPTS FOR LIVING

Electroplex Heights offers a new vision of urban living, a vision that reflects the radical changes affecting our landscapes, our lifestyles, and our notions of "home." Seventy-five years ago, in the heyday of modernism, Le Corbusier regarded the house of the future as a machine for living in. One could argue that we have exceeded Le Corbusier's expectations, and that much of the world itself has become a machine for living in. This is due in large part to the proliferation of digital technologies, causing invisible data streams to increasingly fill the electromagnetic landscape just as "virtual" realities increasingly occupy our minds.

How should we respond? A common strategy is to view the home as a fortress that keeps both the physical and virtual world safely at bay, limiting access to few people and fewer media (TV, radio, the Internet). The intent of this project is quite different. Electroplex Heights embraces the ever more blurred distinction between physical and telematic boundaries. By exploiting the play between the two realms, residents of Electroplex Heights might discover a thrilling new kind of wilderness, a magical hybrid of the electronic and organic that lies right on (and passes right through) the doorstep.

Nowadays, what we think of as "the city" is predominantly fluid and immaterial, a quicksilver space where technological systems and services interact with inscrutable precision. The rough-and-tumble landscape beyond the city limits is (we think) more material, and yet, paradoxically, more alien, more unknown. These unloved stretches, the buffer zones between suburbia and countryside, provide the infrastructure that makes a modern city so seductive: depots, switchyards, processing plants, and so on. However, this landscape has its own unique seductions. And it is the inspiration for, and site of, Electroplex Heights.

There is an obvious environmental advantage in building on land that has already been developed, but would anyone really choose to live in such an inhospitable place? Let's envisage a disparate group of people united only by the fact that all seek a new relationship with their city. What they desire is elusive: although they are loyal to their city—they're not suburban types—they have become disillusioned with the compliant life of the typical urbanite. Behind their disillusion is a growing sense that, due somehow to new information and communication technologies, the city center is losing its pulse. Downtown feels phony. Its vitality as an arena for social exchange and spectacle

is gradually weakening. In sum, their city does not surprise them anymore, and yet the idea of heading for rural isolation seems impossibly anachronistic. Between these two alternatives lies, literally, a middle ground: the no-man's-land of infrastructural space. It's raw, it's intriguing, and it's curiously energizing. The place is both animated and incomplete, and, as such, may offer profoundly new experiences (aesthetic and moral), and thereby bring fresh meaning to urban life.

Largely uninhabited and usually disregarded, these peripheral landscapes are free from aesthetic regulation. They chop and change according to the city's needs. Storage towers, park-and-ride centers, garbage dumps—such things just come and go. Most recently, Internet-based services have acted as a catalyst for this cycle of construction-and-destruction by erecting distribution centers for their online, or virtual, retailers. There is a certain poetry in this. For if there's a physical space analogous to the cyberspace of the Internet, it is surely here, where the crazy jumble of vacant lots is punctuated by zones of ceaseless activity. But the city-limit landscape is not entirely manmade. The brutal geometry of its construction creates pockets of wasteland, which—inaccessible and undisturbed—are much richer in plant and animal life than most urban or suburban parks. And there is another feature of the landscape that often escapes notice—the people. Many thousands of people come through every day, albeit at high speed, intent on their drive in or out of the city.

What would entice our disillusioned urbanites to live out here? What kind of dwelling would most suit this landscape of opposites, so artificial yet untamed, so isolated yet restless? What is needed, we think, is a hybrid architecture—part physical, part electronic. For the resident, such an architecture would present stimulating views outward, and perhaps also inward.

Electroplex Heights is an apartment complex situated in the infrastructure belt encircling a not-too-distant future London. Each apartment building consists of a platform supported by lattice steel columns measuring 15 meters. The platform provides elevated foundations for five to ten apartments, each with a footprint of approximately 8 x 15 meters. Primary access to the platform is via an elevator attached to one of the columns. At a glance, Electroplex Heights resembles a cluster of land-based oil platforms rising out of a sea of low-rise developments.

Because every building straddles its site, and every support column has a small footprint, the complex minimizes

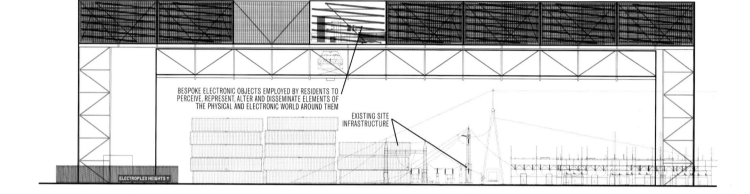

BESPOKE ELECTRONIC OBJECTS EMPLOYED BY RESIDENTS TO
PERCEIVE, REPRESENT, ALTER AND DISSEMINATE ELEMENTS OF
THE PHYSICAL AND ELECTRONIC WORLD AROUND THEM

EXISTING SITE
INFRASTRUCTURE

10 m

SECTIONAL OVERVIEW OF SINGLE APARTMENT
STRUCTURE

ELECTROPLEX HEIGHTS ↑

1 m

disruption to the existing landscape. Life below Electroplex Heights continues, to a degree, as if the buildings were not there. And this life is one of transition. Each apartment building is positioned directly above, or very near, a point where the land changes dramatically—typically a site where an area under development rubs up against a pocket of foliage-rich wasteland. Each apartment thus has two contrasting views: one of tranquil wilderness, one of animated development. The views will alter, of course. That's why an apartment building may have a site lifespan of only a few years: periodically it will be dismantled and reconstructed over a fresh topographical "fault line." Its physical components (as distinct from the equally important, though more delicate, electronic components) have an indefinite lifespan, however, and should survive many relocations.

The diversity of the site is reflected and amplified by the structure of the building. The side facing developed land, therefore more on view, presents a complex arrangement of exposed congregation points and circulation spaces; this side also contains the conduits for the building's services. The other side has few infrastructural components and no communal spaces. If one thinks of the building as an interface—or filter—between its contrasting environments, then the latter side exudes calm.

Residents can augment this building-size interface both by rearranging dividing walls and by deploying a variety of unique electronic objects. These objects perceive, represent, alter and disseminate elements of the physical and electronic world around them. This means that events outside the building influence what happens inside, and vice versa. The small physical footprint of Electroplex Heights is situated inside a large "sensor footprint"—rather like a tree in poor soil, whose roots reach out far beyond the radius of its canopy.

The maintenance of the building's special technology is funded by a service charge, as is the case with communal stairwells and gardens in conventional apartment buildings. Although the technology is moveable, it is considered integral to the architecture, since the part it plays is essential to the experience of living in Electroplex Heights. Electronic media help the residents to communicate with each other (a basic need, since there is no pre-existing resident community here), to commune with the local landscape (physical and electromagnetic), and to relate to the city at large.

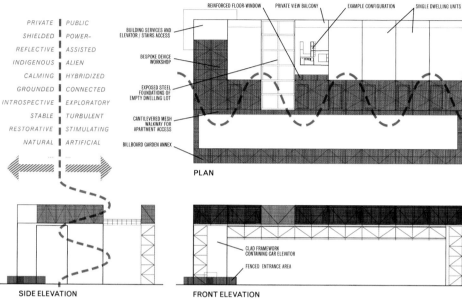

PRIVATE | PUBLIC
SHIELDED | POWER-
REFLECTIVE | ASSISTED
INDIGENOUS | ALIEN
CALMING | HYBRIDIZED
GROUNDED | CONNECTED
INTROSPECTIVE | EXPLORATORY
STABLE | TURBULENT
RESTORATIVE | STIMULATING
NATURAL | ARTIFICIAL
.... | ....

REINFORCED FLOOR-WINDOW
PRIVATE VIEW BALCONY
EXAMPLE CONFIGURATION
SINGLE DWELLING UNITS

BUILDING SERVICES AND
ELEVATOR / STAIRS ACCESS

BESPOKE DEVICE
WORKSHOP

EXPOSED STEEL
FOUNDATIONS OF
EMPTY DWELLING LOT

CANTILEVERED MESH
WALKWAY FOR
APARTMENT ACCESS

BILLBOARD GARDEN ANNEX

PLAN

CLAD FRAMEWORK
CONTAINING CAR ELEVATOR

FENCED ENTRANCE AREA

SIDE ELEVATION

FRONT ELEVATION

10 m

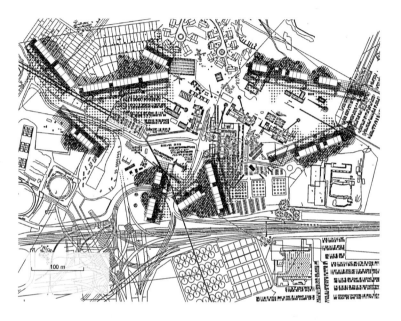

100 m

**LAYOUT AND ELEVATION
OF A SINGLE APARTMENT STRUCTURE**

**SITE PLAN OF ELECTROPLEX HEIGHTS
APARTMENT COMPLEX
EACH APARTMENT STRUCTURE ACTS AS
AN INTERFACE BETWEEN CONTRASTING
ENVIRONMENTS.**

**IMPRESSIONISTIC CROSS-SECTION OF A
350-METER STRETCH OF LONDON'S INFRA-
STRUCTURE BELT SHOWING APARTMENT
COMPLEX.**

50 m

Some of the electronic objects in Electroplex Heights are relatively rudimentary. For instance, there are weatherproof video cameras connected wirelessly to remote display screens. Residents can place the cameras in locations that appeal to them, and also choose where to place the screens. This is not CCTV—not as we currently know it, anyway—because the residents may well decide to put the screens outside their dwelling, so that they form part of the view from a window.

Other electronic objects, though more complicated, are variations on the same principle, and altogether they contribute to a kind of window box "video gardening." The principle is that, should a resident wish it, the view from their apartment should contain elements of the local landscape (such as birds in a tree), the virtual landscape (such as "electronic birds" loosed into the local computer network and projected onto the tree), and also a digital version of the intermingled landscapes (such as video of the two species of bird interacting) which can then be relayed to other residents, thus becoming part of the their virtual landscape … Confusing? But also intriguing. Perhaps even invigorating.

Over time, the residents may develop personal rituals in response to their hybrid view. For instance, someone might take to scattering electronic crumbs in order to attract electronic birds, with the hope that this will, in turn, attract organic birds. Collective rituals may gradually develop, too. Neighborly chitchat about the birds, say, might spark enthusiasm for a website discussing local matters, and this might spawn a local newspaper. In this way, the architecture of the building would encourage a community spirit that is not entirely dependent on physical proximity (as in conventional apartment buildings), nor entirely divorced from the its immediate surroundings (as in internet chat rooms).

Whatever comes of Electroplex Heights, it will never be predictable. Standing as it does at the fault lines in, and between, the physical and telematic landscape—with its feet in an urban no-man's-land and its head in the no-man's-land of cyberspace, as it were—the building is open to the future, and so are its inhabitants.

VIRTUA NEIGHBOR®

ELECTRONIC MEDIA DEVICES HELP THE RESIDENTS OF ELECTROPLEX HEIGHTS COMMUNICATE WITH ONE ANOTHER (A BASIC NEED, SINCE THERE IS NO PRE-EXISTING RESIDENT COMMUNITY HERE), COMMUNE WITH THE LOCAL LANDSCAPE, AND RELATE TO THE CITY AT LARGE. THE MAINTENANCE OF THE BUILDING'S SPECIAL TECHNOLOGY IS FUNDED BY A SERVICE CHARGE, AS IS THE CASE WITH COMMUNAL STAIRWELLS AND GARDENS IN CONVENTIONAL APARTMENT BUILDINGS.

HookerKitchen
Electroplex Heights

Ben Hooker and Shona Kitchen are designers whose work deals with interactive technologies in urban contexts. Their projects typically explore new spatial experiences that are the result of intangible computer-generated "data landscapes" merging with real spaces. Using technology to enhance and enrich rather than distract from the culture and aesthetics of their surroundings, their projects are realized using a network of collaborators: they work with manufacturers on practical commissions such as interactive museum exhibits and retail interiors, with research scientists on more investigational projects that typically culminate in design experiments with particular communities, and with each other on conceptual projects that create foundations for applied design projects to follow.

Ben Hooker's background is screen-based graphic design, but in the last few years nearly all of his projects have centered around collaborations with architects and product designers. As a result he has become particularly interested in finding ways to articulate the overlaps between the phenomenal and ephemeral worlds of materiality and data. He teaches and lectures internationally.

Shona Kitchen studied Architecture and Interiors at the Royal College of Arts (RCA) in London. From 1997 to 2004 she ran KRD (Kitchen Rogers Design, www.krd-uk.com), her own London based design partnership together with Ab Rogers. KRD created a wide range of designs from responsive gallery based installations to commercial design projects, including a new shop for Comme des Garçons in Paris that incorporated automatic moving seating. She teaches in Design Products at the RCA and lectures internationally.

Since their graduation from the RCA in 1997, Ben Hooker and Shona Kitchen have collaborated extensively in various projects. Before Electroplex Heights they worked on a conceptual housing project called Edge Town (www.dataclimates.com/edgetown), which explored related ideas about urban living and formed the foundation for this project.

ATELIER HITOSHI ABE (JAPAN) MEGAHOUSE

Megahouse is a thought experiment that reflects the multiple relationships between technology and urban lifestyles in our media society, with its loss of a sense of place and its ambiguity of boundaries between private space and public space. By the same token, Megahouse is a lifestyle proposal for inhabiting the entire city as if it was one enormous "house." The concept is based on a new timesharing system for unused space in the city that can be made accessible for individual use.

As is true of most post-industrial societies, population in Japan peaked several years ago, and is now in slow decline. Due to this shrinking of society, many gaps have appeared in the urban landscape, and the city is becoming more and more sponge-like. Many spaces, both in office buildings as well as in residential dwellings, are vacant.

Rather than leaving these gaps of unoccupied rooms randomly scattered and unused, Megahouse is a new management system that intends to integrate these spaces, maximizing urban building use, and indirectly elevating the quality of life in a shrinking and mobile society.

The basic technology that constitutes Megahouse is called ZapDoor system. ZapDoor is an access system that will be used to control access to the empty rooms that permeate the entire city. The manufacture of ZapDoor Systems Megahouse Inc. then rents unused spaces, offering them for individual uses.

As Megahouse Inc. offers spaces all across the city, these rooms collectively constitute a "house" for the users. Users inhabit the entire city like one dwelling, walking from one room to the next. This "house" is dispersed and embedded throughout the entire city, and is occupied at different time periods. This leads to a state where the entire city can be used like a big "house": Megahouse.

The online databank of Megahouse contains a great deal of information on registered users, the owners of spaces, available spaces, furnishings, as well as indications on use and reports of past experience. This information is always available by way of the Internet or mobile phone. Users register as Megahouse residents by recording their biometric information in advance. When users access the database from mobile phones or computer terminals, they will be introduced to appropriate rooms that respond to their objectives in terms of location, price, equipment, and design. These rooms are available to the users for differing time-spans, from a short-term use of several hours to a long-term occupation of several months. The users book the room that they prefer and are guided to the reserved room by GPS navigation software. The available spaces are all outfitted with the ZapDoor System. A ZapDoor contains various technologies for identification such as cameras and sensors for biometric recognition by means of fingerprint, iris, or face scans. The ZapDoor connects to the provider server via a digital network, approves the user's identity, and unlocks the doors. ZapDoors can be visually recognized through their unique style.

Megahouse Inc. not only offers empty spaces, but also furnishes them temporarily according to the desires of the users with so-called "fills." There is a choice between standard furnishings (Basic Menu) or many intricate, individual, and expensive variants (Premium Menu). The standard furnishings are multifunctional, so that by using mobile furnishings a tatami room can be used as both a sleeping and living quarters. All fills are equipped with RFID tags providing information about the owner, location, and usage thereby offering a means of control.

People with superfluous furniture, electrical appliances, or other miscellaneous goods can put that domestic dead stock in Megahouse Inc.'s charge and thus offer it for rent. By arranging this stock, Megahouse inc. furnishes the rooms of Megahouse to provide the users a new and sometimes extraordinary life style.

To those not satisfied with the Basic Menu and have additional requirements Megahouse Inc. provides an optional Premier Menu, with features such as BrandRoom, CharacterHouse, and EventBox. Those with a special affection for a particular brand can have the time of their lives in the BrandRoom. If desired, Megahouse Inc. provides products of the favored brand: not only in relationship to the BrandRoom, but in general. Megahouse offers an ideal platform for sponsors that can advertise in the spaces for a certain fee. In the CharacterHouse, the added value is a legend/story relating to the life and styles of certain celebrities. In a space equipped with legendary and personal goods, you can feel like you have slipped into the private life of your favorite celebrity.

The EventBox offers an ideal situation for all kinds of events. The wedding anniversary, birthday or bachelor party can become unforgettable in this room with special decoration, food, bands, and other amenities.

MEGAHOUSE IS A LIFESTYLE PROPOSAL FOR INHABITING THE ENTIRE CITY AS IF IT WERE ONE ENORMOUS HOUSE.

MEGAHOUSE OFFERS AN ONLINE PLATFORM FOR SPACE PROVIDERS, PROVIDERS OF INTERIORS AND SERVICES, AND USERS. ACCESS TO THE SPACE, WHICH BELONGS TO THE MEGAHOUSE NETWORK, IS PROVIDED BY SO-CALLED ZAPDOORS.

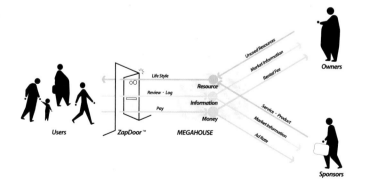

Users

ZapDoor™

Life Style

Review · Log

Pay

MEGAHOUSE

Resource

Information

Money

Unused Resources

Market Information

Rental Fee

Service · Product

Market Information

Ad Rate

Owners

Sponsors

The technical elements required for implementing ZapDoor are already in use. Megahouse is nothing more than integrating existing technical systems into a new way of using technology and an alternative way of using urban space.

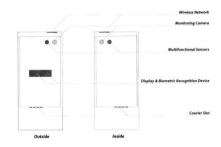

Outside   Inside

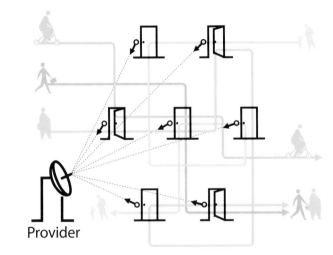

Provider

Bring   Fit   Open

Seamless & Realtime Biometric Recognition

Courier Slot   Media Archive   Monitoring Behavior

ZAPDOORS ARE EQUIPPED WITH A BIOMETRIC SENSOR, POSSESS A COMPARTMENT FOR RECEIVING AND EXAMINING COURIER PACKAGES, AND CAN MONITOR THE BEHAVIOR OF RESIDENTS.

INSIDE AND OUTSIDE OF A ZAPDOOR

ALL ZAPDOORS ARE NETWORKED WITH MEGAHOUSE.

1. Booking   2. Navigation   3. Open Door with Biometrics

User Experience of *MEGAHOUSE*

THE USER CAN BOOK THE SPACES USING HIS MOBILE PHONE. USING A NAVIGATIONAL SYSTEM BUILT INTO THE MOBILE PHONE, HE OR SHE IS DIRECTED TO THE ROOM. ACCESS TAKES PLACE BY WAY OF A BIOMETRIC SENSOR, SO THAT NO TRANSFER OF KEYS IS REQUIRED; AT THE SAME TIME, THE ZAPDOOR REGISTERS WHO IS IN THE ROOM.

BRANDROOM
SPECIAL VALUE IS ADDED TO THE BASIC MEGAHOUSE BY OUTFITTING IT WITH BRAND NAME PRODUCTS. THOSE WHO LOVE A SPECIFIC BRAND CAN HAVE THE TIME OF THEIR LIVES IN THIS TYPE OF MEGAHOUSE.

CHARACTERHOUSE
IN THIS MEGAHOUSE, THE SPECIAL VALUE ADDED IS CELEBRITY. THE ROOMS ARE LITERALLY EQUIPPED WITH THE STUFF OF LEGENDS. YOU CAN FEEL LIKE YOU SLIPPED INTO THE PRIVATE LIFE OF A STAR.

EVENTBOX
SPECIAL VALUE ADDED TO THIS TYPE OF ROOM BY PROVIDING THE STAFF TO MAKING YOUR EVENT PERFECT. YOUR WEDDING ANNIVERSARY OR BIRTHDAY PARTY CAN BE MADE UNFORGETTABLE WITH THE HELP OF A CHEF, A BAND—YOU NAME IT.

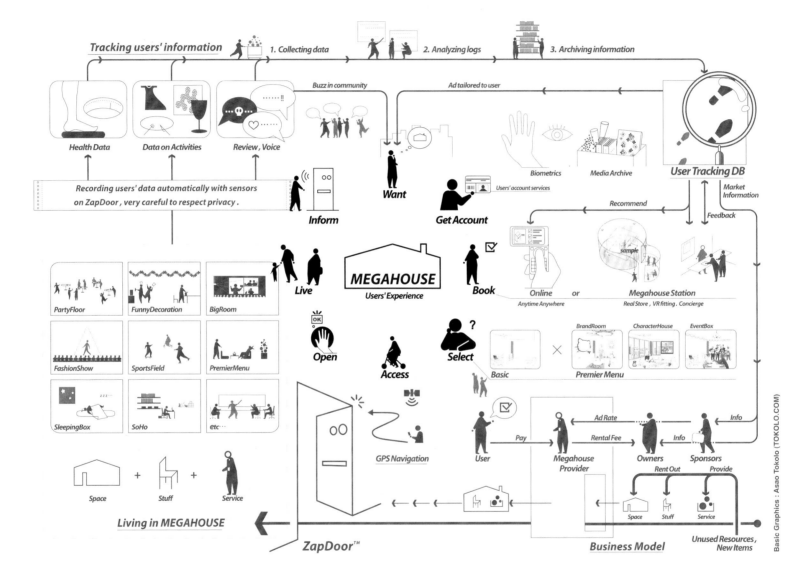

DIAGRAM OF THE OPERATION OF MEGAHOUSE, WHICH MEDIATES BETWEEN SPACE PROVIDERS, SERVICE PROVIDERS, INTERIORS AND USERS

Tracking users' information

1. Collecting data   2. Analyzing logs   3. Archiving information

Health Data   Data on Activities   Review, Voice

Buzz in community   Ad tailored to user

Recording users' data automatically with sensors on ZapDoor, very careful to respect privacy.

Biometrics   Media Archive   User Tracking DB

Inform   Want   Get Account   Users' account services   Market Information

Recommend   Feedback

PartyFloor   FunnyDecoration   BigRoom

FashionShow   SportsField   PremierMenu

SleepingBox   SoHo   etc...

Live   MEGAHOUSE   Users' Experience   Book   Online   or   Megahouse Station

Anytime Anywhere   Real Store, VR fitting. Concierge

Open   Access   Select   Basic   Premier Menu

BrandRoom   CharacterHouse   EventBox

GPS Navigation   User   Pay   Megahouse Provider   Ad Rate   Rental Fee   Owners   Info   Sponsors   Info

Space   +   Stuff   +   Service

Living in MEGAHOUSE   ZapDoor™   Business Model

Rent Out   Provide   Space   Stuff   Service   Unused Resources, New Items

Basic Graphics : Asao Tokolo (TOKOLO.COM)

Atelier Hitoshi Abe
Megahouse

Born in Sendai in 1962, Hitoshi Abe studied architecture at Tohoku University and Southern California Institute of Architecture. Having worked for Coop Himmelb(l)au in Los Angeles for several years (1988–92) he received his Ph.D. in 1993. In the same year he founded his own practice Atelier Hitoshi Abe. Abe also served as associate professor at Tohoku Institute of Technology and since 2002 has been professor at Urban Design Laboratory, Tohoku University.

In his use of new materials and construction techniques, his architecture is known to challenge conventional notions. Some of Atelier Hitoshi Abe's key projects include Miyagi Stadium, Rifu, Japan (2000), Shiki Community Hall, Kumamoto, Japan (2002), SOB (Sasaki-Gishi Prosthetic & Orthotic Services, Inc.), Sendai, Japan (2004), Aoba-tei French restaurant, Sendai, Japan (2005), and SSM sculpture museum, Shiogama, Japan (2006).
His numerous honors and prizes include the 8th World Triennial of Architecture INTERARCH'97, Sophia (1997), the Tohoku Architectural Award for the Michinoku Folklore Museum (2001), the 42nd Building Contractors Society Award for the Miyagi Stadium (2001), the Business Week/Architectural Record Award (2003) for the Sekii Maternity Clinic and the Architectural Institute of Japan Award for the Shiki Community Hall (2003).
Abe's work has also been featured in a number of exhibitions both in Japan and abroad, including the 2000 Venice Biennale.

Masashige Motoe studied environmental science and is currently associate professor at the Department of Architecture, Urban Design and Building Science, School of Engineering, Tohoku University.

Shohei Matsukawa is an architect and interface designer. In 1999 he established his firm 000studio; in 2003 he founded the firm Synctokyo.

Shingo Abe is a visual designer who has worked for w0w Inc. since 2004, while at the same time working independently. In 2005 he won the 9th Japan Media Arts Festival.

Tohru Horiguchi teaches at Tohoku University. He has supervised the work of the two Megahouse student teams at Tohoku University (Hiroaki Miura, Shigeki Honma, Hiroto Nonaka, Yusuke Hayashi, Akira Moteki, Naohiro Sasamoto and Shuhei Yamamura) and at Miyagi University (Shutaro Konno, Tetsuhiko Hanabara, Yusuke Ono, Toshifumi Sato, Atsushi Abe, Keisuke Fukuda, Akira Takahashi, Tomoaki Todome, Takaaki Sugiyama, Rumi Saito, Minami Nagao and Toshiki Oike).

Special thanks to Responsive Environment (Hiroyuki Kamei, Kazuyasu Kochi, Takao Nishizawa, Jin Hidaka, Satoru Yamashiro).

While increased globalization is allowing for a rapid interchange of ideas, goods, and money for some sectors of society, a vast percentage of the world population is being left behind and not reaping the benefits of the global interchange.

Additionally, for the economically disenfranchised, living conditions are comparable to (or below) the standards of pre-twentieth century slums in now industrialized nations. A brief look at the current situation reveals some startling statistics. At the beginning of the twenty-first century, a significant percentage of the world population has no access to safe drinking water (17 percent), sanitation (40 percent), electrical power (31 percent), telecommunications (65 percent), literacy education (15 percent), or decent shelter (15 percent). For this population, both in developing nations as well as in industrialized ones, these basic daily needs are considered luxuries. The advancements of information technology or developments like the "smart house" are unimaginable or irrelevant for people who have never had plumbing or electricity.

But it is possible to overcome these conditions by applying the simple technological advancements made by various disconnected groups (often by the users themselves) scattered throughout the world. Many items such as clay water filters (which effectively screen out the most common types of bacteria), clean fuel stoves (reduce smoke related lung disease), and dome pit latrines (low-cost sanitation) address the critical needs of many communities through inexpensive solutions. Escher GuneWardena's LivingKit project proposes a knowledge distribution system that will make it possible to share such information and develop local expertise, allowing poor communities around the world to improve their physical living conditions and quality of life.

Having identified six basic needs pertaining to a minimum standard of dwelling: water (harvesting, purification, and storage), sanitation (collection and recycling as an energy source), food (storage and preparation), energy (sustainable sources for cooking, lighting, and heating), communication (basic means of access to information and emergency assistance), basic shelter (protection from the elements and provision of security), the LivingKit project would provide a system of access to simple, inexpensive technological solutions that address each of the six needs.

Through existing conduits (such as urban and rural aid organizations, schools, and research groups) and by establis

LIVINGKIT IDENTIFIES SIX BASIC NEEDS THAT NEED TO BE FULFILLED TO ASSURE A MINIMUM STANDARD OF LIVING: WATER, SANITATION, FOOD, ENERGY, COMMUNICATION, AND BASIC SHELTER. USING AN ONLINE CATALOGUE LIVINGKIT PROVIDES A SYSTEM OF ACCESS TO SIMPLE, INEXPENSIVE TECHNOLOGICAL SOLUTIONS THAT ADDRESS EACH OF THESE SIX NEEDS.

LIVINGKIT SHOWS HOW THE MOST BASIC NEEDS CAN BE SATISFIED TO ENABLE A MINIMUM LIVING STANDARD.

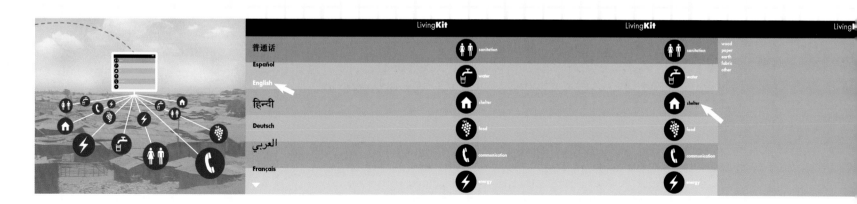

hing new knowledge distribution/exchange posts at application sites, a digital network would connect people and their solutions in one place to others in need in various locations, allowing local adaptability of products and knowledge transfer across continents. The increasing affordability of cell phones, hand-held computer devices, and laptop computers can ease the dissemination of information even to the most remote rural areas.

Such a system of information sharing would further enable a de-centralized, less hierarchical manufacturing and distribution process of the products themselves. The current norm expends a great deal of energy simply on the transportation of goods post-production: a "heavy" system. In the digital network paradigm—a "light" system—much of the production can occur on site or locally, with a minimum of materials and technological ideas coming from afar. For example, a wind turbine for generating electrical energy can be built in South America using technology and digital plans developed in Africa and perhaps a few parts industrially manufactured in China. On the implementation end, a user would first, recognize a need, such as water purification, second, identify the locally available materials, and finally arrive at a solution from the LivingKit catalog in the network. "High technology" could be used to develop materials and products as well as to disseminate information on them to users employing "low technology" materials and "do-it yourself" methods of production. Furthermore, most of the solutions in the LivingKit do not rely on infrastructure, which is usually lacking in rural and urban poor communities. Services such as water access, sanitation, and energy, can be managed individually or by small communal groups to which governments cannot or refuse to provide aid. Once introduced to a community, most of the solutions are self-seeding, providing prototypes easily replicated by those who come into contact with them. The system could be deployed immediately, offering a variety of existing and emerging ideas and products to alleviate the deplorable living conditions caused by poverty or catastrophe in many parts of the world.

While this approach is a shift from the prevailing market-based mode of producer nations selling goods and technology to consumer nations, much information applied to development projects in poor communities is already open source (freely shared by their originators), especially among groups that promote sustainable living. We have the knowledge to enable a better future for more people. The task is to share that knowledge.

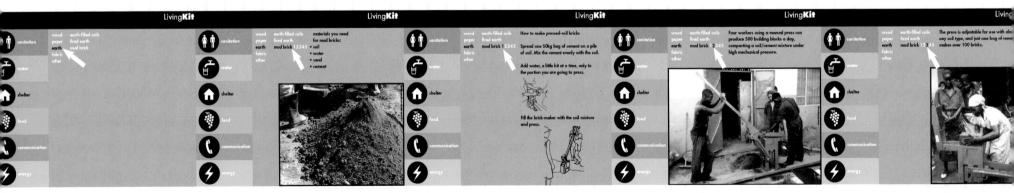

**Escher GuneWardena Architecture
LivingKit**

Team
**Escher GuneWardena Architecture:
Frank Escher and Ravi GuneWardena
Project Team: Bojana Banyasz, Blair El-
lis, Brian Hart, Hillary Jaynes and An-
upama Mann Graphic Design: Judith
Lausten and Renee Cossutta, Lausten
& Cossutta Design
Technology Advisor: John Ingersoll,
P.E., Ph.D., Helios International, Inc.**

Escher GuneWardena's work addresses issues of sustainability, affordability, and
the dialogue between form and construction. They seek simple formal solutions for the complexities presented by
each project, investigating the characteristics intrinsic to the work itself. Their
work, comprising residential and commercial, master planning and institutional
projects, has been done in the United
States, Canada, and Europe, and has been
published and exhibited internationally.
Among their recent projects is Dwell
House II, the winning entry of a
competition sponsored by Dwell Magazine, designed to reconcile issues of sustainability with the aesthetics of modernism.

Frank Escher grew up in Switzerland and
studied architecture at the ETH (Eidge-
nössische Technische Hochschule) Zurich.
He is the editor of the monograph John

Lautner, Architect, (Artemis, London,
1994; Princeton Architectural Press, New
York, 1998). He is former president of the
Los Angeles Forum for Architecture and
Urban Design, and now is a member of
the advisory board. Ravi GuneWardena,
originally from Sri Lanka, was trained at
California State Polytechnic University,
Pomona and in Florence, Italy. He currently serves on the Hollywood Public Art advisory panel of the Los Angeles Community Redevelopment Agency.

Lausten & Cossutta Design, the graphic
design studio established in 1984 by Judith Lausten (MFA, California Institute of
the Arts) and Renee Cossutta (MFA, Yale)
focuses on publication and book design,
informational graphics and signage program design. Their work has received numerous awards from professional design
organizations, both nationally and internationally.

The technology advisor on the project
team is Dr. John Ingersoll, principal of Helios International Inc. This engineering
consulting firm specializes in the development and implementation of sustainable solutions in the built environment
and in transportation, and has extensive
experience in technology research and
development projects in both industrialized and developing countries.

www.egarch.net
www.laustencossutta.com

Open the House! is an alternative concept to living in closed spaces. The house is finally freed from its task of creating an artificial climatic zone, thus liberating the inhabitants of their isolation. Innovative climatic clothing can allow human beings to regulate their own body climate, and the house can open up to external space. This principle enables new kinds of buildings, a more intense social life, and the (re)discovery of a more natural way of living.

Thanks to industrialization and technological progress, the amount of materials needed for building a house has continuously decreased over the centuries. After the establishment of steel construction, the bearing structures and the outer appearance of buildings became lighter, airier, and more transparent. But the energy crises since 1973 have left their traces in architecture, leading to a more frequent use of alternative sources of energy and the sealing of the external building shell with thick insulation facades and triple thermoglazing with airtight frames.

We thus increasingly insulate and isolate our living space from the environment in an attempt to make our lives (seemingly) more comfortable. Already today, people in the industrialized world spend 80 percent of their time in closed, air-conditioned spaces. The consequences of this way of life, divorced from nature, in the so-called developed world are obvious: the experience of nature has become a rarity. People increasingly develop allergies against natural substances. They register the change in season only as an optical change in vegetation and fashion. People living in houses have become mere observers who see their environment, be it the natural or the built environment, through a window, like a framed picture behind glass.

But today, many are looking for a contrast to this world of comfort, air conditioned interiors, and artificial realities. The demand for "adrenaline sports" and vacations in unspoiled nature with simple housing is steadily increasing. Open the House! responds to this situation with a two-fold concept that connects the development of innovative climatic clothing to living spaces that open up to the exterior world.

The convergence of an increased desire for nature on the one hand, and new developments in terms of information and communication technologies, nanotechnology, and the textile industry provides the basis for the development of special climatic clothing. This high-tech clothing is worn inconspicuously like underwear, but warms and cools actively, making the "occupant" more independent of the room temperature around him or her, as long as they lie between 5 and 45 degrees Celsius. So the person wearing this clothing can comfortably be in spaces where the temperature is far below or above what is normally considered acceptable, and yet be dressed only lightly. This clothing has the added advantage that the wearer can control his personal temperature independently of those around him or her.

This fundamental innovation opens up a great variety of possibilities for organizing the way we live, our architecture, and social life. The house can be opened up to the outside, and the clear distinction between inside and outside can be abandoned in favor of a more fluid transition.

The residential house then consists of different climatic zones, ranging from protected and air-conditioned spaces to completely open areas. This zoning is determined by the in habitants according to their habits and ideas about how they want to live. An important advantage of this principle vis-à-vis the traditional forms of building and living is that the individually usable living space is enormously increased additional construction. The integration of the natural surroundings into the living space make forms of living of high aesthetic quality and sensual immediacy possible. Ways of habitation and life that up to now are restricted to regions with a tropical, subtropical, or very temperate climates could now also be realized in areas with a colder climate. The winter in houses without heat in southern countries would also become much easier to bear.

The core of single-family dwellings is now smaller and more compact. But the usable area increases because rooms now extend far into the garden and public areas, living areas can now also be distributed over several buildings that are connected by an open or, depending on the climate, roofed-over living terrace. In multi-story buildings, individual rooms can be changed into conservatories or terraces. Parts of the roof can be removed to create completely open living spaces. Apart from the conversion and rebuilding of existing buildings, this new freedom will also produce new forms of buildings. For example the volume-void house or a modern courtyard building, reminiscent of the southern model. Generous ceiling heights would no longer be a luxury, neither in ecological nor in economical terms.

THE CONCEPT FOR OPEN THE HOUSE! IS BASED
ON THE DEVELOPMENT OF INNOVATIVE
CLIMATE CLOTHING, WHICH MAKES IT POSSIBLE
TO OPEN LIVING SPACE FAR MORE TOWARDS
THE OUTSIDE. EXPERIENCING NATURE AND
EVERYDAY LIFE BECOME ONE.

Ultimately, such architecture leads to a reappraisal of needs, opening up room for a realm of experience thought lost, and spaces for new, yet to be discovered activities.

Since residents are no longer forced to stay indoors in hot or cold weather, urban life will change dramatically. Urban spaces will be used throughout the year. It will be as if the pleasant seasons were extended: in areas with a cool-mild climate, many typical summer activities could also be done during the cold months, cultural characteristics of regions with a warmer climate could be adopted, or new habits will develop. Street cafés would stay open well into the winter, parks frequented throughout the year. Department stores, because of their open ground floors, will feel more like bazaars. Open kitchens on the streets will give city centers an almost exotic flair.

The climatic clothing that makes all this possible is an autonomous system of computer elements and sensors, and consists of alight washable fabric. The clothing will mainly cover the torso, but that will suffice for controlling the temperature of the extremities as well. The elastic fabric, made of comfortable textile fibers capable of transmitting data, is the "textile motherboard" that contains all the technical elements. Wearable electronic systems that are integrated into clothing are already available today. These systems serve purposes of communication and entertainment, but are also used for medical and military purposes, to monitor the body functions of soldiers, for example. These functions are complemented by microscopically small thermoagents for heating and cooling. Highly sensitive sensors, integrated into the fabric and hardly noticeable, continuously measure skin surface temperature, skin humidity, and pulse. The data are transmitted to the textile computer that continuously compares the new data with those saved, and reacts correspondingly.
Neither the weight nor the feel of the fabric is adversely affected by the technologies integrated.

In addition to automatic regulation, the wearer can also control the body heating system manually. Since the computer is capable of learning, it will increasingly recognize certain climatic situations and then know how the clothing should react. The climatic clothing works so inconspicuously that the wearer will quickly become accustomed to it, and will take it for granted in everyday life.

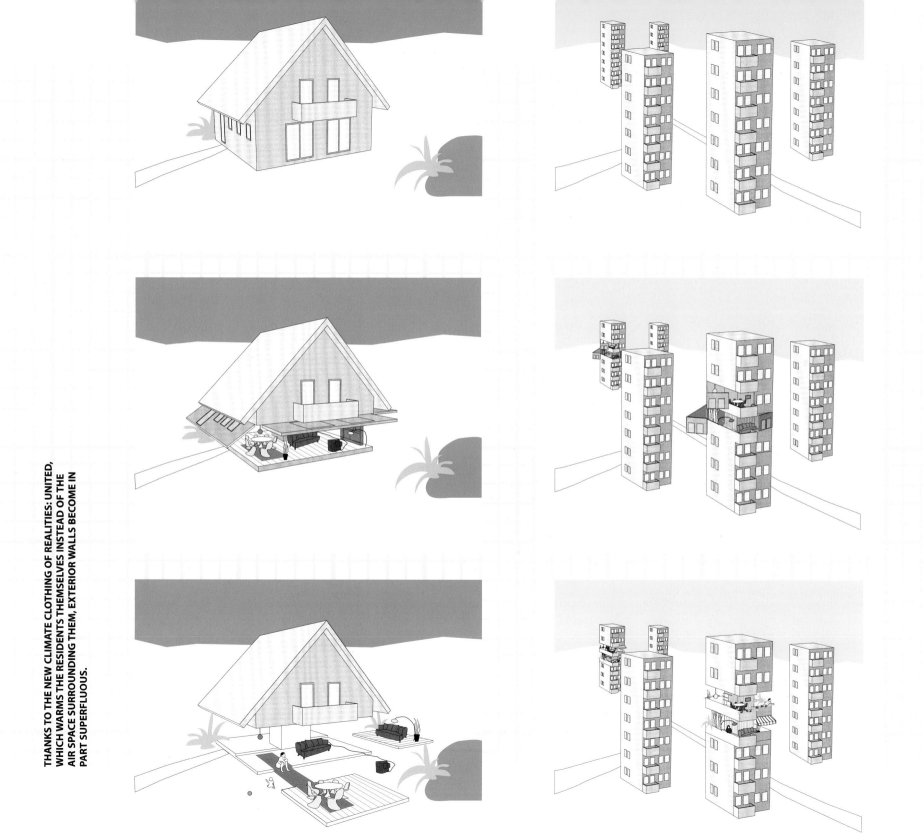

THANKS TO THE NEW CLIMATE CLOTHING OF REALITIES: UNITED, WHICH WARMS THE RESIDENTS THEMSELVES INSTEAD OF THE AIR SPACE SURROUNDING THEM, EXTERIOR WALLS BECOME IN PART SUPERFLUOUS.

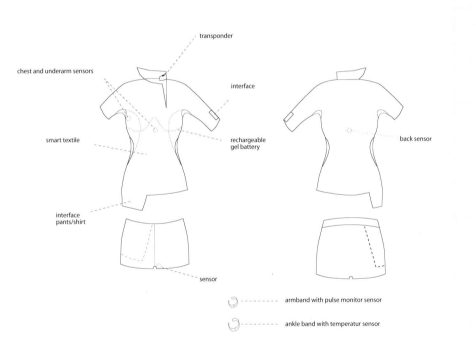

transponder

chest and underarm sensors

interface

smart textile

rechargeable
gel battery

back sensor

interface
pants/shirt

sensor

armband with pulse monitor sensor

ankle band with temperatur sensor

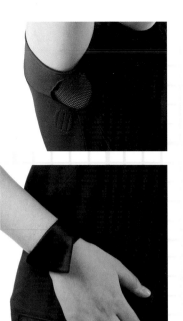

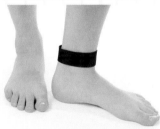

realities:united
Open the House!

Team
realities:united with Milena Monssen
Erik Levander, Andreas Martini
Scientific Advisors: Markus Weder,
Project Leader clothing physiology,
EMPA St. Gallen, Switzerland,
www.empa.ch; Ivo Locher, Wearable
Computing Lab., ETH Zürich,
Switzerland, www.wearable.ethz.ch
Fashion: textile interfaces Alexandra
Baum, Gotha, Germany,
www.textile-interfaces.com

In 2000 the brothers Tim and Jan Edler founded realities:united, a studio for art, architecture and technology. Realities: united studio develops and supports architectural solutions, usually incorporating new media and information technologies. The office provides consulting, planning, and research, also undertaking projects for clients such as museums, architects, and other businesses.

One major focus of realities:united is architecture's outward communicative capacity. Another is the quality of the user experience inside spaces, which in function and appearance are essentially augmented and changed by additional layers carrying information, media content and communication. Some of the firm's projects resemble classical architectural work, but venture regularly into art, design, or technology research. Most projects are intended to serve as a catalyst in a given situation, and are therefore strongly determined by identifying, transforming, amplifying, and combining various existing potentials. In that sense the approach centers on taking advantage of available opportunities, rather than specific skills, procedures, or tasks. Although the majority of the projects incorporate new technologies or experimental approaches in one way or the other, the work always aims to affect actuality, not virtuality.

Strategic initiative and a high proportion of communication and mediation in work processes mark many of the firm's innovative projects. This approach creates the bridge between utopian ideas, abstract conceptions and realizations and has been honored and awarded with several international prizes, lastly the Euro Inspire Award 2005. The projects of Realities: United have been shown at numerous exhibitions in Europe.

Jan Edler studied architecture at the Technische Universität Aachen and at London's Bartlett School of Architecture. Tim Edler studied computer science and architecture at Technische Universität Berlin. Both have lectured and taught at various universities around the world. Milena Monssen studied architecture at the Technische Universität Aachen and Technische Universiteit Delft. Since then, she has worked with different offices in Germany and abroad.

www.realu.de

THE CLIMATE CLOTHING CONCEIVED FOR OPEN THE HOUSE! IS EQUIPPED UNDER THE ARMPITS, ON THE BACK, AND ON THE CHEST, THE HAND AND FOOT, AS WELL AS AT THE GROIN AREA WITH SENSORS THAT MEASURE SKIN TEMPERATURE. A TRANSPONDER ON THE NECK MEASURES THE AMBIENT TEMPERATURE, AN ARMBAND MEASURES THE PULSE.

The great industrial and financial powers produced not only commodities, but also subjectivities.
— Michael Hardt and Toni Negri, *Empire*

How to produce a disalienation process by infiltrating this subjectivity? The Dismiss hypno-chamber is a way to construct a personal relationship, as a "waking up sleeper" with a fictional environment only reachable by hypnosis. The Dismiss hypno-chamber is an open door; a Trans door, in the sense of Dan Simmons, to escape on another layer, an egalitarian layer where the notion of democracy is re-evaluated, as a process of self determination.

Sloterdijk talks about the habitat as a pure machine of acknowledges, a machine of insulation, in the pursuit of Le Corbuiser's *machine à habiter*. We don't want to use technology as a new propaganda of the future but more as a vector of subjectivity, individual and collective, to reintroduce uncertainty, vibes of time, and fears of sleeping comfort. The other is to accept that architecture cannot resolve all human parameter, as a pure objectivization of desire. We will integrate the hypnosis experiment inside the habitat itself, as a new "function." This paradigm includes the way to escape from the human condition, similar to the utopia/dystopia of the Somnambulism movement, as a touchable "star gate." For this we include in our team the hypnosis specialist François Roustang.

Somnambulism
1. Mental activity produced during the phase called waking sleep, or even heightened consciousness. Somnambulism can be characterized by the sensation of an indefinite, uncertain and problematic state, a state of unstable consciousness revealing a new relationship with the world, others and oneself.
2. Historically, the unusual state of the consciousness called hypnosis in the first half of the nineteenth century was an attempt to develop spaces of freedom, egalitarian social projects that could not be perceived and explored except in this state. It could be said that confronted by the impossibility of modifying the mechanisms of the real, tangible, political world, this pre-feminist movement strove, on the contrary, to create a different and distanced layer of existence somewhere out of reach. Although condemned and treated as charlatanism, nevertheless all pre-modern reformist thought drew on this movement. The Dismiss is produced as an indoor chamber, an immersion zone, where a hypnosis session has been registered on individual flat screen. The chamber could be plugged in the wall of any residence, for a family with a maximum of five persons. In front of them the origami, could be stretched as an extension of the wall and used as a home-DVD hypnosis screen to escape from their alienated social condition. The dismiss session last about 15 minutes. After this free time, each family could return to their usual occupation.

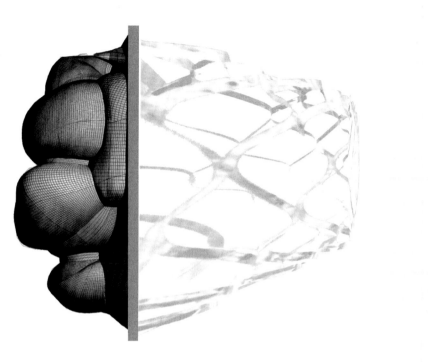

THE DISMISS HYPNOSIS CHAMBER IS AN ORIGAMI-LIKE EXTENSION OF A WALL OF ANY GIVEN LIVING ROOM.

BACK OF DISMISS HYPNOSIS CHAMBER

VIEW INTO HYPNOSIS CHAMBER (MODEL)

François Roustang

Hypnotic chamber:
Please sit down, the chairs are comfortable... have a seat.
There you go. The experience will begin shortly

1. Disconnection/Sensitization Phase

Perhaps you're a little nervous? Let this feeling of unease take you over—it's a natural reaction in the face of the unknown. Let's slide slowly toward that unknown together now. I have to admit that even I was disturbed by what went on there, but at the same time, without understanding why, I had no doubt that there was something there, something that could be... The adventure will be revealed only to those who are willing to risk embarking on it... What are you supposed to do when you find yourself face to face with something unique? First of all, make yourself comfortable on the chair where we're sitting. Do that now. Settle in. You're feeling fine and my voice is easy to listen to. Perhaps you feel a certain tension somewhere in your body, a certain sense of discomfort. Don't do anything special. Let your body take you away. All over your body is relaxed. Your body will take care of the part that's still a little tense all by itself. Don't try too hard to relax, but let your body readjust its position if need be all on its own... You don't need to do anything at all—you don't even need to try to keep from trying too hard. Let yourself by carried away by the soft light and the suspension of time. You don't even need to pay attention to what I'm going to say. You're just going to feel yourself getting heavier, heavy in your chair. And now you feel yourself filling up, swelling until you fill up the whole chair. But don't think about it. Let your mind go where it wants to without worrying about it. You feel heavy, but at the same time you feel light. There's nothing you need to do—just let it happen. You don't need to notice what's going on. Just let yourself drift away.

That's a good way to get ready, to open your mind to a different way of seeing things. Without even realizing it, you're going to open your mind more and more to the uniqueness you've already perceived... You don't have to do anything at all, but if you want you can feel how your back is resting comfortably against the back of the chair, or that your arms are resting on the chair, that your hands are open just like you open your arms and your hands to someone, to something, to something

that happens. You're not trying at all to open anything; you're just letting that opening up happen whenever and however it wants. Your feet are resting comfortably on the floor...

2. Reciprocal Modification Phase

Now you feel solid, you feel at ease, you're ready to face new things. But first we're going to do a little exercise. Close your eyes and you're at home. You're in your bedroom or your living room, if there is one, you're going up and down the stairs of your house or maybe walking through the yard, if there is one. You're breathing in the air of your home, you're letting that atmosphere fill you up, you feel more comfortable, or maybe less comfortable. You realize that you've been transformed by this environment, but on the other hand you can become an actor on this stage as well. A few minutes ago maybe you felt oppressed by the disorder of your home, or just the opposite, by the slightly too rigid order prevailing there. Without thinking about it, let yourself change a few things or move the furniture and other objects around so that your environment goes along better with what you are or what you want to be. Let the environment fill you up by osmosis; you've let your environment act on you and you've acted on it. You're inseparable from it...

Let yourself go further, let yourself be infused by the sensations it brings you and discover a wealth of details you've never noticed before, that you never even suspected. Through the open window the city coming into view is a body, an intertwined, tangled, knotted body... Its curves are like those of a forest with twisted branches and diffused light. The woods guide you, you feel both afraid and protected, childlike and grown-up, this city is an extension of your own body, your arteries, your blood, your genitals, your throbbing body. You are one component in that ensemble, one element coalescing into the whole, something porous with its own respiration and that aspires to be its own environment... You are one of the nerve endings of this body that is a city, you are at the centre where it all interconnects, of a multitude of pulses, and you feel the energy, the substance, you feel the growth of this body that is a city like an extension of your own corporality. No one can make you accept a form that didn't feel right to you at first, and no authority can take it from you. No morality can be dictated from on high... You are this body that is a city and you feel it growing... Mixtures of ugliness and beauty, obstacles

INTERIOR VIEW OF
HYPNOSIS CHAMBER

BRAIN ACTIVITY WHILE HEARING,
SEEING, SPEAKING, DREAMING AND
UNDER HYPNOSIS

and possibilities, waste and efflorescence, threat and protection, technological power and the forces of nature, this body unfolds before your eyes and is your dwelling place... Here everything comes together in a knot. It's all there, in the process of becoming, a never-ending movement... Let yourself go. Don't think. Just let yourself glide into this silky, strange sensation that scares you and caresses you... That scares you and caresses you...

3. Session Closing

Now you can let your eyes open again. Take your time. You can easily forget everything that's happened and even this chair. There might be something different now, but there's nothing to worry about. Gather your thoughts and get ready to stand up whenever you feel ready. If you feel slightly dizzy, just wait a minute until space and time come back to you...

The session is over now. I won't show you out, you know the way...

THE ORGANICALLY GROWING URBAN TISSUE OF I'VE HEARD ABOUT, THE URBAN RESEARCH PROJECT THAT DISMISS IS BASED ON

R&Sie (n)
François Roche, Stéphanie Lavaux,
Jean Navarro
Dismiss

R&Sie(n) is currently working on a
contemporary art museum in Bangkok,
an art center in Korea's DMZ, a hotel in
Belo Horizonte, Brazil, a bridge in Cieszyn,
Poland, a public housing project in
Valencia, Spain, and a private residence
in Nimes, France. François Roche has
lectured at many universities, including
Harvard, Columbia and UCLA. He was a
visiting professor at the Bartlett School in
London, Vienna's Technische Universität,
and ESARQ in Barcelona. Next year he will
teach at the University of Pennsylvania. In
2005, the firm presented the urban planning study I've Heard About at the Musée
d'art moderne de la Ville de Paris. The
self-producing urban structure presented
in this exhibition formed the basis for
Dismiss.

Benoit Durandin
Durandin has collaborated regularly with
the agency R&Sie(n) since 1999, taking
part in its formal research and critical
attitude. His recent work has focused on
modeling unstable environments and
spaces with diminished reality that are
both in flux and fixed. Durandin is member of the editorial board of the
review *Multitudes*.

www.new-territories.com

The Eleven Open House Projects in Context: From Utopian Visions to the Near Future ¶

> SUSANNE JASCHKO

The exhibition Open House: Architecture and Design for Intelligent Living ventures to provide a glimpse of the future of home living. In face of the growing role played by technology in daily life, the curators explored the question of which technologies and associated housing concepts have the potential to change our lives for the better in the years to come. Eleven architects and designers responded to this

"It was Panasonic's birthday or something and they had a party at your place."
"Everyone was supposed to come to your house and have a look at something."
"At what?"
"How it worked."
"So how did it work?"
"Well, not like a house. Not like a party. It wasn't like we were dancing or anything. We just looked at how the house worked."

René Pollesch: *Smarthouse* (1-3), excerpt

124

question with their individual proposals in the context of the exhibition, taking into account the relevant social, economic, and technological developments that have already yielded an impact or are clearly soon forthcoming.

Architecture, especially housing construction, is a reflection of social, economic, and technological processes. Although it appears certain that some of the processes evident in the present day will continue into the future, it is difficult to predict whether other linear-seeming developments will end up coming to a halt while new processes are set in motion. Technological innovation in particular is not linear but occurs in leaps and spurts, making its future development difficult to predict. In the following, I will seek to trace the most important developments currently shaping the deliberation on and formulation of future forms of living and housing, and locate the eleven architectural proposals within this context.

The Intelligent House: The End of a Vision?

The era of the "intelligent house" might seem to have passed, yet a good number of information technology engineers and producers are apparently still possessed by the notion of a fully computerized home. For most, however, the utopian vision of an "intelligent house" intended to simplify the life of its occupants through the far-reaching integration of reactive systems has become more of a dystopia. In René Pollesch's 2001 play *Smarthouse (1+2)*, for instance, the actual protagonist is the house itself, a product of the Panasonic corporation. Originally designed to provide an ideal, self-regulating home environment, the house grows increasingly out of control and begins to terrorize its occupants. The play—as always in Pollesch's work—presents man as a powerless victim of social and technological development.

A similarly critical perspective on the proliferation of technology in the home environment is taken by Rich Gold, an artist and researcher at Xerox PARC where Mark Weiser developed his theory and research on ubiquitous computing. In an essay published back in 1994, Gold pondered, "How smart does your bed have to be, before you are afraid to go to sleep at night?"[1]

Daniel H. Wilson, who has carried out extensive research on the use of sensor technology in the home, seems to be responding to Gold's question with this ironic advice to potential occupants of a "smart house." "Choose an escape route. Starting from your safe place, outline a path to the outside. Make sure there are few sensors along this path, and no effectors (robot arms, etc.) Discuss the route with your family and agree to meet at the safe place during an emergency. (Be sure to have this conversation away from your snooping robot house.)"[2]

The fully computerized house of the future is a product of research in the late 1980s and early 1990s, a time when the personal computer began its triumphal march through the home and technology manufacturers set about upgrading household appliances, once analogue and mechanical machines, into microprocessor-based systems. The development of "intelligent houses" is linked to the hope that invisible, computer-based systems can be integrated into all areas of the home, greatly simplifying life for the occupants. Generally speaking, an "intelligent house" is developed as a complex whole able to autonomously recognize and respond to situations, by and large without the direct intervention of the occupants. A second line of development emerged in the 1990s with the "smart systems" and "smart materials" that emphasized the "interface" between individuals and technological systems and thus took up the idea of direct regulation and control by occupants.

Even though these developments have certainly not run their course, the visions of a total permeation of technology in our living environment have not been fulfilled to date. Moreover, they have not only met with criticism but have also long since hit up against the boundaries of the sensible. Some initial doubts about the usefulness of a highly computerized home were already raised by the TRON House developed and realized in Tokyo from 1988 through 1993, with over 1,000 computer systems in an area of about 200 square meters controlling the air conditioning and atmosphere of the house and monitoring the security and the health of its occupants. In view of such a project, questions were bound to come up regarding the longevity and susceptibility of complex systems, the social ramifications of the surveillance technology, and the actual level of comfort in a fully automated environment.

From today's perspective, the TRON House and subsequent projects seem less like pioneering models of future housing, and more an expression of their time. In the 1990s, the post-industrial age culminated in the information society, shaped by the expansion of the global communication and information system of the Internet. The possibility of locally and globally linked computer systems that can be activated and controlled from anywhere in the world or that react autonomously and dynamically to complex changes and needs was joined by the notion that computer systems are becoming increasingly invisible with their integration in our everyday surroundings. In 1996, Mark Weiser predicted that computers would be integrated over the next twenty years in the most trivial objects, such as clothing, coffee cups, light switches, and pencils, and that in such a world we would no longer just interact with computers, but dwell and live with them.[3]

Mobility versus Fixed Location. Indeed, the progressive miniaturization of hardware components and the parallel gains in computer performance have allowed technology to penetrate our habitat ever more deeply, bringing about clear social and economic transformation. The model of our age is the mobile individual who adapts to this transformation via means of communication and production independent of location and who operates in a global network within which they distribute their products and services. In the post-industrial service society, this way of living has achieved a presence though not yet among a majority of the population, which still understands mobility as the disliked daily commute to the workplace.

Vilém Flusser—himself forced to lead a nomadic life—described the ambivalence of humanity, on the one hand genuinely nomadic and on the other on the longing for a sense of home and homeland. The first half of this dichotomy can be seen in the incessant rise of travel activity around the globe. Travel seems to fulfill the need of many individuals for stimulation, escape from everyday life, and demonstration of affluence. In a US study on the meaning of domestic materiality by the psychologist Mihaly Csikszentmihalyi in the early 1980s, 70 percent of those surveyed said their greatest desire was "a trip."[4]

On the other hand, a number of Western states including Germany have registered a decline or at least no increase in residential mobility, despite the dramatic worsening of the labor market. The geographic flexibility and mobility that society and the marketplace demand of those looking for work almost as a matter of course runs counter to the core human need to create a familiar environment, an enduring sense of home.

It is important to remember here that forced migration has been a constant throughout the history of humanity. Today natural disasters and political and economic conditions still continue to trigger large-scale migratory movements. Yet society has developed behavioral patterns and housing forms that make this forced mobility more bearable and allow for conclusions to be drawn about the psychological significance of the domestic environment.

Home = Relationship to the World. Flusser was of the opinion that the home is a primary human need, even more important than having a homeland. He understood living space as a vital shelter, a small cell constituting one's immediate personal environment: "The Parisian clochards live under bridges, the gypsies in caravans, the Brazilian farm workers in huts, and as appalling as it may sound, people dwelled in Auschwitz….[W]ithout the protection of the customary and the habitual, everything we encounter is noise, nothing is information, and in a world without information, in chaos, one can neither feel nor think nor act."[5]

The home defines the physical as well as the psychological space that individuals shape according to their needs. For instance, an eight-year-old boy in Csikszentmihalyi's survey responded to the question of what the objects in his home meant to him: "They make me feel like I am part of the world."[6] Each of the belongings in his domestic environment represents a certain part of the world as he perceives it. Clearly the personal interpretation of the outside world is reflected in the home and reveals the individual life goals of occupants: "For most people, the home is a church in that it is the place where ultimate goals can be culti-vated, sheltered from the intrusions of public life."[7]

To reflect on the future architecture of residential building, it is not enough to consider technological and formal possibilities; we also need to address the question of how individuals will relate to a potential future world.

Standardization Versus Individualization. The human is being engaged, throughout his life span, in an unceasing struggle to differentiate himself increasingly fully, not only from his human, but also from his nonhuman environment, while developing, in proportion as he succeeds in these differentiations, an increasingly meaningful relatedness with the latter environment as well as with his fellow human beings. —H.F. Searles[8]

As long as there are still geographical, economic, and religious differentiations among groups and societies, the world will continue to exist in a state of heterogeneity without yielding any sort of uniform worldview. In fact, lifestyles are becoming more and more pluralized. In this context, individualization means increasing self-determination in all areas of life. For individualization to proceed, it is hence necessary to eliminate hierarchical structures and replace them with more open, network-like systems that individuals can make use of according to their particular needs and requirements.

It remains to be seen whether individualization is in fact just a phase on the path to a new form of social existence, as posited by Antonio Negri and Michael Hardt. In their view, individualization will be displaced by a new structure of power and action, the multitude, which entails among other things the dissolution of nation states and establishment of world citizenship.[9] For the near future in any case, such a social reorganization seems out of the question against the background of the continuing expansion of networks, globalization, and the inherently associated trend toward individualization.

The progressive differentiation of society increasingly directs attention to individual housing needs in different phases of life and in the context of various life models, subsequently leading to the development of new housing types. The realization of these new housing concepts is slow to occur, however, as such steps toward future housing have to be supported by a gradual change of the economic system on which housing and building are based. At present, changing one's residence and building a home are both associated with relatively significant financial expenditures. As a result, it is relatively rare that people move to a new residence or repeatedly build new homes for themselves despite the increased demands on individual mobility and changing needs in terms of living space throughout the course of life.

Moreover, the theoretical abundance of non-standardized forms of architecture is opposed in many places by standardized regulations, norms, and construction techniques. At the beginning of the last century, with the rise of modern architecture, the incipient industrial production of building components led to an increased in the formal and functional similarity of buildings. In particular, the building codes for public housing from the 1950s through the 1970s that established minimum standards in Germany for things like the size of windows and baths had an impact on the uniformity of private homes.

City Versus Family Zone. Technological and formal standardization is always conspicuously accompanied by a simultaneous social shift. In the transformation from the subject tied by strict social structures to an individual with more self-determination, conventional living and housing models tied to tradition exist alongside innovative, future-oriented concepts. It can be observed that many of older ideals of living continue to have an impact on the present, and will continue to do so in the future, as they are based more on social models than actual human needs.

For instance, the majority of the German population adheres to the desire for a freestanding single-family home or two-family duplex even though a long-term commitment to this form of property ownership conflicts with the altered constellations of households and families and the greater inconstancy over the course of life.[10] Undoubtedly, one of the key reasons for this ambition is the social status represented by having one's own house in a preferably idyllic setting. This ideal of a family domicile away from the hustle and bustle of the city was dominant in Germany the 1960s and 1970s and led to a process of suburbanization, the establishment of a "family zone"[11] on the outskirts of urban areas.

The strong drive to own a home in the open countryside has been viewed critically since the 1960s, and with the continued accumulation of suburban development came under renewed public scrutiny in the 1990s in the Netherlands and elsewhere. In particular, it was criticized that sprawling development outside cities was swallowing up large swaths of the landscape and destroying the ecosystem. In addition, it as also led to new segregation and increased mobility. Yet the public discussion regarding the ecological and social disadvantages of the private home has had no impact whatsoever on construction activities: current forecasts estimate that private home building in the Netherlands, for example, will rise to 30 percent of overall building production in the coming years.[12] While this trend remains undiminished in countries like the Netherlands and the US, a countermovement back to cities can be witnessed elsewhere. The advantages of urban life are clear in times characterized by the dissolution of traditional family structures: the level of infrastructure in urban spaces affords single persons, single parents, and younger people with moderate incomes with a high quality of life. The transformation from an industrial society to a service society furthermore contributes to a densification of cities where services are in great demand. The city moreover offers a "public lifestyle,"[13] a shifting of many formerly private activities and pursuits into the public sphere, which in contrast to the past is now linked to a higher social status. In a society that assesses social status based on access to the material and the immaterial, different life concepts can achieve high social standing parallel to one another. For example, the social status of a family in a suburban home can be the same as that of a single person in an urban apartment. The social standing within a group is ultimately decided by the ideals that emerge in the group and the associated degree of difficulty in attaining these values. For even the individualized self is not free from norms but operates within the norms of the respective network.

Self-Organizing Systems. In the industrialized world, the social upheaval of the 1960s and 1970s led to fundamental reflection on the future of architecture and the organization of social existence. Architects turned their attention to the cities as dynamically changing living spaces and spheres of activity. Although the radical urban utopias of this period went unrealized, they left their mark on contemporary architecture and city planning with an impact that is still felt today. The then-innovative concept of the city as a living organism or even as a metabolism, as a self-organizing system and megastructure, continues to develop and evolve today under the influence of several factors: research advances in biotechnology and artificial intelligence as well as current theories of global societal transformation are bringing about a renaissance of architectural concepts oriented to the structure and functioning of living organisms.

Molecular nanotechnology seems to open up new paths for the independent production of stable structures. Today the vision of using nanotechnology to produce nearly every conceivable stable chemical structure, as put forward by the physicist Richard Feynman in the late 1950s, has become reality, at least in part. Scientists are already able to genetically "program" bacteria to produce human hormones. While this is still far removed from the creation of stable, autonomously growing structures, it is currently an area of intense research activity.

One line of research in this field concentrates on systems that are supposed to "build" the molecular structures. According to K. Eric Drexler, these construction systems of the future are not biological in nature but rather mechanical nano-computers with communicative capabilities that can act in combination to fabricate complex biological structures. These nano-machines are tiny factories the size of a single cell and connected with the organic cell material. They have arms that allow them to build replicas of themselves or other structural elements. Compared to the natural reproduction of cells, the mechanical replicators would be able to produce structures in a much shorter time, with more deliberate and precise targeting and with greater variance. [14]

This technological vision serves as the foundation for the project Dismiss by R&Sie(n)

DISMISS, R&SIE(N)
→ PAGE 116

ORGANICS (WILLIAM KATAVOLOS, 1960)

architects, in the broadest sense a part of the project I've Heard About. I've Heard About is an architectural utopia that does not focus on feasibility but rather represents a realm of possibility. I've Heard About rejects the concept of the singular residential building and contrasts it with an interwoven dynamic urban organism in which the individual parts can be utilized as living space. The architecture is generated by a reactive system, consisting of a biochemical organism and nano-machines.

The project distantly recalls the idea devised by William Katavolos in 1960 of houses that would "organically" grow from chemical substances. In his text "Organics," he spoke of powders and liquids that form volumes and harden while remaining forever adaptable in regard to the desired strengths, predetermined orientations, and estimated periods of time.[15]

In these concepts, the image of the designing architect and an institutional hierarchy is abandoned in favor of self-organizing, self-producing architecture. The occupants of the structure imagined by R&Sie(n) constitute a non-hierarchical society in which the individual can determine his or her personal level of society-building and environment-building work. Yet this future vision of human action seems to run counter to the history of humanity, which shows it is easier to establish hierarchies than to create dynamic networks. Such a reshaping of social structures thus requires a change in consciousness, centering on the transformation of the individual into an active, autonomous member of a decentralized and networked group. In order to achieve this, Dismiss includes a hypnosis chamber to mentally prepare us for such a role. The diversity of the project is matched by the multiplicity of its architectural history references. Among others, R&Sie(n) cites Chaneac as an inspiration, who developed prefabricated living

modules in the 1960s that could be joined together to form private houses or entire developments. Yet Chaneac also envisioned expanding conventional apartment buildings by fixing his living modules onto the exterior façade. Similarly, the hypnosis chamber of Dismiss seems to protrude from of the existing boundaries of the living space. The components of consciousness expanding that Dismiss plays with evoke associations with Haus-Rucker-Co's Mind Expander (1967): a pneumatic helmet in the form of an oversized insect head that was supposed to transport the two persons simultaneously wearing it to another state of consciousness. Dismiss seems to be both a symbiosis and a resolutely contemporary continuation of such historic visions.

Homo faber—man as maker, exploiting the world with the aid of tools—appears in this future scenario as both inhabitant and programmer with access to the source code of the nano-machines. The concept I've Heard About responds actively to the error proneness of highly complex technological and biological systems with the "open source" principle. The open source movement originally demanded the disclosure of programming codes with the goal of continual improvement of these codes. Meanwhile, the demand has expanded to encompass other areas of creative work and intellectual property as well as to equal global access to information and knowledge. The movement is founded on the belief that technological innovation should not be proprietary but should be available to the entire world for humanitarian and ethical reasons.

EscherGuneWardena's Living Kit project adopts this demand for the disclosure of knowledge and seeks to establish a self-organizing network of competence. The conceptual basis of Living Kit is the distribution of information about creative, sustainable, and technical solutions of basic living needs in the non-industrialized world. Living Kit facilitates access to individually designed, non-standardized, and non-industrially produced equipment and building components that can be recreated as needed. While the scenario designed by R&Sie(n) architects points to a quite distant future, Living Kit seems to be within reach as all the prerequisites for implementation are fulfilled: both the communications technology (Internet and telephone) as well as the basis of the distribution network (the infrastructure of locally operating non governmental organizations and local schools) are already in place. The practicability of self-organizing knowledge networks has been demonstrated in the recent past with the emergence of non-commercial information databases like Wikipedia. A requirement for the development and maintenance of such systems is a new understanding on the part of the user that departs from a pure consumer role in favor of active participation.

Life in a Global Network. In the 1990s, the period when current information and communication technology proliferated, many prophesied the end of cities, global democratization, and the rise of a new economy. In fact, no workable new economic concept has managed to establish itself to date and important developments have proceeded in seeming contradiction to one another. While certain occupations and regions have seen a rise in decentralization, cities continue to become more concentrated as physical nodal points in cyberspace despite broadband connections and real time flow of data. The Internet facilitates the development of new, less hierarchical and decentralized groups, yet at the same time old economic systems are also gaining in power and impact, inevitably leading to increasing social and economic segregation at the local and global levels.[16] Living Kit counters this negative development by offering a network-based distribution concept that attempts to balance out the disadvantages of globalization, in this case increasing segregation, with its advantages: the rapid dissemination of information via communication networks.

Communication networks also serve as the basis for the Megahouse scenario developed by Hitoshi Abe and Tohru Horiguchi. While this initially constitutes a local distribution system for living space in Tokyo, it is theoretically capable of being expanded into a world-encompassing system. As with Living Kit, the focus of the Megahouse concept is not on the design of new architecture but on the intelligent use of existing technologies and infrastructures to optimize quality of life. Vacant spaces in the city are made available for temporary usage, allowing system users to move within the urban space as if in a large building and to explore this space according to their own individual needs. In contrast to Living Kit with its foundation on non-commercial principles, the economic system of Megahouse, while operating through online booking, is otherwise a traditional commercial trading system.

This quite practicable concept is especially interesting in view of its manifold implications: it envisions a user who is extremely mobile and maintains a profoundly specialized lifestyle that cannot be entirely satisfied by private living quarters or by public space. In particular, the two furnishing variants of the spaces to be rented—BrandRoom and CharacterHouse, representing artificial worlds—can be interpreted as indications of a pseudo-individualization, as critically identified by the sociologist and philosopher Georg Simmel back in 1903 in regard to urban society.[17] The pluralism of

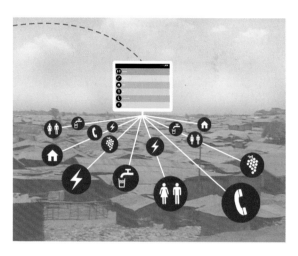

LIVINGKIT, ESCHERGUNEWARDENA ARCHITECTURE
→ **PAGE 106**

MEGAHOUSE, HITOSHI ABE
→ **PAGE 100**

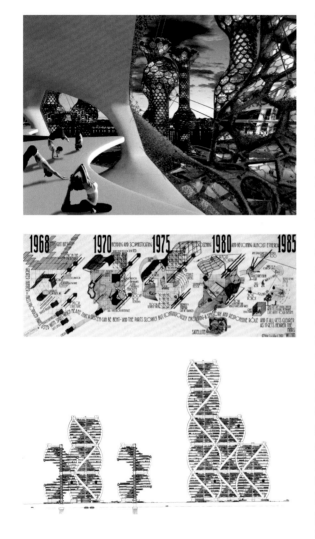

SEOUL COMMUNE 2026: RETHINKING "TOWERS IN THE PARK," MASSSTUDIES
→ PAGE 56

CONTROL AND CHOICE (ARCHIGRAM, 1968)

MANIFESTO OF METABOLISM KISHO KUROKAWA, HELIX CITY PLAN FOR TOKYO, ELEVATION, 1961

lifestyles furthered by the city, accompanied by a cultivation of the subjective, can lead to an artificial individuality under the pressure of urban complexity and the lack of creativity, which is channeled in the adaptation of brand and star images. Megahouse thus describes one of the drawbacks affecting not only urban life but also globalized, media-defined society in which the individual has to choose from a vast, nearly incomprehensible multitude of options.

Living in the Local Community. To the same extent that Megahouse reflects the problems of a mobile and media-saturated society, the project offers answers to a wide range of contemporary developments in the industrialized world that will continue into the future, such as the vacancy of buildings due to decreasing population or fluctuation within the city. Another evident trend is the need for ever-larger living space despite the shrinking size of households. In principle, this continuous increase in housing space paired with declining birth rates and the growth of single households does not constitute a spatial problem, though it could result in problems of a social nature. Large numbers of the population in the Western world already live alone during long periods of life and these phases are becoming even more prolonged with the further dissolution of traditional family structures and the overall increase of life expectancy. The phase between moving from the parental home and establishing one's own family is becoming longer; the same is true of the late phase of life in which older people are often left alone without a partner.

The social isolation that can ensue from such solitary living situations is treated by the project Seoul Commune 2026: Rethinking "Towers in the Park" by Massstudies, which foresees the communal use of living space. In its assumption that the classic home model is unable to fulfill the varied living space needs of occupants, Seoul Commune 2026 is certainly related to Megahouse. The important difference is that the former envisions a newly constructed high-rise complex to provide the different spaces instead of using the extant structure of the city. Seoul Commune 2026 also utilizes existing communication technology as the management system for the collectively used living areas.

Seoul Commune 2026 combines architectural visions of the 1960s, like Archigram's "Control and Choice" and the megastructures of the Metabolists, with the goal of sustainable and above all socially effective architecture. The concept again contains the idea of a self-organizing community with the help of new technologies. Private space is restricted to a small unit in the core of the buildings and the high-rises feature a broad spectrum of semi-private and public spaces that are open to all residents. The subdivision of the buildings into modular units makes it possible to adjust the living area to changing spatial in the course of a lifetime and thus supports the coexistence of the different generations.

Opening of the Floor Plan Versus Privacy. This modularization of living space and the associated distribution of living areas and activities in a multitude of rooms and spaces, as proposed on a small scale by Seoul Commune 2026 and with greater magnitude by Mega-house, can be seen as an alternative to the principle of the open floor plan. The open or free floor plan goes back to Le Corbusier and refers to a functional organization of space that treats the entire enclosed volume as a coherent continuum and not as a combination of self-contained sub-areas or uses. One goal of this "flowing" space is its multifunctionality and the flexible use of the different areas. The aesthetic advantages of the open floor plan are offset by the problem of simultaneous use of the space by multiple occupants, which can lead to acoustic, visual, and olfactory disturbances among the residents. Depending on the radicalism with which the principle is implemented, the opening of the floor plan can also mean the loss of private retreat areas for residents, which are actually of central importance for such community-based models of living.

Csikszentmihalyi established that in most cases children prefer to spend time in their own room while women feel most comfortable in the kitchen and men in their workroom.[18] This research finding undoubtedly represents a small segment of a population with a conservative lifestyle. Nevertheless, it allows general conclusions to be drawn about the importance of spaces that offer the possibility of retreat while also being the site of favorite activities. The existence of a space seen as private, individually designed according to personal notions and preferences, seems to be a basic requirement for transforming living space into a home.

It remains to be seen whether increasingly mobile lifestyles will cause these private refuges to be stripped of their physical existence and replaced with immaterial, media-based representations. The first steps toward a dematerialization and de-privatization of the private can be recognized in the phenomenon of blogging and the success of public-private photo sharing databases like Flickr. In a time when the PC not only serves as a gateway to the world but also in a figurative sense as a workplace, hobby room, and personal archive, the physically tangible symbols of home might gradually lose their significance.

A clear differentiation of the home into private and public spaces did not occur in Europe until the eighteenth and nineteenth centuries. Previously, from fifteenth to the seventeenth century, mobile furniture like folding tables and portable bathtubs facilitated the multifunctional use of rooms. It was common practice to receive visitors in the main room of the house, which also served as a bedroom. There was no such thing as a personal room for the individual occupants. It was only once greater value was placed on the individuality of each family member that living space became personalized.[19]

The compact bath with toilet and bathtub in one room that constitutes the current standard in homebuilding did not even come into being until the mid-nineteenth century in the United States. In today's extremely complex and fast-paced world, the bathroom is more and more becoming a highly private realm, a domestic oasis of wellness, and perhaps a health centre as well in the near future thanks to digital diagnostic technology. The project Thinking Ahead by Rojkind Arquitectos places a bathroom with expanded medical functions in the center of the home, both spatially and conceptually. In this conception of a house that continues to meet the needs of occupants in old age, the bath constitutes a private core and retreat area in an otherwise open and spatially flowing living environment. The proposal reacts to the fact that the average time spent in the bathroom increases with age while physical mobility becomes more diminished. The standardized bath, usually built without handrails and other aids for the bathtub or shower and characterized by smooth and thus potentially slippery surfaces, is generally unsuitable for older people: in a Swiss survey on living spaces, 60 percent of respondents 65 to 74 years of age indicated that their own bathrooms were problematic for them.[20] At present, the altered bath-

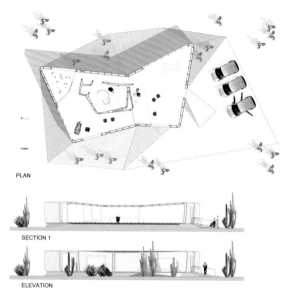

PLAN

SECTION 1

ELEVATION

**THINKING AHEAD!,
ROJKIND ARQUITECTOS
→ PAGE 80**

room needs of elderly occupants can only be accommodated by undertaking extensive remodeling or by moving to a new residence. It is precisely older individuals, however, who have difficulty getting used to a new living space and new technologies.

Experience Architecture. A major challenge faced by architects, designers, and the consumer electronics industry in the twentieth century is balancing the relationship between sensory stimulation from dynamic media presentations and spatial situations on the one hand and the feeling of security and well-being that arises from the constancy of the living environment on the other.

In the traditional domestic architecture of the twentieth century, home meant a constant, steady environment into which media like radio and television gradually found their way, but without really influencing the fundamental architectural conception. Changes in the living space remained limited to refurnishing and redecoration. A stimulation of the senses or the mind with art and other intensive processes of reception occurred primarily outside the home in the public sphere.

In their potential implementation in architectural elements as well as their ability to generate atmospheres, networked digital media make it feasible to achieve a continuous dynamization of living space. The discipline of architecture in the twenty-first century is challenged not only to integrate these "technologies of stimulation" in a sensible way but also to redefine the relationship between the spatial experience of built form, up to now at the fore, and the experience of media. The use of audio-visual media to positively influence the atmosphere of interiors is nothing new. In the 1930s, some American dental practices began to play

a continual stream of music to soothe and distract the patients. During the Second World War, background music was piped in to motivate the workers in the British munitions factories. Muzak was an American company founded in the 1920s that explored the stimulatory value of music for creating an optimal work atmosphere, subsequently developing an unobtrusive, largely repetitive musical program that would be described today as "ambient." Musical numbers that got an especially positive response and were actively requested by listeners were consistently deleted from the play list to create an atmosphere maintaining a uniform level of stimulation.[21]

Of course, individuals create environments that they find pleasant. While the visual quality of private architecture is generally accorded great value, the aural tone and harmony within the architecture is only gradually becoming the subject of focused attention. In creating garden architecture as well as in shaping the light situations in buildings that change over the course of the day, dynamic processes are staged to enable an ever-variable aesthetic experience of the surrounding environment. In addition, changes in the surroundings are important chronological and spatial reference points in psychological processes like memory. People typically link situations they experience with the sensory stimuli of that particular environment.

Architects are increasingly paying attention to the design of dynamic processes in architecture by developing buildings that make use of new technologies as time-based and dynamic systems. Through the slowly changing patterns and the alterations of the light and colors in the building's external skin, the Jellyfish House by IwamotoScott follows the principle of an understated environment made dynamic

by incorporating media elements. The limited variance of the manifestations and the smooth transitions between the different states allow both deliberate, selective observation as well as passive, unconscious perception.

This choice is also available to occupants of the Mix House, a concept based entirely on the generation of tonal experiences. The team of Joel Sanders, Ben Rubin, and Karen van Lengen has conceived a house devoted to the linking of the auditory and visual. The acoustic design creates spaces within the building and areas with different tonal qualities. In addition, the house is outfitted with a number of media-based tonal channels that are linked together in the interior and exterior spaces. These can be adjusted to have more of a background presence or to temporarily command the focus of perception. It is fully up to the occupants to decide how they wish to use the system on a daily basis and what external sound sources they want to welcome into the home.

In this context, a radical concept is presented by the project Electroplex Heights from Ben Hooker and Shona Kitchen. Issuing forth from a similar idea, a linking of the interior and exterior through media, Hooker and Kitchen developed a scenario in which the perception of an urban industrial environment can be accepted as an aesthetic experience and processed using different electronic media. The resulting dynamization of the space recalls Constant's New Babylon as well as Nicolas Schöffer's kinetic architecture. And like Ville Spatiale by Yona Friedman, Hooker and Kitchen propose a residential complex erected on stilts over an area that is already built-up to a certain degree. With the difference that Hooker and Kitchen's Electroplex Heights makes a new housing zone out of the industrial and commercial areas intersected by motorways, power lines, and

SUSANNE JASCHKO

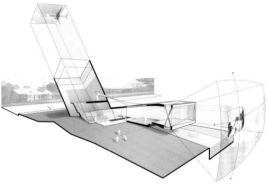

10 m

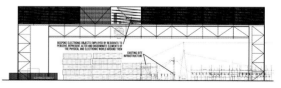

ELECTROPLEX HEIGHTS ↑

**NEW BABYLON (CONSTANT
ANTON NIEUWENHUIYS, 1971)
VIEW OF NEW BABYLONIAN
SECTORS**

SUSANNE JASCHKO

antenna towers that surround today's urban agglomerations. In the digital age, the project thus supplies a contemporary counterpart to the galleries and lofts in former factory buildings that came into fashion in the 1970s and 1980s and have long since led to the gentrification of formerly industrial districts within the city. As odd as it may seem, we already view certain artificial surroundings as aesthetically attractive. For instance, we commonly find visual appeal in the lights of the city, the blinking of a television tower, and the flow of automobile taillights.

The energy flows form a space that is dynamic and heterogeneous, in contrast to structural space. The theory of energetically formed spaces, with campfires being one of the first examples, goes back to Reyner Banham. [22] Light, warmth, and sound are capable of forming energetic spaces; modern media can channel, bundle, and intensify these energy flows. The systems of Electroplex Heights and Mix House thus act to create spaces within a structural space through energy. The solid structure of the built architecture is certainly still a subject of the design process, although a dynamic architecture of energy flows is added to this static framework.

Both projects represent a media-based form of transparency that distances itself from modern glass façade architecture while also taking it further with the help of digital technology. Considering the buildings currently being realized, the glass façade is still a popular standard of respectable architecture. The principle has not become established in residential building, for it runs counter to the existential human need for privacy in living quarters. If applied deliberately and selectively and not throughout the entire building, transparency can enhance the spatial experience, enrich the

perception of the surroundings, and stimulate the senses.

With awareness of this effect, Japanese architecture in the sixteenth and seventeenth centuries defined a type of space that simultaneously joins and separates the interior and exterior: *en* is a veranda that encircles the building, serving as a transitional zone for interaction and the interface between the architecture and its surroundings. With the two planes defining the space (building wall/exterior environment) and the different partly overlapping and variable layers, the veranda enables highly differentiated and flexible shaping of vistas, privacy from outside, and protection from the elements. [23] With paper screens that can be shifted horizontally, bamboo roller blinds that move up and down, and other features, the space can be easily adapted to the varying needs throughout the different seasons of the year.

realities:united's Open the House! attempts the opening of the structural space to allow an intensive experience of interior and exterior space on the basis of new technologies. With the aid of a new type of "climatic skin," a mobile, energetically shaped space, the occupant is freed from the inhabitation of closed spaces. Opened up to the exterior, the resulting living areas offer a realm for interpersonal interaction and intensive sensory impressions similar to the Japanese en generated through closer contact with the dynamically changing surrounding environment.

Sustainability and Development of Organic Architecture. In the 1960s, Buckminster Fuller and Athelstan Spilhaus still envisioned a complete or partial roofing over of the city to make the inhabitants less dependent on weather, raise their level of comfort and, as a side effect, to

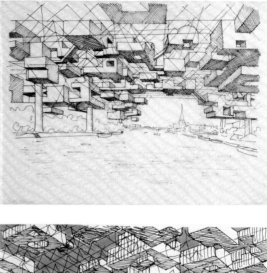

PARIS SPATIAL (YONA FRIEDMAN, 1960)

VILLE SPATIALE (YONA FRIEDMAN, 1960)

OPEN THE HOUSE!,
REALITIES:UNITED
→ PAGE 110

DUNEHOUSE, **SU11**
ARCHITECTURE+DESIGN
→ PAGE 70

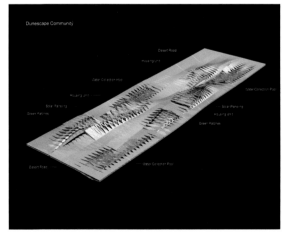

save on energy costs. Today, however, the constantly rising consumption of energy, the finiteness of fossil fuels, and global climate change are prompting an intensive search for energy-conserving systems and autonomous energy cycles. The project Open the House! seeks to apply "intelligent" textiles to keep the spaces that need to be heated and therefore require energy as small as possible. This is an intuitive solution when considering that each person has his or her own sense of thermal comfort and that temperate climate zones have seen a historic development toward ever-increasing room temperatures. [24]

Sustainability in no way means a minimization of comfort, as was often misinterpreted in the mid-1990s. Instead, the term sustainability stands for the abolishment of a conventional way of thinking rooted in industrialization in favor of a stronger adherence to natural systems, with the aim of increasing the quality of life and comfort of society today and in the future. Against this backdrop, it becomes apparent that today's development of sustainable architecture is closely linked with the modes of operation and forms of organic systems. Biomimicry, the application of principles that come from nature in the designing of systems, increasingly serves as the basis of architectural design. This trend is rooted in the conviction that natural biological systems have been shaped "intelligently" by evolution. In addition, the orientation to organic systems results in an aesthetic that itself allows new experiences of space. The molecular growth upon which I've Heard About and Dismiss are based yields biomorphous forms.

In designing the building's outer skin as a load-bearing structure, Dunehouse and Jellyfish House both refer to natural systems. With similarities to a cellular organism, the modular

SUSANNE JASCHKO

structure of Dunehouse by su 11 enables the design of a building that fits in smoothly with the natural surroundings. The basic shape of Dunehouse derives from the geomorphous forms of the surroundings and changes depending on the site of the building.

The shell of the Jellyfish House is derived from the membranous skin of the jellyfish, taking this as the model for its active, constructive composition. In a similar fashion, the functional building shell of Primitive Hut for the 21st Century by Sean Godsell Architects refers to the functions of human skin and acts as an interface between the extreme climatic conditions of the surrounding environment and the interior. The shell is formed from tubular segments that evenly enclose the entire building like cells. Solar cells and sprinklers integrated into the outer skin allow for sustainable use of resources. The exterior structural elements of Dunehouse and Jellyfish House are likewise outfitted with a variety of existing heating and energy conversion technologies as well as others that are still in development, all intended to make residential buildings less dependent on fossil energy sources.

In all cases, the building's outer skin is much more than just a functional element, but rather a form of expression and a mode of communications. Upholding Frank Lloyd Wright's fundamental precept that architecture should be organic and adapt in form and material to the circumstances of the building site, the forms of Dunehouse and Jellyfish House respond to the natural surroundings. They not only enter a formal relationship with their environment but also make use of its specific characteristics to produce energy and raw materials in an ecological manner, representing a resolute development of organic architecture on the path towards sustainability.

Façade as Interface. The term façade can be etymologically traced to the Latin word facies for face. And in the same way that the face acts as the medium of human expression, the façade can be understood as the means of expression and communications. Today's innovative light and visual media and the dynamic real time control and regulation of such provide for new possibilities of expression in the façade. These are currently being explored as a medium by artists, architects, and designers; an early example of this, the Tower of the Winds project, was already presented as a trendsetting concept in 1986. For an underground shopping centre in Yokohama, Toyo Ito developed a ventilation tower with a façade that reacts to such factors as the speed of the exiting exhaust, thus using abstract visualization to communicate otherwise invisible internal process to the outside world. The Jellyfish House uses this principle as its point of departure. Here the visual manifestation of the façade changes according to the conversion of energy occurring within the building shell, making these internal processes visible to neighbors and passers by.

To an even greater degree than a glass façade, the media façade communicates the dynamic internal processes and thus conveys an impression of activity. In addition, façades are conceptually designed as large projection walls that play a constant stream of animated images. In all cases, these media façades have a tremendous impact on the immediate context and users of the space, as the expansive dynamic surfaces inevitably become the focus of attention. Against the background of the theory of energetically shaped rooms, a building with a media façade modulates the entire surrounding environment, as the energetic space reaches far beyond the borders of the structural space. The perception of such a building makes it a central

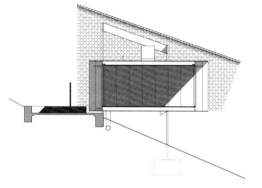

PRIMITIVE HUT FOR THE 21ST CENTURY , SEAN GODSELL ARCHITECTS → PAGE 76

TOWER OF WINDS, KANAGAWA, JAPAN (TOYO ITO & ASSOCIATES, ARCHITECTS, 1986)

focal point within the urban space, both up close and at a distance.

Summary. Contemporary apartment construction and homebuilding are confronted with the major challenge of developing new typologies of residential building from among the many given technical and formal possibilities in a way that fulfils current and future needs of occupants better than present-day standard architecture. As much as the diversity of life patterns and personal values calls for individual concepts, it is also important to consider the economic reality of residential construction, which requires developing new basic concepts capable of being adjusted to individuals as needed.

In this context, the designs presented in the exhibition should not be merely viewed as individual solutions but rather as points of departure for new typologies of living and housing. Even though the projects of Open House point in different conceptual directions, this is no way rules out of the fusion of concepts: architecture geared toward sustainability, for instance, can and should take into account all basic needs of the modern individual whenever possible. This holistic approach is already evident in many of the projects presented.

Interestingly, the current rapid spread of technology in our everyday lives with the need for constant updates and continuous accessibility seems to be producing two diametrically opposed trends: on the one hand, a complete acceptance of this development expressed in the integration of technology in all areas of life and objects and on the other hand a turn away from a technology-permeated environment and the search for more natural ways of life. The majority will position themselves somewhere between these two extremes on the spectrum. For them, the concepts presented in the context of Open House offer reference points for examining their own needs and beliefs and a basis for making more conscious lifestyle and housing decisions.

SUSANNE JASCHKO

1 Rich Gold, "How smart does your bed have to be, before you are afraid to go to sleep at night?", *Ars Electronica 94, Intelligente Ambiente*, Vol. 1, Vienna, 1994, p. 187.

2 Daniel H. Wilson, *How to Survive a Robot Uprising: Tips on Defending Yourself Against the Coming Rebellion*, New York, 2005, p. 53.

3 Mark Weiser, "Open House," *ITP Review 2.0* (March 1996), p. 3.

4 Mihaly Csikszentmihalyi and Eugene Rochberg-Halton, *The Meaning of Things: Domestic Symbols and the Self,* Cambridge (UK), 1981, p. 148.

5 Vilém Flusser, Bodenlos: *Eine philosophische Autobiographie*, Düsseldorf/Bensheim, 1992.

6 Csikszentmihalyi and Rochberg-Halton, *The Meaning of Things*, p. 139.

7 Ibid., p. 123.

8 H.F. Searles in Csikszentmihalyi and Rochberg-Halton, *The Meaning of Things*, p. 39.

9 Antonio Negri and Michael Hardt, *Empire*, Cambridge (Mass.), 2000.

10 Nicole Schneider and Annette Spellerberg, *Lebensstile, Wohnbedürfnisse und räumliche Mobilität*, Opladen, 1999, p. 167.

11 Ibid., p. 73.

12 Bart Lootsma, "Individualisierung," *Arch +: Zeitschrift für Architektur und Städtebau*, 158 (December 2001), p. 42.

13 Hartmut Häußermann and Walter Siebel, *Neue Urbanität*, Frankfurt am Main, 1987, p. 15.

14 K. Eric Drexler, *Engines of Creation: The Coming Era of Nanotechnology*, New York, 1986, Chapter 4, "Engines of Abundance".

15 William Katavolos, "Organics," *Programme und Manifeste zur Architektur des 20. Jahrhunderts*, ed. Ulrich Conrads, Frankfurt, Berlin, 1964, p. 157.

16 See Manuel Castell's "The Information City is a Dual City: Can it be reversed?," *High Technology and Low-Income Communities: Prospects for the Positive Use of Advanced Information Technology*, eds. Donald A. Schön, Bish Sanyal, and William J. Mitchell, Cambridge (Mass.), 1998.

17 Georg Simmel, "Die Großstädte und das Geistesleben," *Aufsätze und Abhandlungen 1901–1908, Gesamtaufgabe* (Vol. 7) Frankfurt/M., 1990.

18 Csikszentmihalyi and Rochberg-Halton, *The Meaning of Things*, pp. 136 ff.

19 Witbold Rybczynski, *Wohnen: Über den Verlust der Behaglichkeit*, Munich, 1987, pp. 45, 126 (original title: *Home*, 1986).

20 Francois Höpflinger, *Age Report 2004: Traditionelles und neues Wohnen im Alter*, Zurich, 2004, p. 82.

21 AUDC/Robert Sumrell and Kazys Varanelis, "The Stimulus Progression. Muzak and the Culture of Horizontality," *Conditioning; The Design of New Atmospheres, Effects and Experiences, (Verb. Exploring the Potentials of Architectural Identity in the Age of Real Artificiality*, vol. 4), Barcelona, 2005, pp. 106–21.

22 Philipp Oswalt, "Die Architektur intelligenter Gebäude," *Thesis: Wissenschaftliche Zeitung der Bauhaushochschule Weimar* (1997). Oswalt refers in his text to Reyner Banham and the theories he developed in the book *The Architecture of the Well-Tempered Environment*.

23 Matthias Loebermann, "Transparenz heute," *Arch+ Zeitschrift für Architektur und Städtebau*, 45. 144 (December 1998), p. 100. Loebermann in turn refers to Günther Nischke, "en – Raum für Interaktionen," *Daidalos*, 9.33 (1989).

24 Wolfgang Feist, *Das Niedrigenergiehaus: Energiesparen im Wohnungsbau der Zukunft*, Karlsruhe, 1989, p. 129

New Spaces, New Materials ¶

> CHRISTIANE SAUER

Technology Transfer. The classic activity of the architect has been the creation of built space. Yet in recent years, the element that defines this space—the boundary—is steadily moving into the focus of architectural interest. New technologies and developments are continually expanding the design repertoire. The traditional building materials—glass, steel, stone and wood—are no longer exclusive categories: composites, sandwich materials, and other hybrids that unite the positive properties of several different substances in one product are proliferating. Aluminum foam, "liquid wood," and translucent concrete are no longer tomorrow's vision, but today's reality.

These innovations are attracting a great deal of attention, yet for technical reasons many aesthetically interesting surface materials still have very limited applications in the building sector. Façade cladding must meet especially stringent standards with regard to fire resistance and UV absorption. Experimentation is more feasible in the design of interiors and individual objects, since the issue of durability does not have the same priority in these areas.

Designers have shown an interest in innovative materials long before now, often testing the limits of conventional materials and making new discoveries. Charles and Ray Eames, for example, constructed their DAX Dining Armchair in 1948 with a material that was at that time unfamiliar in the field of design: fiberglass-reinforced polyester resin. They first encountered this material in the aeronautics industry; during the Second World War, radome nose cones for military aircraft were made of fiberglass. The Eameses embraced the industrial aesthetic and left the surface of the chair unupholstered, so that the layered strands of glass remained visible.

The development of innovative materials typically takes place in industries other than the building sector. The financial and technological capabilities to generate experimental materials are found in the domains of aviation, space, automobiles and the military. The process usually follows a similar scheme: initially, a new material is developed for a very specific purpose at a high investment cost. After the product has proven itself in the high-tech industry, it is "spun off" and adapted for broader commercial applications. For this reason, many of the so-called "new"

DAX ARMCHAIR (CHARLES AND RAY EAMES, 1948–50; COLLECTION VITRA DESIGN MUSEUM)

AEROGEL, AN EXTREMELY LIGHT AND HIGHLY INSULATING MATERIAL, WAS ALREADY DEVELOPED IN THE 1930S AND WAS USED BY NASA SINCE THE 1970S.

materials are not really new at all, but have been established in other market segments for decades. For example, the super-insulating, high-tech nano-material aerogel was invented over 70 years ago. The first silica aerogels were developed in the aerospace industry; NASA has used aerogel as insulation for space suits and spacecraft since the 1990s. The material is made of as much as 99.8 percent air, which is enclosed in nano-scale pores, making it an ideal insulator. Aerogel has recently been processed in granular form for building applications—after a lead time of more than half a century. Architects are discovering not only the technological advantages of such innovations, but also new design options. A façade with aerogel combines the properties of insulation, light transmission and the delineation of space in a single lightweight building element.

Not only new materials, but also new forms have been prominent topics in the architectural discourse of the past decade. The formal experimentation of the 1990s was similarly aided by groundbreaking technologies from other industries. The office of Frank O. Gehry has adapted the software CATIA, produced by a French aircraft manufacturer, to an architectural platform in order to facilitate the digital modeling of Gehry's complex aesthetic visions. An amorphous design vocabulary has been used especially by the younger generation of architects in their exploration of the "free form" and flowing spaces. The "blob"—as the complex, transmutable and biomorphic forms of digital architecture have come to be called—has attained the status of a new architectural style.

There is still a great discrepancy between what can be calculated and visualized on a computer and what can be built. The challenge lies in the physical realization of digital images. What material can be used to create a free-

flowing space and simultaneously serve as a floor, wall, ceiling, and furniture? The conventional building industry has yet to offer marketable solutions to such questions. Architects in pursuit of suitable materials must be prepared to search off the beaten track.

That is precisely what Maurice Nio has done. In 2003, the Rotterdam-based architect designed a 50-meter-long bus station. He envisioned a strongly emblematic structure that would contrast with the dry pragmatism of the building's function: a curving organic form, both mystical and modern at the same time. The monolithic structure was developed with 3D computer software. Initially, Nio considered the classic medium of concrete for the realization of his building; however, this proved too expensive due to the complexity of the formwork that would be required. The architect finally discovered a suitable material in the field of boat construction: the finished form was carved out of polystyrene foam and coated with fiberglass-reinforced polyester, similar to the construction of a surfboard. For the purpose of handling, the form was digitally divided into 100 individual components. These data were transmitted to a five-axis CNC milling machine, which produced the load-bearing foam core. Additive hierarchical detailing was unnecessary: all of the furniture elements were carved out of the overall shape and manufactured in a single step as part of the load-bearing structure. The individual pieces were assembled on site, glued together, and again covered with a protective polyester skin. The result is the world's largest building structure to date made completely of synthetic materials.

While new processing methods are affecting the utilization of various materials, experimental research is leading to changes in their actual properties. An adept combination

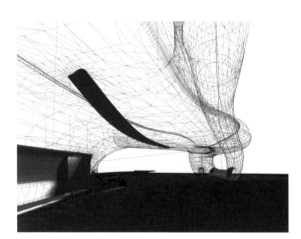

< HOOFDDORP BUS STATION, HOOFDORP, THE NETHERLANDS (NIO ARCHITECTS, 1999–2003) MEASURING 150 X 30 X 15 FEET, THE BUS STATION IS THE WORLD'S LARGEST STRUCTURE MADE OF PLASTIC.

ARTIST'S RENDERING OF HOOFDDORP BUS STATION, HOOFDDORP, THE NETHERLANDS (NIO ARCHITECTS, 1999–2003)

DETAIL, HOOFDDORP BUS STATION, THE NETHERLANDS (NIO ARCHITECTS, 1999–2003)

ELECTRONICALLY-CONTROLLED MILLING MACHINE WORKING ON POLYSTYRENE FOAM FOR USE IN HOOFDDORP BUS STATION

of materials can produce new surfaces with versatile functions and a novel aesthetic appearance. Translucent concrete is a much-touted example: a material long familiar as a densely solid, opaque mass now glows with light. The layering of glass fibers into the concrete matrix allows the finished product to transmit light, giving it an elegant, lightweight appearance. Since only four percent of the concrete is replaced by glass, it still retains its strength and load-bearing capability, but has a completely different visual effect.

Innovations in the realm of nanotechnology, invisible to the naked eye, follow a completely different concept. Indeed, one of the most exceptional qualities of such new functional coatings is that they cannot be seen. The engineer Werner Sobek is exploiting these super-thin materials to realize his vision of transparent, ecological architecture. In Case Study R 129, a project for a multi-purpose structure, all of the functions of the building envelope, such as sun protection, heat regulation and energy supply, are controlled by nano-scale films and coatings. Thanks to the application of an electrochromic film, the transparent façade can be darkened or made completely opaque either in sections or as a whole. The visible architecture merely comprises a self-supporting transparent skin in the shape of a dewdrop and filigree carbon frame structures for the elements that open. Like a soap bubble, the building envelope is reduced to an absolute minimum.

The concept of the façade as a functional system of layers has gained increasing relevance in recent years. Like the human skin, the building envelope of the future should be capable of performing various tasks: a filtering membrane that is both protective and porous, and that reacts to diverging temperatures and other external climate conditions. Another worthwhile

aim in the development of façade systems is autonomous renewal at specified intervals or self-repair in case of damage. The respective technologies already exist.

Smart Materials. The adjective "smart" or intelligent" is often encountered in connection with new developments in the area of materials technology. No material is actually "intelligent" in the sense that it possesses cognitive abilities. Rather, the term refers to the capacity of a material to respond to certain signals from the surrounding environment. The reaction is not controlled by an electronic system, but is initiated by the material itself on the basis of its inherent properties or chemical composition.

Surfaces that can change their color or degree of transparency by means of photochromic or thermochromic coatings present interesting design options. A photochromic coating reacts to ultraviolet radiation by darkening, due to a change in its molecular structure that causes it to selectively absorb or transmit certain wavelengths. A thermochromic film, on the other hand, is heat sensitive, and changes color or becomes transparent depending on the ambient temperature. A small electric current functions as a switching mechanism for electrochromic coating that control the degree to which light is absorbed or reflected.

These are enticing possibilities, especially in the context of architectural applications. It is easy to imagine a sun-blocking glass that darkens at the push of a button, or a building that changes its color according to the outside temperature. There is still a considerable amount of development work to be done, however, before such scenarios become reality. As of yet, such coatings tend to degrade upon prolonged exposure to UV radiation, and the technologies that control them are susceptible to malfunc-

LITRACON™: A LIGHT-TRANSMITTING CONCRETE INVENTED BY THE ARCHITECT ÁRON LOSONCZI IN 2002

> HOUSE R 129, STUDY (WERNER SOBEK AND MAREN SOSTMANN, 2001)

CHRISTIANE SAUER

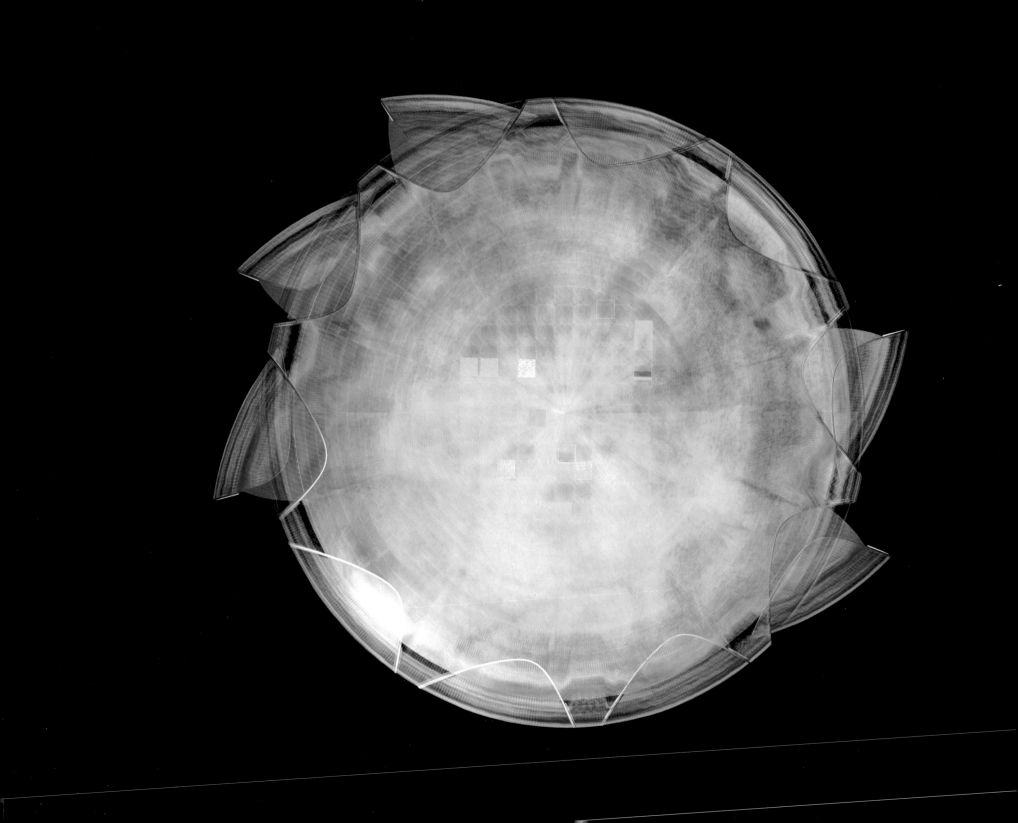

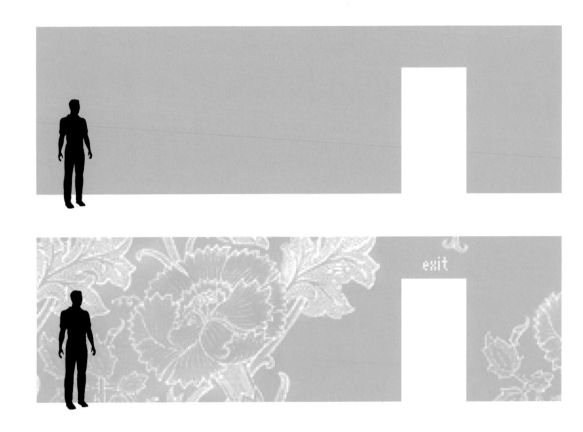

PIXELPAPER (SIMON
HEIJDENS, 2006)

tion. Architects will have to exercise patience with regard to the availability of practical building products. But in the areas of interior architecture and product design, a number of prototypes and marketable products with intelligent surfaces have already been introduced.

Pixelpaper, a transmutable material that can change the designation or mood of a room, was conceived by Simon Heijdens in 2005. This "moving wallpaper" can reproduce any photograph or graphic image by means of pixels measuring 2.5 x 2.5 centimeters that are capable of changing color. The functional concept is based on thermochromic pigments that are activated by a thermally conductive backing. The idea is comparable to a computer monitor, except that this material is flexible and available in standard wallpaper dimensions. Individual pixels require approximately two seconds to change their color, which creates flowing transitions between images and makes it possible to create an interior with constantly changing patterns. Supplemental light sources are unnecessary, because the thermochromic transition is determined by the structure of the pigments. It is precisely the apparent simplicity of the transformation that makes this project so enticing.

A collaboration between the interactive media agency ART+COM and the Berlin-based architectural office Hoyer Schindele Hirschmüller + Partners also explores the activation of surfaces that define spatial borders. ART+COM has devised dynamic and responsive LED ceilings for the Reactive Gap House, a residential building project of this architectural firm. The "floating" structure is to fill a gap between the upper stories—the ground floor will remain open—of a typical nineteenth-century housing block. The three-to-five meter wide passage is a common feature of Berlin city

CHRISTIANE SAUER

blocks with peripheral residential structures surrounding a large interior courtyard that serves as a playground or park-like space for residents. The architects have already completed a similar project in the Berlin neighbourhood Prenzlauer Berg. The advantage of this concept is that the utilization of "airspace" between otherwise contiguous buildings, which are often located in central areas, is much less expensive than building on a normal site. A challenge to the architects is presented by the long and narrow shape of the passageway, which greatly restricts exposure to natural light. The narrowness of the "inserted" structure also requires the longitudinal (and therefore sequential) disposition of rooms across the depth of the building. For this reason, ART+COM have proposed floor/ceiling assemblies between stories with integrated monochromic LED panels covered by translucent glass. This would create a homogeneous, dynamic surface that could respond to the position and movements of occupants or passers-by with the aid of a videotracking system. The system would offer either constant, evenly distributed lighting or directional lighting that "follows" occupants through the rooms. In a manner analogous to Pixelpaper, it would also be possible to animate the LED ceilings. For the new BMW Museum in Munich, which will open in 2007, ART+COM have designed responsive LED walls with a surface area of 600 square meters based on the same principle as the Berlin case study.

Another option for changing the properties of materials is liquid crystal technology. Liquid crystals—as the name indicates—are an intermediate phase between crystalline solids and isotropic liquids. When an electric current is applied to a "smart" window (or suspended particle display), the liquid crystals in the intermediate layer assume a parallel

REACTIVE GAP HOUSE, BERLIN (HOYER, SCHINDELE, HIRSCHMÜLLER & PARTNER, AND ART+COM, 2005)
THIS IMAGE, PART OF A STUDY FOR THE 6TH ARCHITECTURE BIENNALE IN SAO PAULO, DEMONSTRATES THE ANIMATION POSSIBILITIES OF THE LED CEILINGS.

REACTIVE GAP HOUSE, BERLIN (HOYER, SCHINDELE, HIRSCHMÜLLER & PARTNER, AND ART+COM, 2005)
THE LIGHT OF THE LED CEILING WOULD BE CAPABLE OF FOLLOWING PERSONS MOVING THROUGH THE APARTMENT.

PRADA EPICENTERS (REM KOOLHAAS/OMA, 2001/2004) INTERACTIVE CHANGING ROOMS WITH SGG PRIVA_LITE® GLASS VERTICAL PARTITIONS, WHICH CHANGE FROM TRANSPARENT TO OPAQUE-WHITE WHEN STEPPING ON A BUTTON BUILT IN THE FLOOR

alignment, which allows light to pass through and makes the panel appear transparent. In the absence of an electric field, the liquid crystals are randomly oriented, absorbing light and making the panel translucent. The transition from clear to milky takes place instantaneously—at the push of a button.

This technology has already found numerous uses as a temporary privacy screen: in conference rooms, restroom facilities, and changing rooms in clothing stores. Rem Koolhaas takes advantage of the "peep-show" effect of liquid crystal technology in his stores for Prada in Los Angeles and New York: the glazed changing rooms are located in a central zone of the store, and the on/off transparency of the booths draws the attention of customers.

Microcapsules can also be used to invest materials with new properties. Microencapsulation enhances the handling and applications of many different core materials. NASA developed microencapsulated phase change materials in the 1980s as thermal protection systems for spacecraft. In changing to a liquid state, the minuscule particles absorb excess heat from the surrounding environment; when the external temperature falls, stored thermal energy is released. The switching temperature of a PCM is alterable and can be set during the production process; the material solidifies in the cooled state, and the cycle can begin again. This principle is used in the textile industry for athletic apparel, since PCMs have a cooling effect when the body produces heat, and a warming effect as the body cools down after physical exertion. Such high-tech textiles store ten times the thermal energy that can be stored by conventional fabrics.

Under the name of Micronal, microencapsulated PCM has been adapted as a thermal regulator for use in the building industry. Microscopic polymer capsules with a wax core are inserted into gypsum wallboards or stucco finishes to increase the thermal storage capacity of interior surfaces. Three kilograms of PCM per square meter can effectively moderate the temperature of a room: a 15-millimeter thick wallboard has the heat storage capacity of a 9 centimeter thick concrete wall or a brick wall 12 centimeters thick. This presents completely new perspectives for lightweight building—complex and costly air conditioning systems become unnecessary and resources are conserved.

Microcapsules can be used not only for PCM applications, but also to embed healing agents in synthetic composites. A self-repairing structural material would represent a great advancement for the building industry, especially in engineered components where maintenance is hindered by poor accessibility. The field of medicine has also seen the introduction of implants and artificial joints that can autonomously repair tiny fissures. This is made possible by so-called self-healing polymers, which are embedded, together with a catalyst, as microcapsules in the structural composite matrix. If the material is damaged, cracks in the matrix rupture the capsules, thereby releasing the healing agent through capillary action. Contact with the catalyst triggers the bonding process of polymerization at the place of damage. Analogous to the healing of a wound in the human body, material is released and replaced *in situ*. The longevity of structural materials can be increased by as much as three times when microcracks are immediately repaired before moisture and dirt are able to penetrate and accelerate the process of degradation or corrosion.

Shape memory alloys also equip structures with self-protective properties. These metal alloys can be bent into various shapes, but will resume their original, or "parent" shape when cooled or warmed to a set transition temperature ranging between -50° C and +100° C. Nickel-titanium alloys, under the generic name Nitinol, have proven to be the most useful of SMAs. Nitinol is highly resistant to corrosion and material fatigue. When heated, it will fully recover its original shape following mechanical deformations in the cool phase; it can also reverse stress-induced deformations of up to eight percent (superelasticity). The behaviur of such metals can be controlled by the concentrated application of electric voltage. SMAs can counteract the effect of external forces on structural systems or compensate for deviations in the length of critical components.

The Dutch designer Marielle Leenders has exploited this phenomenon in the development of her Moving Textiles. Thin Nitonol wires, which are woven or stitched into the fabric, cause a fabric sample or piece of apparel to alternately contract and expand. In addition to various applications of this technique in the production of clothing, its use is also conceivable for window coverings that would automatically unroll in response to heat and sunlight, and contract when the temperature falls again.

The response of a material to vibration can be influenced by the presence of Nitinol. For example, by applying stress to Nitinol rods incorporated in a bridge construction, the resonant frequency of the bridge could be shifted to avert structural failure in the case of dangerous vibration levels. Even the early development of Nitinol was motivated by its mitigating effects on vibration: in the 1960s, it was utilised as a dynamic insulation material for submarines and warships to avoid detection by acoustic emission. Today, the material is finding increasing use in the construction of robotic devices,

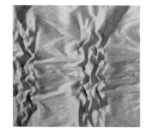

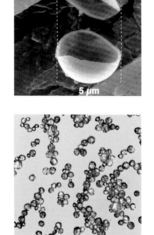

MICRONAL® IS A PHASE-CHANGE MATERIAL DEVELOPED BY BASF CONSISTING OF MICROSCOPICALLY SMALL POLYMER CAPSULES CONTAINING A PURE WAX STORAGE MEDIUM AT THEIR CORE.

THE DESIGNER MARIELLE LEENDERS WEAVES NITINOL WIRES INTO HER MOVING TEXTILES. THANKS TO THIS "MEMORY METAL," THE TEXTILES ARE CAPABLE OF CHANGING THEIR SHAPE.

MARIELLE LEENDERS, MOVING TEXTILE: BY WAY OF THE INTEGRATED NITINOL WIRES, THE CURTAIN AUTOMATICALLY ROLLS ITSELF UP WHEN BEING HEATED.

SEMITRANSPARENT THIN LAYER MODULE OF PHOTOVOLTAIC PANEL WITH STRIPE PATTERN

THESE PHOTOVOLTAIC PANELS, DEVELOPED BY PVACCEPT IN COLLABORATION WITH THE COMPANY WÜRTH SOLAR, CAN BE PRINTED ON.

since it can mimic the smooth movements of human muscles.

As we have seen, shape memory alloys have an astonishingly broad range of applications, from textile design to robotics to bridge safety.

Functional Surfaces. Building surfaces have never represented a physically neutral delineation of space. Throughout the history of architecture, the protective envelope of a building has been assigned additional functions and aesthetic qualities. Colors and textures, for example, have indicated the inhabitants' social position or the function of a building. Lighting and ventilation have also played a central role—one needs only to cite the delicate latticework of wooden windows in Arabian homes or the whitewashed façades of Mediterranean towns.

Today's functional surfaces take advantage of advanced technologies, but they are still concerned with the energy-related, protective, or communicative functions of the building envelope. Coatings are important precursors of future developments. Functional elements are reduced to mere micrometres and can be applied to practically any substrate, offering ideal conditions for myriad uses. On an even smaller scale, namely a millimicron (one billionth of a meter), nano-thick coatings exploit the fact that nano-particles exhibit different physical characteristics than solids. Due to their chemical composition, nano-composites can be fabricated to possess almost any chemical, physical, electrical or optical property. It is possible to manufacture magnetic liquids, ceramic films and self-cleaning glass. The use of such materials will foster collaboration between previously unrelated disciplines: the chemist will become the architect's new engineering consultant. One of the most promising future topics is the energy-producing façade. For several decades now photovoltaic systems have been on the market that convert solar energy into electrical power using semiconductors that operate on the basis of negatively and positively charged electrons. The individual solar cells, which are connected in series to form modules, are embedded between layers of glass. However, large arrays of silicon-based semiconductors have not enjoyed widespread success. Along with the critical issue of efficiency, this may be due to the fact that many architects and building owners dislike their appearance—and tend to regard an unattractive surface as the price to be paid for the production of clean energy. Only a few studies have so far addressed the design potential of this technology.

One interesting new development—especially from an aesthetic perspective—is thin-film photovoltaic technology. Ultra-thin layers of semiconductor material are applied directly to a substrate. Because the photovoltaic cells are directly connected within modules, visible conductors and welds are eliminated, achieving a homogeneous black surface. A European project consortium coordinated by Berlin's Universität der Künste, entitled PVACCEPT, is researching the design potential of thin-film technology and experimenting with manipulations of PV surfaces. Etching, milling, and laser scribing techniques have been used to fabricate semi-transparent test modules. The standard black surface can also be altered by printing pixel-based colored images onto it. The surface area covered by ceramic screen printing should comprise no more than 10–20 percent of the entire surface area to retain an acceptable level of solar efficiency, since printed areas do not generate electricity. This technique makes it possible to combine photovoltaic panels with informational graphics. The exposed surface can also reproduce a wide range of images by means of selective applications—for example, the surface could imitate the material concealed by the PV modules (brickwork, masonry). These promising initiatives represent a creative approach to PV technology that could promote broader acceptance on the part of consumers.

In addition to the growing interest in innovative sources of electricity, manufacturers are also focusing increasing attention on the potential of luminescent surfaces. It is no longer necessary to illuminate a surface or an object by means of a separate light source (i.e. lamp fixture); rather, the surface itself can emit light.

Electroluminescence will play a key role in the future of lighting. Some electroluminescent materials also make use of semiconductor technology. A luminescent semiconductor is sandwiched between electrodes. When an electric field is applied between the electrodes, electrons and holes are injected into the luminescent layer, causing it to emit light in relation to the intensity of the current. Light-emitting diodes and electroluminescent films are based on this principle. Flexible EL-films use luminescent pigment powders, are very thin and can be cut into almost any desired shape with a pair of scissors or a cutting device. Due to the relatively low intensity of emitted light, they have most commonly been used as backlighting for display panels or LCD monitors.

Light-emitting diodes, which have found widespread applications, also comprise a luminescent semiconductor material between positive and negative electrode layers. Since LEDs do not contain any short-lived components—in contrast to the classic light bulb with its delicate filament—they can last for up to 100,000 hours. For this reason, it is possible to integrate LEDs in fixed, sealed, or enclosed superstructures.

OLED (organic light-emitting diode) technology is based on semiconducting polymers. A composite film is made of an anode layer on a transparent substrate, a layer of emissive polymer and a cathode layer. An applied voltage causes the sandwiched luminescent polymer to emit light. The chemical structure of the polymer, which is variable, determines the color of the light. OLED films are very bright and could potentially be manufactured in the form of flexible roll-up monitors or large display panels.

Photoluminescent materials do not require the application of an electric current. They absorb incident energy from an external light source and then emit light at a lower wavelength (sometimes with a delay). The Boston-based architectural firm Kennedy & Violich has experimented with fabrics that take advantage of this phenomenon. Their Give Back Curtains "recycle" incident light by means of photoluminescent pigments that are integrated in synthetic or natural fibers. The fabric absorbs ultraviolet radiation from daylight and fluorescent ambient lighting and then emits it as colored light. Different pigments, whose luminescence varies in intensity, colour and duration, create dynamic patterns that change over a period of several hours. Chameleon Cloth, a second-generation prototype textile by Kennedy & Violich, has a flexible circuit of LED strands woven into the fabric, which enhances the control of light emissivity, color, and pattern. The result is a multi-functional textile that offers alternative options to the fixed location of conventional partitions and lighting systems. The efficiency of semiconductor technology and the ability to use photovoltaic-generated electricity presents new possibilities for lighting and visual communication. The radiant energy of light can be harvested, stored

TRANSPARENT INVISIBLE PRINTED CIRCUIT BOARDS IN THE PVB-LAMINATED GLASS ARE EQUIPPED WITH ELECTRONIC DEVICES, IN PARTICULAR WITH LEDS.

GIVEBACK CURTAIN
(KENNEDY & VIOLICH
ARCHITECTURE, 2000)
AT THE HEADQUARTERS
OF WALL INTERNATIONAL,
THE CURTAINS SERVE AS
TEMPORARY ENCLOSURE
FOR MEETING ROOMS.

CHAMELEON CLOTH
(KENNEDY & VIOLICH
ARCHITECTURE, 2002)
THE PHOTOLUMINISCENT
TEXTILES HARVEST NATU-
RAL DAYLIGHT, LATER
EMITTING IT.

CHRISTIANE SAUER

and supplied to lightweight, portable and flexible textural surfaces.

The Parcel project of the Stockholm research group Krets explores ways of combining off-the-shelf packaging technology and consumer electronics in an interactive, digitally animated wall surface based on ambient sound. A recombinable wall-paneling system is constructed out of pre-punched plastic sheets that are folded into volumetric shapes. Each module is equipped with a local digital circuit, so that the combined structure comprises an integrated network. The behavior of each individual unit is dependent on its variable position in the system and interaction with other modules. Surrounding sounds are picked up locally through microphones and then dispersed throughout the network. The sound signal is transformed by microcontrollers and emitted as "white noise" through loudspeakers and LED lighting, establishing local environments within the structure. White noise comprises all of the audible frequencies and is perceived by the human ear as a quiet, uniform hum or rushing sound. Ambient sound from white noise and human conversation is constantly picked up, transformed and redistributed, thereby creating a textured, atmospheric wall with tonal and optical impulses moving in waves across the structure and into the surrounding space. The Krets group is currently working on kinetic elements made of shape memory alloys that could also alter the physical properties of the surface, thereby extending reactive characteristics to shadows and reflections of light.

The word "parcel" refers to the simple and inexpensive manufacturing methods used to produce the modules. Cut and fold lines were established in a standardized production pattern; after punching, the sheet is folded into box-like units. Electrical components are based

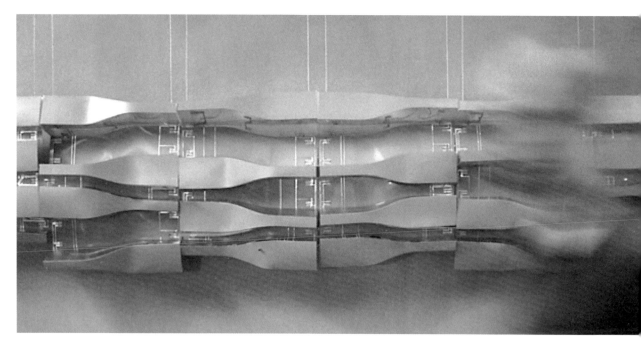

KRETS RESEARCH GROUP, PARCEL, A PRESENTATION AT STOCKHOLM CONCERT HALL ON THE OCCASION OF THE ARTS+SCIENCE FESTIVAL 2004

ONE SINGLE UNIT OF PARCEL INTEGRATING PRINTED CIRCUITS, MICROPHONES AND LED

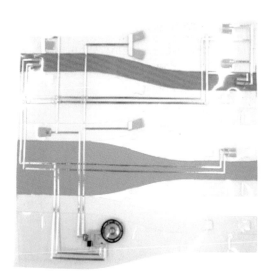

on inexpensive consumer products. Consequently, the Parcel system meets mass-production criteria. It is an object with disposable qualities, as it were, since it is so easy to disassemble and discard. This product could be used to create temporary, inexpensive "instant environments" that bring an element of interpretative performance to a space.

The architecture and design firm Formorf is developing space-enclosing envelopes that can alter their shape, while individual layers of the envelope serve different functions. Similar to the human skin, the exterior surface of the spatial structure Corpform can adapt to changing environmental conditions. Its inventors describe the state of the structure as "inconstant." This small-scale architectural object demonstrates analogies between the built environment and living organisms—yet Corpform is not a representative of organic architecture; rather, it could be described as a constructed organism.

The outer layer, a scaly structure made of insulating ceramic material, is equipped with flexible photocells that provide an autonomous energy supply. The next layer is a textile with a low-emissivity coating that reflects most of the thermal radiation from external sources. Beneath this layer is a lighting system, comparable to the nervous or vascular system of living organisms, which glows through the skin. A PCM membrane serves the purpose of thermal absorption and storage. This layer compensates for the climatic disadvantages of a lightweight construction and protects the internal space from extremes of heat and cold. The thermal storage capacity of the membrane is comparable to a solid wall. A pneumatic construction in the interior supports the shape of the object. Because its volume is alterable, the form can expand and contract. The multi-layer envelope is only a few millimeters thick. Functional details such as

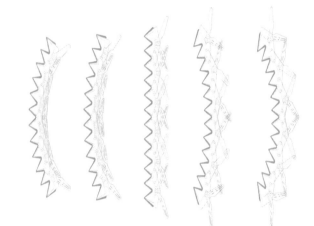

STUDIES REGARDING SHAPE AND PERFORMANCE OF THE NEW SPLINE GRAFT PROTOTYPE, DEVELOPED BY KRETS FOR THE EXHIBITION OPEN HOUSE

CORPFORM – LEBENDIGE ARCHITEKTUR, 2005: LAYERING (FORMORF, ENGINEERS MARCO HEMMERLING AND MARKUS HOLZBACH) © FORMORF

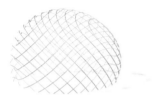

**CORPFORM (FORMORF,
MARCO HEMMERLING AND
MARKUS HOLZBACH, 2006)**

**PAUL, ADAPTIVE TEXTILE
BUILDING SKIN, INSTITUT
FÜR LEICHTBAU ENTWER-
FEN UND KONSTRUIEREN,
UNIVERSITÄT STUTTGART
(MARKUS HOLZBACH, 2004)**

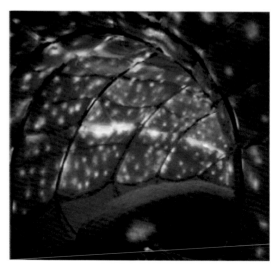

hook-and-loop fasteners, clip closures and zippers are borrowed from the textile industry.

SmartWrap, a high-performance polymer compound developed by the Philadelphia architectural firm Kieran Timberlake, integrates and compresses the segregated functions of a conventional wall structure and auxiliary building systems. For the flexible protective substrate, the architects combined polyester and its derivative PET (polyethylene terephthalate), a robust and inexpensive plastic that is widely used as a packaging material in the food and beverage industry. Printed and laminated layers of "smart" functional elements are roll-coated onto the polymer film: organic photovoltaic cells to generate electricity, ultra-thin batteries and organic thin-film transistors and circuits for energy storage and distribution, OLEDs to provide lighting and information displays, an electrochromic coating, and entrapped pockets of phase-change material (aerogel) to regulate the transmission of heat and sunlight. By virtue of this production process, a SmartWrap façade could be mass-manufactured according to individual requirements.

The goal of innovative approaches to complex spatial and technological interactions is the creation of buildings that are capable of autonomous adaptation to environmental conditions—without relying on computerized management systems. The technological features of the layered building envelope can make it possible to create an individual and dynamically alterable architectural identity.

Structural Materials. The functional and aesthetic considerations of new materials have received a great deal of attention, but builders and planners are also challenged by their structural potential. Many innovative compounds have originated in the automotive and aeronautics industries, which have manifold uses for strong lightweight materials.

The structural components of the human body—the bones—are excellent examples of a material that combines light weight with high tensile strength, thanks to their sponge-like internal structure. Material and structural unity has been a motivating principle behind the construction of open-cell metal foams. The high specific surface area accomplishes an even distribution and transfer of loads. The density of foamed metals is roughly 10 percent relative to the solid base metal; pores measure between 1.5 to 4 millimeters in diameter; components are 100 percent recyclable. Possible machining operations include cutting, milling and lathing. Fittings and additional elements can be incorporated in the molding process for seamless bonds.

Foamed metals were developed in the filter industry since they offer an extremely large surface area, ideal for filters. They are used in the automobile industry because of their noise-reducing properties and high level of deformation energy absorption; in the case of an impact, energy is evenly distributed throughout the continuous ligament structure of a foamed metal component as it compresses.

Advanced pore morphology (APM) is a newer development in metal foam technology. The properties of APM foams can be precisely tailored to individual structural specifications by adjusting the size of the spherical foam elements and thickness of exterior walls or sheeting. APM elements, which are granular in shape and have a foam core, are poured into a mould or hollow structure and thermally bonded with an adhesive coating. Large-scale structures and complex shapes can be achieved with this "foam-in-a-foam" process. Researchers and ar-

chitects have collaborated on a futuristic design for a monolithic bridge made entirely out of a similar compound comprising small hollow metallic spheres mixed with a synthetic bonding agent. The combination of hollow or foamed aluminum granules and a synthetic adhesive yields a compound with unique properties. The spherical metal elements absorb energy and provide structural stiffness; the synthetic adhesive creates a strong bond between the elements themselves, and also between the granular fill and shells or surface sheeting.

Similar composite materials have been utilized in the construction of aircraft, automobiles and other vehicles for quite some time. Primary structural parts of the new Airbus A380 are being manufactured out of high-performance carbon-fiber reinforced plastic. To produce a CRP (or CFRP) part, a weave of super-strong carbon fiber threads is laid into a mould, saturated with epoxy resin and heat or air cured to produce the desired shape. Connecting parts can be interwoven and moulded together, making other types of joint attachment unnecessary.

Californian architect Peter Testa, working together with the engineering firm Arup & Partners, has applied this technology to a visionary design for a forty-storey circular office tower made entirely of composite materials. The building's shell consists of bands of carbon fiber hundreds of feet long, winding in a helicoidal pattern around the cylindrical volume. The thin bands run continuously from the bottom to the top of the building and take the entire vertical compressive load. An external ramp system winds around the structural helix and provides lateral bracing. The floor plates between stories are tied in to the external structure, resulting in a homogeneous, interdependent tectonic system based on tension rather than

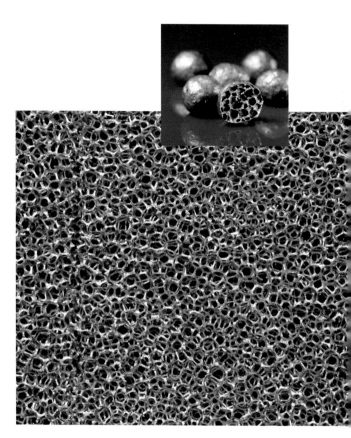

< SMARTWRAP™, KIERANTIMBERLAKE ASSOCIATES LLP
THE MASS CUSTOMIZABLE PRINT FAÇADE IS CAPABLE OF TRANSFORMING SUN LIGHT INTO ENERGY, OF STORING AND CONDUCTING THIS ENERGY. IN ADDITION, IT IS A GOOD INSULATOR.

SECTION THROUGH AN ALUMINUM FOAM SPHERE THE DIAMETER OF THE HOLLOW SPHERES RANGES FROM 0.8 MM TO 20 MM WITH A WALL THICKNESS BETWEEN 10 µM AND 100 µM.

PANELS OF ALUMINUM FOAM CAN BE MANUFACTURED WITH DIFFERENT PORE WIDTHS.

VISION OF A BRIDGE MADE OF STABILIGHT®
THE COMPOSITE OF HOLLOW METALLIC SPHERES AND AN ADHESIVE COMPOUND WAS DEVELOPED IN 2003 BY THE COMPANY OF THE SAME NAME AND THE FRAUNHOFER INSTITUT IN DRESDEN. THE DESIGN FOR THIS BRIDGE WAS CREATED IN COLLABORATION WITH THE UNIVERSITY OF BATH.

> PETER TESTA, CARBON TOWER, PROJECT, 2005
FORTY STORIES HIGH, STRUNG TOGETHER BY CONTINUOUS CARBON FIBER STRANDS, ABOUT 1 INCH WIDE AND NEARLY 650 FEET LONG, WHICH ARE WOVEN TO FORM A STRUCTURE THAT DISTRIBUTES ITS LOADS OVER ITS ENTIRE SURFACE, AND WHICH ARE ARRAYED IN A HELICOIDAL (CROSS-HATCH) PATTERN.

on the structural hierarchies of conventional architecture. The efficient construction process would save not only material resources, but also energy. Manufacturing carbon fiber and resin requires only about half the energy of steel; in addition, the low weight of source materials and other components would reduce transport costs. Only a bundle of fibers and plastic would be needed for the on-site production of core elements: robotic pultrusion machines would work their way up the building, forming the continuous helical bands by passing raw strands of carbon through a resin bath and an extrusion die. A transparent synthetic membrane would form the skin of the building, so that the rising structure would be realized without using steel, concrete, or conventional glass.

Composites are considered highly promising materials, due to the fact that they can be adapted to specific building types. In addition, their properties can be altered according to the required structural function. Researchers at the DLR Institute of Structural Mechanics (Deutsches Zentrum für Luft- und Raumfahrt) are experimenting with environmentally friendly alternatives to petrochemical resins, which are difficult to recycle. Natural fibers embedded in a biodegradable matrix can replace traditional fiber-reinforced plastics. The so-called biopolymers or biocomposites are embedded in a matrix system on the basis of vegetable starches from corn, potatoes, wheat or other grains and reinforced with flax, hemp or jute fibers. The strength of such materials is comparable to their non-renewable and unecological predecessors. Industrial safety helmets and vehicular paneling elements are already in series production.

In the boat building industry, the capillary effect of glass fibers has been used to develop a hybrid material that is both sandwich and composite. This type of cored material

CHRISTIANE SAUER

comprises a three-dimensional mat of woven glass fibers between two cover layers. The dry sandwich is placed in a mould and saturated with resin. The capillary effect draws the resin through the fine glass fibers to the point of maximum impregnation. In this way, the core of tiny glass ligaments rises to a pre-set height determined by the vertical piles of the glass weave, so that the cover layers harden at an exact distance in a precisely shaped panel.

Other sandwich materials are also distinguished by the reduction of material in the core and stabilizing deck layers. Countless possible combinations of different materials for the core and exterior surfaces can be adapted to individual specifications. Foam, woven piles or a honeycomb fill can be sandwiched between deck layers made of aluminum, aramid, plastic, glass or paper in large-scale panels. Even natural stone facing is used in combination with an aluminum honeycomb core for lightweight, resilient stone panels. Sandwich technology makes it possible to redefine the properties of classic building materials.

Transparent-faced sandwich composites with a honeycomb core have a fascinating appearance; they oscillate between solid and transparent, depending on the viewing angle, and transform the outward view into a pixeled image. The aesthetic effect can be further manipulated by the selection of colored, transparent, or patterned deck layers. A mass-produced industrial product from the automotive industry becomes an individually tailored product.

Material Mania? Smart materials, structural surfaces, functional layers—potential applications seem almost limitless. And yet the best technological solutions are meaningless without people who are ready to embark on new paths by putting them to use. This requires a

FOR ORGANIC COMPOSITES
THAT ARE MORE ENVIRON-
MENTALLY FRIENDLY THEN
PETROCHEMICAL PLAS-
TICS, VEGETABLE STARCH
IS REINFORCED WITH
HEMP OR JUTE FIBERS.

FOR THIS HYBRID OF
COMPOSITE AND SAND-
WICH MATERIAL, TWO
FLEXIBLE OUTER LAYERS
ARE JOINED BY A THREE
DIMENSIONAL WEAVE AND
THEN SOAKED WITH RESIN.

SANDWICH MATERIALS
COMBINE STABILITY WITH
LIGHTNESS AND, IF
DESIRED, TRANSLUCENCE.

CHRISTIANE SAUER

committed group of planners, owners, manufacturers and technicians. Innovative materials face many obstacles: building codes, long-term testing requirements, fire safety certification and, last but not least, the reception of challenging spatial and visual qualities. Many of the projects mentioned here owe their realization to the visionary, adventurous individuals who have conceived and pursued them.

Purely ornamental façade elements have enjoyed a renaissance during the recent past. Does the abundance of available materials bear the danger of arbitrariness and mere decoration? Façades and interior walls can be adorned with large patterns in a variety of techniques—printing, mill-cutting or etching. How stylish should a surface be?

This invariably brings up the question of "honest" materials. Yet to the same extent that materials are not really "smart," they also cannot be "honest." The proponents of classic modernism who defined this term eventually carried it to the point of absurdity. Sheathing materials and mixed structures were common among modernist architects from Le Corbusier to Rietveld. Ultimately, it has always been the design intention that matters most.

If one defines "stylish" in a positive sense, meaning "appropriate to the time" or "transient," then this might even inspire new solutions for the spatial envelope, i.e. building façade. The concept of sustainable architecture, for example, addresses the interaction of short-term and long-term building components. Individual structural systems (e.g. tectonics, utilities, cladding/ envelope) have different life spans and must be renewed or replaced at certain intervals. The age of a building is no longer a fixed quantity, but a dynamic process of renewal. The outermost layer has been liberated from the tasks of structural support or even environmental seal-

ing, and the elimination of such fundamental technical functions allows a much greater freedom in the choice of façade materials and treatments. It is now conceivable to install inexpensive, "alternating" façades at periodic intervals.

The new fascination for materials can also be explained by a rediscovered yearning for sensual experiences. In a society dominated by a ceaseless barrage of mostly visual information, by monitors, screens and displays, there is a growing desire for physical—especially tactile—sensations. Surfaces are the physical interface between architectural structures and human beings. The surface is the place where one comes into contact with a building, touches it, uses it. The properties of a material are central to this experience. It is not merely a matter of "styling" or superficial qualities, but has to do with atmospheric, spatial and conceptual perceptions. This is precisely what characterizes an interesting space, regardless of its stylistic references or the personal tastes of the person who encounters it. Architecture is the transformation of a design idea into space and matter, whereby the chosen materials can either reinforce or undermine the spatial concept. Architects who work not only with space, but also with the qualities of its boundaries, will be inspired by the wide range of innovative materials to expand their design vocabulary—or perhaps even to learn a new language.

Pragmatic Futurism: Forecasting the Home of 2026 ¶

> DANA HUTT

A better innovation approach is to switch attention from science-dominated futures to social fictions in which imagined new contexts enrich an otherwise familiar world. Design scenarios are powerful innovation tools because they make a possible future familiar and enable the participation of potential users in conceiving and shaping what they want. —John Thackara[1]

* THE NUMBERS REFER TO
THE PORTRAITS OF THOSE
INTERVIEWED ➔ PAGE 183

168

Introduction. For anyone other than a professional visionary, describing the future "house" or dwelling and how we will live in the future can be a perilous undertaking. For an architectural historian, the act is practically tantamount to transgression: speculation is for real estate, not the august practice of history. Besides, as any shrewd architectural observer will tell you, most proposals about the future of architecture have turned out to be completely wrong. However, learning what architects think about when they engage in future-forecasting can be extremely useful. In this way, not only can we begin to detect present trends in design and culture, we can also gain insight into the meaning of the house itself as well as the motivations and influences that drive these creative individuals.

"The future may be unknowable, but it's not unthinkable," a popular saying goes. And while futurism and pronouncements about the "future" may be doomed to a certain failure, forward thinking is always worthwhile. As John Thackara points out, "social fictions" set in a "possible future" can serve as valuable tools that enable potential users to participate meaningfully in the design process.[2] With this purpose in mind, this essay will survey currents in architecture anticipated in the next 20 years as forecast by a number of prominent architects, educators, critics, and technology experts from around the globe. A baseline of 20 years, roughly a generation, was selected to ground the discussions in reality and avoid, as much as possible, purely fanciful futuristic impulses.

Even within the frame of 20 years, forecasting the future at the beginning of the twenty-first century is fraught with uncertainty—especially when it comes to technology, which is nearly inseparable from the future house. The velocity of technological innovation, with

17*

its proliferation into all aspects of global production and everyday life, is transforming design and culture. Twenty years ago, few could have predicted the prevalence today of mobile phones, laptops, and iPods. It remains an open question how today's technological trends—such as miniaturization, wireless interconnectivity, mobility, RFID-tag integration, and personalization—will evolve and what influence they will have on the design, fabrication, structure, space, and systems of the future house and how we will live.

Future Challenges. Our house, or wherever we make our home, is a microcosm we make of the world. So it is not surprising that questions about the future of domestic architecture—how the contemporary house will change and how it will change our way of life—lead to broader concerns about the future of the world. For Craig Hodgetts, these include global population explosion, scarcity of resources, and higher urban densities. Making reference to both Buckminster Fuller and Le Corbusier, Hodgetts states, "The stuff that seems to me to be really meaningful and provocative would be, how do I pack more people per square foot into a housing development and still give them a sense of space and access to fresh air."[3] Werner Sobek rephrases the question, advocating that the contemporary house *should* change, particularly in light of the global dependence on fossil fuels and their future scarcity, as well as the dwindling supply of other natural resources, such as steel, aluminum, and copper. Sobek says, "What has been totally forgotten in the last 30 years, when architecture was dealing with postmodernism and deconstructivism and all those more or less formal discussions, was that architecture has to give an answer to those upcoming problems. But there is no answer on

the table, so we have to develop that answer."

Shifting populations and social patterns will also shape the house in the next 20 years. "What's interesting to me is, if you really look at the larger trend in housing, we can't really isolate issues of homes and houses from issues of urbanism and urbanization in a global sense," Toshiko Mori points out. Citing cities in China, Spain and South America, she asks, "How do you house areas of fast growth in population?" In addition, the future retirement of the baby boomers, the growing number of senior citizens, and ongoing daycare and childcare needs will also affect housing requirements. Alluding to the implied gadgetry of the "smart house," Mori states, "Issues of survival, issues of shelter and protection become so much more important [than] having a gadget in the kitchen." Indeed, the disconnect between matters of basic shelter at one end and hi-tech devices in an individual home on the other is huge. In this context, the idea of technology-laden house appears elitist and absurd, indeed raising questions about how technology, if at all, can best serve human needs and the future house.

Architecture vs. Technology. In the past two decades, technological innovation has rapidly transformed sectors of the economy from information (transistors, microprocessors, fiber optics, and lasers) to health care (antibiotics, transplants, biotechnology).[4] For architecture, however, progress comes slowly: the design and construction process is lengthy, the costs involved are huge, and building codes and liability limit creativity and unconventionality in design. Architects and critics, therefore, express deep skepticism about whether technology will truly change the house. "In 20 years, 99 percent of houses will look very similar to what they look like now because of the incredibly conservative construction industry, especially when it comes to residential work," Blaine Brownell notes.

"Smart" technologies for the home and "smart houses" generally elicit derision and doubt from the architecture community. "Being smart is not necessarily being intelligent," argues Mori, who sees those houses as wasteful and superfluous. "I don't think that technology will change the way we live at all," says Aaron Betsky. "I think that technology changes our ability to organize our activities and to obtain information, but when it comes to the home, the whole point is to quite literally domesticate technology, to make it something that you want to live with." For Thackara, the notion of an "ambient intelligent environment (which in the United States tends to be called 'ubiquitous computing' or 'pervasive computing')" in which people will be surrounded by networking technology embedded in everyday objects is flawed because it is based on implausible assumptions. "No technology delivered by computing private companies will ever be 'seamlessly' integrated."[5] Nor can human beings or systems be expected to be perfectly reliable. Nonetheless, corporations are steadily working toward fully integrated home-technology environments, and according to recent news reports, that reality may already be here.

The fact is that most of us upgrade our homes incrementally, with new and old technologies coexisting side by side. As Deyan Sudjic observes, "In Europe, houses 100 years old are very commonplace. They've been through probably four or five different technological shifts in that time, and the house has still got the same form. And the stuff has been stripped out and replaced time and again… I'm not convinced that technology does really change houses, because so much of what the house is

remains a kind of archetype in our heads or dream about the way we live or an antidote to movement or change so that the house is a solace. And to design a house around technology seems to be missing the point."

Evolving Concepts of Home

Any definition of home today must consider how new attitudes and values come up against the familiar; how our needs are served by what we know, as well as by what we remember.
—Akiko Busch[6]

…Home is not household, as a social group and something to be perpetuated; home is not an abode. Sedentariness and rootedness are linked with a conservative view of the world that doesn't encompass changes at work — economic and social changes, not to say the dissolution of what is called the household unit. The home is a place of strategic application in the formulation of positions with regard to problems connected with the effects of globalization.
—Béatrice Simonot[7]

Defining the future house is impossible without rethinking what constitutes a home today. At its most basic level, is a home the repository of your belongings, the place where you sleep, the center where your family gathers, or something more—or less—than that? "As designers we still can't escape the image of our home," says Michelle Addington. "Home is the most difficult question of all." It may be true, as Béatrice Simonot asserts, that associating "home" with values like "rootedness" is outmoded. However, for many like architecture writer Akiko Busch, the home still retains long-standing associations with memory as well as

12

identity, status and comfort. "A house is always going take with it aspects of ritual and tradition because very few people are going to throw everything away," Thom Mayne points out. "Even in today's peripatetic culture that lives more like nomads, you're going to bring a trunk; you're going to bring a couple of pictures of your parents or your grandmother—something connected to your history, and it's private and personal, and it's going to have the sum notion of tradition or conserving." It is one of the intriguing ironies that the building type we most invest with symbolism about stability and memory also serves as the foremost laboratory for architectural research. Recalling time spent sleeping in a tree house, in a cave, and on a beach under the stars, Mayne says, "The house has always been extremely interesting. It has a history of being a model for design experimentation precisely because what we call 'home' is so incredibly elastic."

7

Even so, each generation will formulate its own new values for the home. Looking ahead 20 to 25 years, Neil Denari states, "I don't think we'll see a brand new landscape of housing, but there's another world of generations who are going to live differently and be raised differently, who will have different desires and less and less nostalgia for place and more for just momentary needs, a culture that's more connected to interfaces and images." In this time of transition, what appears most certain is that the home will keep the few vestiges that retain meaning as we race toward new products, new conditions, and even new architecture.

Features of the Future Home

A series of recent interviews with notable architects and others from the worlds of architecture, design, and technology reveals a number of overlapping interests and likely future directions for domestic architecture. As Geoffrey London writes about the twenty-first century house, it is no longer possible to "claim such a powerful single instance of a broadly supported approach" as in the Smithsons' "House of the Future."[8] Today's architects are not so much compelled by a "dream of salvation by technology" than the following qualities and features they anticipate in any future-house scenario.

Comfort and Sanctuary. While the idea of the house as a place of sanctuary or retreat is not new, there will be a heightened desire for these qualities in the future home. "I believe in a kind of super-living in the sense that we need to start to think of how you can bring to the house far more comfort than we are doing right now," says Ben van Berkel, architect of Living Tomorrow Amsterdam, a temporary building and exhibition that shows how innovative technologies and appliances can be integrated into daily life and work environments. Van Berkel believes people in the future will have much more time at home to work and will want more leisure in or close to their homes. Nearby services will be more clustered and part of a critical package of programs connected to the house to provide much more comfort. Van Berkel says, "My belief is that the house and living in the future should be more like holiday."

2

While also a center of connectivity, the house will become more and more like a sanctuary where you can escape from hyperconnectivity, think quietly, and be with your family, according to William McDonough. "I think that the pressures of modern life are so dramatic that we're going to be looking for stress reduction. Certainly in the countries that are crowded, it matters a lot to get away from the hustle and bustle." Among his current projects are cities in China, for which his architecture firm is designing new building systems based on the concept of silence, with wall systems and floor systems that also serve as lightweight insulators to minimize sound. He further explains, "A house that can breathe, a house that knows how to sleep, is the kind of thing that we're going to want to do. I think there will be a whole set of things that are essentially transparent to experience, but are actually life-support systems instead of simply comfort-support systems or entertainment."

In response to higher levels of stress, production, and speed, the house will serve as a health spa, refuge, and "stress-reliever concept," suggests Neil Denari. Home becomes the place where you seek new ways to rest and regenerate. "The body, after all, is the one thing that doesn't change," he notes. In addition, the house will help to edit, filter, and control information, becoming a new kind of refuge for the mind as well. He adds, "The house doesn't need to get thicker walls or become heavier or become a bulwark of resistance. Maybe it just needs to change in the way in which it works for you so you can live to the highest potential." Perhaps achieving that potential will mean reconnecting to nature, as Toyo Ito writes, "Houses in the twentieth century intently moved towards the 'White Cube' isolated from the nature, in other words, creating a man-made environment. But I believe the direction we are taking in the twenty-first century is to recover the relationship with nature as it was before modern times.

A variety of technologies should be developed towards such a recovery. Air conditioning technology, for example, must be much more energy saving and at the same time provide comfort in a sensitive way."

Above all, it is essential that the house enhance domestic life. We need to "postpone as long as possible the shape of the box—and indeed the shape of the inside of the box—and to look first at the kind of activities that that box is supposed to support," advises John Thackara. "On the contrary, the vast majority of houses in developed countries are put up according to formulas about future uses that are either out of date or just plain wrong. And this is because people are no longer looking or thinking about the changing patterns of domestic life and also the changing structures of the changing combinations of people who will live in them." He continues, "The reason that people feel that they're the victims of a too-fast society is that we fill the world full of systems that have their own logic, which is not the same logic as human comfort."

Flexibility. The notion of flexibility also has a longstanding tradition in modern architecture, with multiple meanings and applications. Citing flexibility as "one of the holy grails of architecture," Neil Denari raises a primary question, "Do people want more and more to have a rooted concept called home or do they want something that is simply a shell, both physically and conceptually, that supports something that's constantly changing? Flexibility seems to be the question about how can architecture perform more like the product world, which is upgradeable, changeable."

Flexibility will allow room designations to change according to whim or function. Peter Cook says, "The famous thing the parent says to the kid—'You treat this place as a hotel'—is in a way very telling, because in a sense, you have two, three, four, five, six people, inhabiting a house, who each treat it as their own mental hotel, or even physical hotel." In contrast to the regulatory spaces he once designed in accord with an official housing manual, Cook believes we will live with more elasticity. "If you said any window of your house could be effectively a screen or a view of the world so that you can decide at that moment, whether plugging something in or not, oh, I seem to be in this room, and I feel like watching a movie. And, I'll mosey into the other room, depending how Auntie Maude is in that room. So, I'll sit here, and here we go into the movie. Rather than saying, traditionally, this is the room in which I eat; this is the room in which I watch a movie; this is the room in which I bathe; this is the room in which I sleep. So I think there's that whole aspect, which is to do with the transferability of association between space and activity."

The designations of rooms in the future house are likely to be interchangeable, relaxed, and spatially fluid. Toyo Ito also anticipates great flexibility in the use and configuration of the house. He notes that the family—formerly the smallest unit in the social structure—is no longer stable and is now becoming a variable assemblage of individuals. To accommodate these societal changes, the private house will no longer have the function of a living room or dining room at its center, but instead contain a collection of private rooms. In an alternative scenario, Ben van Berkel suggests a plan of "endless living," as seen in his 1998 design for the Möbius House, which draws upon the concept of a Möbius strip and was inspired by Kazuyo Sejima's circle house, Villa in the Forest (1994), and Toyo Ito's White U House (1976).

"I believe that this is essential that there are no dead ends in the house," Van Berkel says. "The Möbius House is also endless. It's endless living. I do believe in this cycle of living in time, that you have a smoothness in it, and that is creating continuously in this smoothness, unexpected experiences."

Urbanity. For some, the future of the house will depend upon its relationship to the city and a larger urban context. Yung Ho Chang says the city offers freedom in housing choices, lifestyle, and mobility and the benefits of density. "In an urban setting, high density is not only not a problem, but rather it's an advantage, because there's a much greater offering of retail, commercial, and cultural activities. Look at Hong Kong—that's a city with a really rather high density and, in fact, it's pretty convenient and comfortable to live in. Urban living quality is based on density, and a lot of cities in Asia aren't dense enough." Noting the end of the single-family house as a concept for future living because of its vast inefficiency, Thom Mayne sees vitality in new urban models. "Probably the most interesting direction is various hybrids, where you look at denser organizational structures that can accommodate some of the uses and rethink how you can keep the attributes of the single-family house, and put those within a more ethically driven logic that you can defend in biological, ecological terms." For Deyan Sudjic, how housing is connected or built in groups is more critical to the future than new technology. "Maybe the question is not much the house of the future as the community of the future."

Urban densities facilitate the networks of services and shared resources that make a city vital and sustainable. John Thackara writes, "The integration of private and common space

5

is enabling the creation of communities of people who choose to live together on the basis of shared facilities such as kitchens, laundries, do-it-yourself workrooms, children's play areas, guest rooms, gardens, and garden tools. In Hong Kong, the majority of recent buildings have been constructed to incorporate this kind of sharing."[9]

Like the house, the city of the future will be transformed by technology. Mizuko Ito, a research scientist who studies the effect of digital technologies on structures of social and cultural life in Japan, says that mobile phones and text messaging now allow young people to construct virtual spaces and deepen relationships, often at the expense of engaging in serendipitous exchanges in urban space. She predicts that this process will continue in the future. As Japanese youth now make arrangements to meet their friends using the mobile phone, their previous cultivation of neighborhood landmarks, bars, and shops as places to encounter friends by happenstance has changed, Ito suggests. "I think that there's probably some relationship between that and the growth of more impersonal chain-type restaurants and cafes as a much more pervasive presence in Tokyo. There are a lot of reasons why there are Starbucks on every corner and there's a lot more of these franchises that has a lot to do with aesthetics and design. There's obviously a lot of factors. But I think it converges with the desire for people to have kind of generic spaces that they can appropriate as opposed to urban locations that rely on personal relationships."

Technology will also create a new connection to the city. "One of the things we're seeing in urban environments is that the sense of place is disappearing rapidly because people and information are moving very quickly," says Brenda Laurel. "They don't stick long enough for 'placeness' to happen. The things that do stick are things that stick everywhere like Burger King and Gap, so it all looks alike in some ways. There are ways that we can use media and technology to illuminate the invisible architecture as a place and give you back that sense of comfort that you get from real places that still have a character, so there's an overlay." As Malcolm McCullough notes, "In our age of technological saturation, response to place becomes the most practical adaptation strategy of all."[10]

Solutions for Urban Nomads. Populations for whom the idea of a single home is impractical will be provided with new housing solutions in the next twenty years. The trend of nomadism applies to families with more than one place of residence, people who need to work in different locations, and families who migrate from one building type to another every few years to accommodate overall population growth. Toyo Ito predicts the emergence of a new building typology that could accommodate this group. "Any clear-cut distinction between an apartment and an urban hotel will become blurred; in other words, an apartment hotel will establish itself as one possible urban lifestyle." Toshiko Mori describes a housing policy in Spain that treats the entire population as nomads. "As they grow, in terms of family and then age group, they will migrate from one housing type to the other." Single people begin with a small 30-square-meter unit, then migrate to larger and smaller units as they marry, begin a family, become empty-nesters, and then retire. Mori notes, "If you look at the cyclical nature of housing, it's much more resilient in a responsive way to the need. You can build a variety of housing types, and then looking at the growth in population; they can actually peak and then ebb."

As more and more people around the world work outside the city, outside their home country, new housing solutions will be necessary for these modern nomads, suggests Werner Sobek. His office is now exploring how to individualize a hotel room. "What we are thinking about is, are there materials which are multifunctional, modifiable, so that you can transfer? Is there modifiable furniture? Are there modifiable functions? Is there deployable furniture that can appear and disappear?"

Sustainability. At the beginning of the twenty-first century, the notion of sustainable or "green" architecture has gained wide acceptance as a goal. "For me, any building from now on has to really take on that issue," says Yung Ho Chang. Most architects believe that sustainability has simply become a given—one among many performance requirements for buildings. Environmental and energy concerns in the 1960s and 1970s spawned earlier versions of green architecture, often associated with organicism, solar energy, biodegradability, use of recycled materials, and communal social experiments. Today's sustainable architectural movement, however, places a premium on high performance and aesthetics. For a successful building, "there's a merging between the form and performance, in a way it doesn't when it starts with form or starts with performance," notes Thom Mayne. One of the foremost examples of the high-performance sustainable house to date is the R 128 House (2000), designed by Werner Sobek. The glass-and-steel four-story family house in Stuttgart is entirely recyclable, emission-free, and energy self-sufficient (through solar cells), using systems and appliances controlled by touchless microwave sensors. Sobek explains, "With this building I wanted to show that outstanding formal, aesthetical qualities do not conflict at all with recyclability, and because R 128 does not need any energy, it has no emissions; it has no chimney. So it's totally environmentally friendly while it is run, [and] this does not conflict with high and outstanding aesthetical qualities."

In the United States, where sustainability has become almost a marketing requirement, more and more public and corporate clients commission buildings with the goal of a LEED (Leadership in Energy and Environmental Design) rating. Developed by the U.S. Green Building Council, this voluntary national standard outlines the broad tenets of high-performance green buildings: "state of the art strategies for sustainable site development, water savings, energy efficiency, materials selection, and indoor environmental quality." [11] One of the leading proponents of sustainability in the United States, William McDonough, goes even further, advocating what he calls "the next industrial revolution," in which building components and consumer goods are redesigned so they can be fully reused or recycled in a "cradle-to-cradle" model.

For the future house, it is likely that sustainability will be achieved through new approaches to renewable energy production and use; biomimicry; intelligent materials and processes, as will be discussed below, and shared resources. Energy will no doubt determine the form of the individual dwelling and its locality. "What I'd like to see is some of what [Jeremy] Rifkin posited [in *The Hydrogen Economy*], having to do with widely distributed, more locally autonomous centers of energy production and distribution with renewable technologies: geothermal, bio-mass, solar," says Blaine Brownell. "The house of the future would obviously be formally affected by incorporation of these technologies, whether they're building integrated photovoltaics, or some other means of being semi-autonomous or off the grid. The idea is that our neighborhoods can be interconnected through energy and resources in a web structure that mirrors the Internet." In addition to lowering the energy usage of individual households, architects also seek to exploit building processes and building materials that use less or no energy. For a project in China, McDonough explains, "We're looking at a new material made from gypsum and sand that uses a new constant discovered by a French chemical engineer where we can produce a limestone-like material without energy… What we're looking for are new materials that have very low embodied energy, are highly insulating for both sound and thermal effects, and very inexpensive."

Biomimicry also offers potential solutions for sustainable housing. Popularized by Janine M. Benyus's 1997 book of the same name, biomimicry—the science of seeking innovation through emulating natural processes—suggests a means of making building materials without using or generating huge amounts of energy or toxic products. One of the book's compelling examples is a spider's "dragline" silk, which is ounce for ounce five times stronger than Kevlar, the material used in bulletproof vests. Spiders make this silk through biochemical processes, using no heat or pressure.[12] "If we could turn the industrial project on its head, it would be a complete change in thinking." Brownell continues, "We have to make things smarter. We have to make things without a ton of embodied energy and also create things [without] petroleum-based sources, plus all the nasty synthetic chemicals that aren't really fully tested in the lab and end

up persistent pollutants." And Brenda Laurel concurs with this view. "As we get real about what's happening to our climate and our environment here on earth, we'll begin to see much more technology that's modeled after biological systems. So the whole realm of biomimicry as a design method for thinking about solving hard problems will become more and more obvious in the shapes and mechanisms that we encounter in our daily lives."

For John Thackara, the way we design houses influences everything related to a sustainable future. "The kind of houses that we design will have impacts on the kind of patterns of mobility, the way that people use energy, the materials that they use in their lives, how they take their children to school." Furthermore, he sees sharing resources as central to sustainability. "I think that it's tremendously important that we look for ways to share spaces and facilities and equipment far more actively than we do now, because one of the big problems of this sustainability of houses is that you have large numbers of people, possessing and using equipment in a kind of individualistic way, which is a very wasteful way to do that…. Just thinking about the home as one box for one family or one person is too limiting a way to think about home."

New building materials, products, and ideas.
A renewed interest in new materials and technology for architecture, a veritable "materials revolution" is now afoot, says Blaine Brownell, who surveys the profusion of recent products in the 2006 book *Transmaterial*.[13] Stimulated in part by the sustainability movement, a growing number of architects and designers are conducting materials research as well as collaborating with manufacturers and scientists to develop new materials and products. Promising

building materials for the housing industry include vacuum-insulated panels, which are ten times as effective as conventional insulation products and will enable thinner walls and ceilings; sophisticated photovoltaics that will be embedded in fabrics or paint; and numerous recycled materials, ranging from agricultural waste to plastics.

An exciting area of future materials research is what Brownell terms "transformational materials," which includes smart or dynamic high-performing materials with intelligence that mimics structure inspired by nature or adapts or can be adapted to different situations. Smart materials and technologies, as defined by Michelle Addington and Daniel Schodek, exhibit the following characteristics: immediacy (real-time response), transiency (response to more than one environmental state), self-actuation (intelligence internal to material), selectivity (discrete and predicable response), and directness (local response).[14] Architects are only now exploring potential applications of "smart" materials, assemblies, and systems. One example of a widely available smart product is SensiTile, which Brownell suggests could be used to provide more privacy in open-plan houses. Developed by an electrical engineer/architect, SensiTile responds to objects that cast shadows on it by migrating light through its matrix of acrylic polymers, so that the "shadow" disappears or creates other dynamic effects.[15]

Another significant application of responsive technologies is intelligent building skins. As Werner Sobek has already demonstrated in the R 128 House, it is possible to realize zero energy usage through building envelopes and skins of high quality materials and high technology that senses the exterior environment—temperature-wise, rain-wise, wind-wise, and humidity-wise—and responds by changing the interior conditions. Depending upon whether you are home or not, or the number of people in the house will determine how conditions will change. Sobek contends, "The building's skin should not have, as all building skins actually have, constant physical properties." And Neil Denari agrees with this view. "Intelligent skins and operable skins and looking more at envelopes rather than where walls are going is probably the investigation of the future."

Microclimates controlled by individually responsive controls are likely to revolutionize environmental design, according to Toshiko Mori. Instead of using tons of energy to heat or cool an entire room or house, software is being developed to provide microclimate control for the individual human body. Microclimates will eliminate the need for generic room temperature and thus greatly reduce energy consumption. Mori points out that what is important is the person's direct environment; for that is where comfort matters. So traditional modeling of environmental volume is completely wrong; microclimates, in contrast, will be tailored to each individual through a control system regulated close to a body that moves your environment from one place to another, she explains. "That's definitely the future of environmental controls." Michelle Addington also suggests that micro- and mini-heat exchange devices, already used today in electronics, could completely change our domestic thermal environments.

Light emitting diodes—LEDs—could also radically transform what we see and how we reset our hormonal systems, according to Addington. LEDs will in the future have the greatest potential as a new material for the home, especially as they require almost no infrastructure. They are low power, discrete, highly directional, have specific control of wavelengths and therefore spectrum, and fit into our understanding of the neurobiology of the eye, as Addington points out. The full potential of LEDs has yet to be realized. Instead, they are seen as substitutes for existing technology, being force-fit into a standard conception of lighting: white, housed in fluorescent tubing, and placed on the ceiling. "And that it takes not a single one of the advantages of LEDs and uses them in a very disadvantaged way, except if we think about how we might really want to use them, which would probably be more peripherally, very discreetly located," says Addington. "What we're not doing is stepping back away from the technologies and really asking what it is that we want to create."

One of the frontiers of materials science research in architecture is perception: specifically, the idea of separating the representation of physical environments from their reality through small imperceptible devices. "We've been caught up in this idea of representation and physical object as being one and the same since the Renaissance, since the development of orthographic projection. I don't think we're quite prepared yet for where that splitting apart could possibly take us," says Addington. "Now if we're decoupling physical phenomena from the building, then we're also sort of decoupling the physical space from its surroundings as well." Unlike 1990s cyberspace, where virtual worlds were built on computers, it is projected that a new world of embedded information technology—sensors, actuators, microchips, microprocessors—will surround us everywhere in everyday life.

"In the next twenty years things are going to change so much you and I cannot imagine," says Brenda Laurel. "In my experience, for about ten years things look kind of familiar and then, wham, it's all different, like when laptops appeared or when cell phones appeared. I think we're coming up to another one of those [dramatic periods of change] with sensor activated environments." Laurel forecasts radical changes in daily life as well as in how industry works, from keeping track of inventory being shipped to managing huge distributive networks. She says, "That is all going to change really fast—overnight, I think. In the next five years we're going to see big phase shift because of sensor technology and sensor networks and what they can provide to us in terms of information." How sensors will be applied to the dwelling is yet to be seen.

Today, it appears we will live in increasingly ambient environments of pervasive computing or what Malcolm McCullough in the book *Digital Ground* calls "interaction design." [16] To extrapolate from these developments, we can see the potential of creating unique environments in response to a single individual through computationally-shifting perception. "You can begin to imagine walking through this space, [and] at certain moments, certain physical things or certain behaviors are triggered and take place a centimeter away from the body, but they could be distributed throughout huge space," Addington explains. "Each step might activate one of these interactions or exchanges." Here we arrive at the outer limits of architecture: the ability to create any environment or the appearance and feeling of any environment that we choose. In this case, as Bruce Mau asks at the beginning of the exhibition catalogue *Massive Change*, "Now that we can do anything, what will we do?" [17] Or, if buildings are free to be anything, what do we want the home to be?

Conclusion. Without a doubt, accelerated technological innovation is coming to the future home and will transform it sooner than we think. Although it is still uncertain *how* the home might look in 2026 consumers and designers alike have a crucial role to play in shaping it. As John Thackara posits, "The critical issue—for people, organizations, and governments alike—*is knowing where we want to be*. The imaginary, an alternative cultural vision, is vital in shaping expectations and driving transformational change. Shared visions act as forces for innovation, and what designers can do—what we can all do—is imagine some situation or condition that does not yet exist but describe it in sufficient detail that it appears to be a desirable new version of the real world."[18] A large portion of the criticism directed at recent industry-commissioned, engineer-developed "smart" houses derived from the absence of architectural imagination in these projects and a failure to understand the nature of human needs. Clearly, creative collaborative vision is crucial for planning the future home. It is also essential to look for inspiration around the world for how we can live in the future in a more creative and sustainable way. Global collaborations that bring together architects and the creative community with people and leaders in science, technology, business, and government, will make a truly intelligent home possible.

1   John Thackara, *In the Bubble: Designing in a Complex World,* Cambridge, The MIT Press, 2005, p. 219.

2   Ibid.

3   Unless otherwise noted, the comments of designers and architects are taken from interviews with the author (or with the author and Richard Koshalek) between August and December 2005.

4   Michael J. Mandel, "This Way to the Future," *Business Week* (October 11, 2004), p. 94.

5   Thackara, *In the Bubble*, p. 204.

6   Akiko Busch, *Geography of Home: Writings on Where We Live*, New York, Princeton, 1999, p. 20.

7   Béatrice Simonot, "Strategies and Tactics," *ArchiLab's Futurehouse: Radical Experiments in Living Space*, eds. Marie-Ange Brayer and Béatrice Simonot, New York, Thames & Hudson, 2002, p. 10.

8   Geoffrey London, "The 21st Century House," *Houses for the 21st Century*, ed. Geoffrey London and Patrick Bingham-Hall, Singapore, Periplus, 2004, p. 12.

9   Thackara, *In the Bubble*, p. 19.

10 Malcolm McCullough, *Digital Ground: Architecture, Pervasive Computing, and Environmental Knowing*, Cambridge, The MIT Press, 2004, p. 213.

11 www.usgbc.org.

12 Janine M. Benyus, *Biomimicry: Innovation Inspired by Nature*, New York, William Morrow and Company, Inc., 1997, p. 132.

13 Blaine E. Brownell, "The Leaders of the Latest Materials Revolution," *Architectural Record Innovation* 193 (November 2005), p. 36.

14 Michelle Addington and Daniel Schodek, *Smart Materials and Technologies for the Architecture and Design Professions*, Oxford, Architectural Press, 2005, p. 10.

15 Brownell, "The Leaders of the Latest Materials Revolution," p42.

16 McCullough, *Digital Ground*, p. xiv.

17 Bruce Mau with Jennifer Leonard and the Institute without Boundaries, *Massive Change*, London, Phaidon Press Limited, 2004, p. 15.

18 Thackara, *In the Bubble*, p. 26.

1

MICHELLE ADDINGTON IS ASSOCIATE PROFESSOR OF ARCHITECTURE AT HARVARD GRADUATE SCHOOL OF DESIGN. TRAINED AS A MECHANICAL ENGINEER AND AN ARCHITECT, SHE PREVIOUSLY WORKED AT NASA AND IN THE CHEMICAL INDUSTRY BEFORE TURNING TO ARCHITECTURE. SHE IS CO-AUTHOR OF *SMART MATERIALS AND TECHNOLOGIES FOR THE ARCHITECTURE AND DESIGN PROFESSIONS* (2005).

2

BEN VAN BERKEL IS CO-DIREC-TOR OF UN STUDIO IN AMSTERDAM, A NETWORK OF SPECIALISTS IN ARCHITECTURE, URBAN DEVELOPMENT AND INFRASTRUCTURE. RECENT PROJ-ECTS INCLUDE THE MERCEDES BENZ MUSEUM IN STUTTGART, HARBOR RE-DEVELOPMENT IN GENOA, A MUSIC CENTER IN GRAZ, AND A MASTERPLAN FOR ARNHEM, THE NETHERLANDS.

3

AARON BETSKY IS DIRECTOR OF THE NEDERLANDS ARCHITECTUUR INSTITUUT, ROTTERDAM. HE WAS CURATOR OF ARCHITECTURE AND DESIGN AT THE SAN FRANCISCO MUSEUM OF MODERN ART, AND INSTRUCTOR, SOUTHERN CALIFORNIA INSTITUTE OF ARCHITECTURE. HIS LATEST BOOK IS *FALSE FLAT: WHY DUTCH DESIGN IS SO GOOD* (2004).

4

BLAINE E. BROWNELL IS AN ARCHITECT AND A SUSTAINABLE BUILDING ADVISOR AT NBBJ, BASED IN SEATTLE. HE IS AUTHOR OF *TRANSMATERIAL: A CATALOG OF MATERIALS THAT REDEFINE OUR PHYSICAL ENVIRONMENT* (2006) AND EDITS A WEEKLY ELECTRONIC JOURNAL ON INNOVATIVE PRODUCTS.

5

YUNG HO CHANG IS HEAD OF THE DEPARTMENT OF ARCHITECTURE AT THE MASSACHUSETTS INSTITUTE OF TECHNOLOGY, PRINCIPAL OF ATELIER FCJZ IN BEIJING, AND HEAD OF THE GRADUATE ARCHI-TECTURE PROGRAM AT PEKING UNIVERSITY. ATELIER FCJZ HAS CURRENT PROJECTS IN CON-STRUCTION IN CHINA, KOREA AND JAPAN.

6

PETER COOK FOUNDED THE EXPERIMENTAL MAGAZINE AND ARCHITECTURE COOPERATIVE ARCHIGRAM. RECENTLY HE DESIGNED (WITH COLIN FOURNIER) THE KUNSTHAUS IN GRAZ. HE IS PROFESSOR OF ARCHITECTURE AT LONDON UNIVERSITY'S BARTLETT SCHOOL OF ARCHITECTURE AND AUTHOR OF *THE CITY, SEEN AS A GARDEN OF IDEAS* (2003).

7

NEIL DENARI IS PRINCIPAL OF NEIL M. DENARI ARCHITECTS, LOS ANGELES AND PROFESSOR-IN-RESIDENCE IN THE ARCHITECTURE AND URBAN DESIGN DEPARTMENT AT UCLA. HIS PRACTICE AND TEACHING FOCUSES ON THE COMPLEX RELATIONSHIPS BETWEEN ARCHI-TECTURE, DESIGN, AND CONTEM-PORARY LIFE. HE IS AUTHOR OF *GYROSCOPIC HORIZONS* (1999) AND *NOTEBOOKS 1990-2006* (FORTHCOMING).

8

CRAIG HODGETTS, PRINCIPAL OF HODGETTS AND FUNG IN LOS ANGELES, IS AN ARCHITECT, URBAN SCENARIST, INDUSTRIAL DESIGNER, AND THEORIST WHO SYNTHESIZES ARCHITECTURE, ART AND TECHNOLOGY IN WORKS SUCH AS THE RENOVA-TION OF THE EGYPTIAN THEATER IN HOLLYWOOD. HE IS PROFES-SOR IN THE UCLA DEPARTMENT OF ARCHITECTURE AND URBAN DESIGN.

9

MIZUKO ITO IS RESEARCH SCI-ENTIST AT THE ANNENBERG CENTER FOR COMMUNICATION AT THE UNIVERSITY OF SOUTHERN CALIFORNIA, LOS ANGELES, AND CO-EDITOR OF PERSONAL, *PORTABLE, PEDESTRIAN: MOBILE PHONES IN JAPANESE LIFE* (2005).

10

TOYO ITO IS THE FOUNDER AND PRINCIPAL OF TOYO ITO & ASSOCIATES, ARCHITECTS IN TOKYO. WHILE RENOWNED FOR CONCEPT BUILDINGS THAT MERGE THE PHYSICAL AND VIR-TUAL WORLDS, SUCH AS THE SENDAI MEDIATHEQUE (2001), HE IS NOW SEEKING A NEW ARCHITECTURE FOR THE TWENTY-FIRST CENTURY THAT REFLECTS NATURE AND CREATES JOYFUL AND PLEASANT SPACES FILLED WITH LIFE.

11

BRENDA LAUREL IS A DESIGNER, RESEARCHER AND WRITER, WHOSE WORK FOCUSES ON INTERACTIVE NARRATIVE, HUMAN-COMPUTER INTERAC-TION, AND CULTURAL ASPECTS OF TECHNOLOGY. SHE IS CHAIR OF THE GRADUATE MEDIA DESIGN PROGRAM AT ART CENTER COLLEGE OF DESIGN AND DISTINGUISHED ENGINEER AT SUN MICROSYSTEMS. HER NEWEST BOOK IS *DESIGN RESEARCH* (2004).

12

THOM MAYNE—2005 PRITZKER-PRIZE LAUREATE—IS PRINCIPAL OF MORPHOSIS ARCHITECTS IN LOS ANGELES, CALIFORNIA, AND PROFESSOR OF ARCHITECTURE AT UCLA. CURRENT PROJECTS INCLUDE FEDERAL BUILDINGS IN SAN FRANCISCO, OREGON, AND MARYLAND, EDUCATION BUILD-INGS FOR NEW YORK'S COOPER UNION AND CALTECH IN PASADENA, AND INTERNATION-AL PROJECTS IN MADRID, SHANGHAI, AND GUADALAJARA.

13

WILLIAM MCDONOUGH IS FOUNDING PRINCIPAL OF WILLIAM MCDONOUGH AND PARTNERS, ARCHITECTURE AND COMMUNITY DESIGN IN CHARLOTTESVILLE, VIRGINIA. HE IS ALSO CO-FOUNDER AND PRINCIPAL OF MBDC AND CO-AUTHOR OF CRADLE TO CRADLE: *REMAKING THE WAY WE MAKE THINGS* (2002).

14

TOSHIKO MORI IS CHAIR OF THE DEPARTMENT OF ARCHITECTURE AT HARVARD GRADUATE SCHOOL OF DESIGN. SHE IS ALSO PRINCIPAL OF TOSHIKO MORI ARCHITECT IN NEW YORK. SHE IS AUTHOR OF *IMMATERIAL/ ULTRAMATERIAL: ARCHITECTURE, DESIGN, AND MATERIALS (2002) AND TEXTILE/TECTONIC: ARCHITECTURE, MATERIAL, AND FABRICATION* (FORTHCOMING).

15

WERNER SOBEK—ARCHITECT, ENGINEER, AND AUTHOR— FOUNDED WERNER SOBEK INGENIEURE, A GLOBAL STRUC-TURAL ENGINEERING AND DESIGN CONSULTANCY. HE IS PROFESSOR OF ENGINEERING AT UNIVERSITÄT STUTTGART, WHERE HE ESTABLISHED AND LEADS THE INSTITUTE FOR LIGHTWEIGHT STRUCTURES AND CONCEPTUAL DESIGN.

16

DEYAN SUDJIC IS THE DIRECTOR OF THE DESIGN MUSEUM IN LONDON. HE WAS ARCHITEC-TURE CRITIC OF THE LONDON OBSERVER AND DEAN OF KINGSTON'S FACULTY OF ART, DESIGN AND ARCHITECTURE. HE WAS EDITOR OF *DOMUS* AND EDITORIAL DIRECTOR OF *BLUEPRINT*, OF WHICH HE WAS ALSO FOUNDING EDITOR. HE HAS PUBLISHED SEVERAL BOOKS, INCLUDING *THE EDIFICE COMPLEX* (2005).

17

JOHN THACKARA IS DIRECTOR OF DOORS OF PERCEPTION, A DESIGN FUTURES NETWORK THAT INVOLVES VISIONARY DESIGNERS, BUSINESS, THE PUBLIC SECTOR AND GRASSROOTS INNOVATORS IN COLLABORATIVE PROJECTS. HE WAS THE FIRST DIRECTOR OF THE NETHERLANDS DESIGN INSTITUTE. HIS MOST RECENT BOOK IS *IN THE BUBBLE: DESIGNING IN A COMPLEX WORLD* (2005).

The Future of the Future ¶

> BRUCE STERLING

Our ideas about the future are period artifacts. The passage of time is a feature of the universe, like gravity. Cultural formulas about time, history, and progress are temporary notions. The clock always continues to tick. We find that intellectually inconvenient, but the clock doesn't care what we think about the future. It just brings some.

If you're a contemporary furniture designer, anything called "modernity" has to feel painful and musty today. "Postmodernity" has a very

1980s tang for present-day furniture mavens, since it's so Superstudio, so Memphis, so Italian plastic laminate. "Supermodernity" sounds new and terrific, but it has no conceptual traction as yet. I love the idea of being or becoming "supermodern," but that term will likely have an even shorter shelf life than "modern" and "postmodern." And what would follow "supermodern? "Ultramodern?" "Hypermodern?" How would we be made to care?

People like a popular consensus about futurity, because they can focus creative efforts around a common line of advancement. To fully share an ideological future vision gives one a warm, cozy, unified, bravura feeling. Unfortunately, that doesn't necessarily help us to deal with the physical fact that time is passing. We always advance into the future at the unaltering rate of one second per second. We can call ourselves progressive or retrograde, Communist or Free World, futuristic or antiquarian, but the rain falls on the just and the unjust alike, and the dust of the cosmos settles on everybody at precisely the same rate.

A truly useful vision of futurity would be one that could assure us of having an actual future, not just ideas about it. As long as we human beings have a plentiful supply of time, plus energy and resources, we can generate any number of enticing theories about futurity. "Without vision the people perish," as the Bible has been saying for millennia, but every generation sprouts a crop of visionaries. Visions of the future come pretty cheap and are mostly recyclable. They're generally knitted up of rags and tatters of previous visions of the future, in the way that, say, the Bauhaus was a Machine Age steel-and-glass remake of the outworn Arts and Crafts Movement.

We're not likely to run out of ideas about time, but we might well "run out of time" in a more pragmatic sense. We might well have "no future" because we were foolishly over-committed to obsolete and dangerous methods of manufacture that can no longer be carried out. A civilization will collapse catastrophically if it fails to get its material act together. If flows of material and energy stop, civilization collapses. The Mayans, the Easter Islanders, and the Vikings on Greenland had no future for their future. The Bauhaus had a short lifespan. It didn't fail because its modern ideas became passé; the Bauhaus was physically padlocked by Nazis and then bombed flat after the professors scattered.

Avoiding collapse means achieving "sustainability." "Sustainability" is an ambitious set of ideas. Like "modernity," "sustainability" wants to become an entirely comprehensive way of thinking and acting in the interests of the future. Sustainability means keeping a wary eye on the mounting threats and the dwindling resources, and contriving ways to survive the long-term consequences of our previous technical successes. The future of the future must be some form of sustainability, because time is on its side. We may not crash into the "limits to growth" or explode a "population bomb" when we first hear the zealots moaning. But unless we redress their grievances, all we need to do is wait a while. When you're doing something that can't go on, sooner or later you have to stop.

"Modernity," while it lasted, was exciting, motivating, and different. "Sustainability" is scary, stunningly tedious, hectoring, conformist, and dull. Sustainability is about posterity, about the mindful struggle to bequeath a future to our imperiled descendants. However, sustainability has never felt, even in the least bit, futuristic. That's why people hate it.

Modernists may have been often wrong but were rarely in doubt, whereas sustainablists

186

are alarmist scolds, incoherent and often mystical, people who sound like they gave up all sense of taste in order to live on their last resorts. As noted chair designer Mike McCoy points out, "Nobody gets up from a meal and says, 'Thank you dear, that was very sustainable.'" "Modern" is a glowing term of praise. "Sustainable" has the sweaty reek of communes, lifeboats, ration-systems, and fall-out shelters.

However, we can't achieve a future by permanently doing things that physically can't be continued. Many of the speculative problems that sustainability wrung its hands about back on Earth Day 1970 are real as concrete now. Parisians have died of summer heat in thousands; New Orleans was under water; bioaccumulative toxins are piling up in our lungs and livers; the poles are missing chunks of ice the size of Texas, while tropical storms with Greek letters for names roam the Caribbean. Those are symptoms of unresolved, growing civilizational problems; we are still far from the crux of the crisis there. The game plan? We're blithely heading toward a planet crammed with 10 billion urbanized people who plan to burn oil that will not exist. When "mechanization took command," the much older world of handicrafts melted away in a hurry. Imagine the swift and ugly fate of mechanization when it flips its power switch and nothing happens.

A compelling future of the future would be a sustainability that somehow manages to feel modern. We don't know how to get there from here. Modern sustainability will be based in technologies, innovations, and ways of thought that we haven't mastered yet. At the moment, it's unimaginable. However, it's also entirely necessary. So it will be imagined, and, more or less at the same time, it will be done in practice. Like the transition to modernity, sustainable modernity won't get done everywhere, all

at once, or with comprehensive success. The proof will become visible on the ground, in bits in pieces, in hints and trends. People and places that manage this transition will be living in a way that is currently unimaginable. People who fail to do it will have lives that are unthinkable.

Let me drag my thesis closer to home here by discussing furniture. Let's consider two tables. Like all human artifacts, these two tables are a frozen set of technosocial relationships. They embody two radically different design philosophies, so they have scarcely anything in common. One table is an Eileen Gray's Adjustable Table E-1027, a bedside table. The other table, radically different in most every way, is also an Eileen Gray Adjustable Table E-1027. However, one is modernist while the other is sustainable. They are tables from two different conceptual worlds.

First, we'll approach that "modernist" table, because a modernist table is glamorous, revolutionary, exciting and really compels reader interest, plus, people are willing to buy them. To become as modernist as possible, we'll assume that we're the mother of this table; the year is 1927, the place is southern France, and we are Eileen Gray.

Our heroine, Miss Gray the furniture designer, is a well-to-do Scots-Irish émigré who has done so much hands-on furniture craft-work that she has contracted "lacquer disease" in her aching fingers. Eileen has good reasons to be fed up with the older ways of hand-crafting furnishings. By dint of sharing the continent with pioneers like Mies, Breuer, Le Corbusier, and Charlotte Perriand, and her own Union des artistes modernes, Eileen has quietly converted to the revolutionary modernist cause.

Modernism is a comprehensive revolution in thinking about objects. Modernism means death to handicrafts, and surrender to the command of mechanization. Modernism is on a social mission to bring clean, functional, designed possessions and surroundings to mass populations. These mass objects will be rationally made of mass-produced materials, cheaply.

Also, Eileen's sister badly needs a new table, because it's her habit to eat breakfast in bed.

So, Miss Gray has a methodology, a client, means, motives, materials, and opportunity. Despite her painful mastery of Japanese lacquer work, she's jumping ship for the glass-and-chrome contingent. Prying herself from the stifling coils of tradition, she re-thinks a bedside table from its first principles. She takes a rational, minimalist approach to the functional challenge of coffee and biscuits suspended over a mattress.

Her result is the E-1027. This contraption looks radically ahistorical. The E-1027 is truly a breakthrough table. It is radically emancipated from all vernacular bedside-table traditions. Eileen's unprecedented table is clean, sleek, mechanically manufactured sheet-glass and chromed steel. Eileen's sister probably expected something like a teakwood tea trolley. She's gotten a creation whose closest relatives are a microscope slide and a trombone.

If Eileen Gray had successfully troubled some mass-scale manufacturers, she might have made and sold a million of E-1027 tables for approximately eighty dollars each. Unfortunately, Eileen Gray was painfully shy and never mass-market-oriented. So rather than achieving wide adoption for her table, she modestly slid into a deep creative obscurity. Her Paris apartment was bombed flat in World War II, destroying much of her legacy.

Shortly before her death at a remarkably advanced age, design journalists rediscovered her "modern" E-1027 table. It emerged from the darkening mists of encroaching history and became a period *objet*. Licensed reproductions of the E-1027 are currently available for four hundred dollars plus shipping, thanks to the aptly named ClassiCon outfit in Munich. The E-1027 now thrives far better than it ever did while its creator lived, not because it's "modern," but because it's retro-modern and elegantly antiquarian.

So much for the "modernist" Eileen Gray table. Now we'll consider our "sustainable" Eileen Gray table. This E-1027 table was, unfortunately, bombed in World War II. The glass was shattered to bits. The steel tubing is warped beyond recognition. All the chrome has flaked off. There's not a tinge of romantic lore or Walter Benjamin aura left to this table. It is garbage; refuse, rubbish, and it will stay that way.

With its useful lifetime long since over, it has been sitting in a French landfill since the late 1940s. There it is foully surrounded by other outworn possessions of the traumatic twentieth century. Though they no longer have any modernist cachet, these dead objects are still very much part of our biosphere. This French landfill is fermenting, offgassing dangerous methane, and leaching its decaying contents into the European water table.

The "sustainable" table's brief period in daylight lasted a mere twenty years or so. No longer useful or beautiful, it has since become a well-nigh permanent environmental hazard. Unless we take deliberate remedial action, it will remain a menace for generations to come. That is its future. This sustainable table, this defunct relic, gives us no pleasure, but rather a lively sense of active loathing. That broken glass could slash our feet. The rusty iron could give us tetanus. This snarled wreck of artsy modernist ambition is a gloomy, rusting tangle of technological downsides. We'd pay good money not to have to look at it.

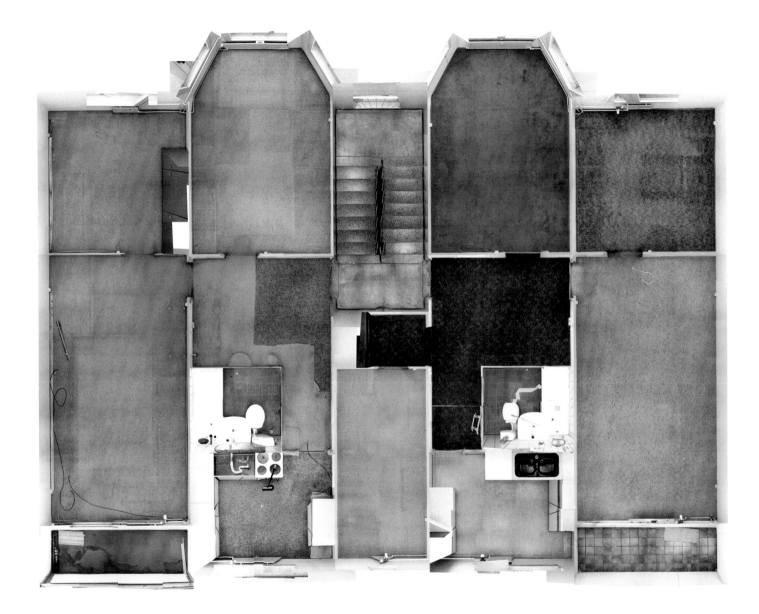

ANDREAS GEFELLER,
*UNTITLED (PLATTENBAU
1-4)*, C-PRINT/DIASEC,
110 X 133 CM,
EDITION OF 8, 2004

COURTESY THOMAS
REHBEIN GALLERY,
COLOGNE

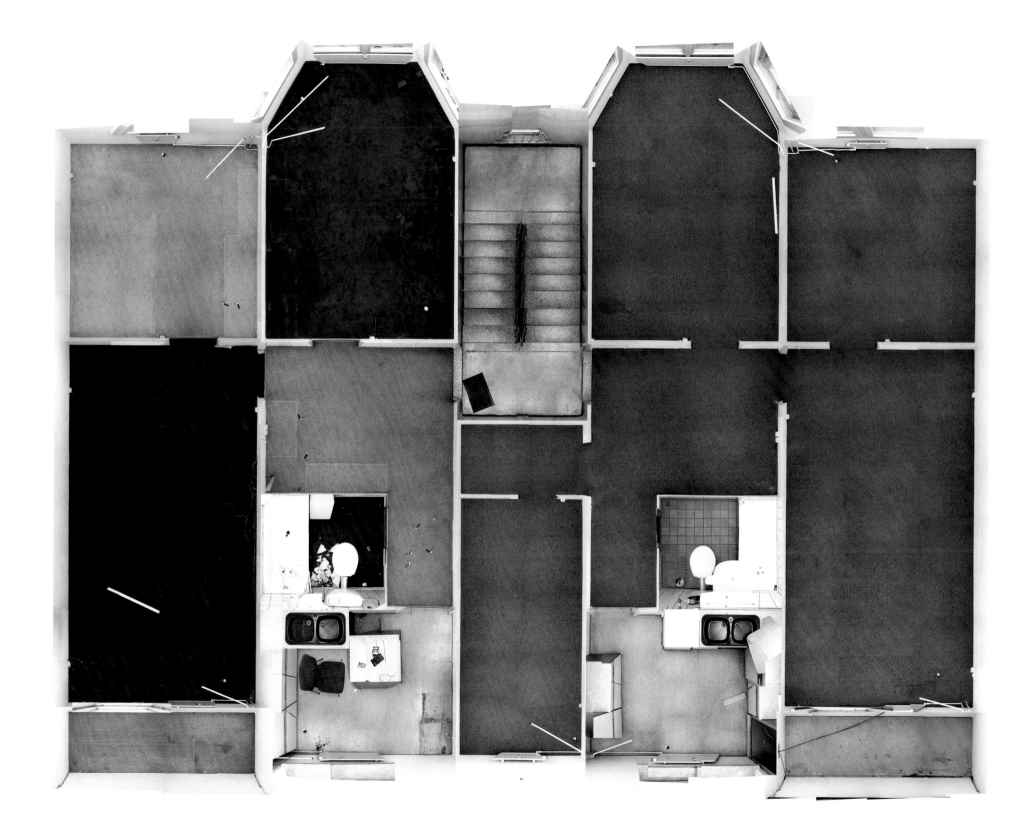

There is one minor advantage: steel and glass, properly handled, are recyclable. So if we're sufficiently dutiful, mindful and voluntarist, we might pry the dead E-1027 of its matrix of French rubbish and send it to a smelter somewhere. It's too bad that this wasn't done long ago, but as advocates of sustainability, we're never ahead of industry's game. We're always following the elephants' parade with bucket and shovel.

No wonder we sustainable types hate consumers so. Our unease grows acute if we abandon the works of Eileen Gray and walk into IKEA, a triumph of modernity writ large. IKEA features interminable, Wal-Mart-scale lots of cheap, thoughtful, machine-made objects. Unlike Eileen Gray luxury *objets*, IKEA is genuinely cheap, mass-market, and proletarian. We sustainabilists can wearily search all over IKEA, and, admittedly, it's hard to find any object in IKEA that is "badly designed"—that is, from a modernist perspective.

IKEA's wares are crammed full of Scandinavian rationality. They're clean lined, sleek, minimal, "timeless," and even relatively durable commodities. They're useful, safe, low maintenance, cheap, nice-looking and have a high sales appeal.

However, these manifest modern design virtues don't make us Sustainable types any happier. Heavens no. We're possessed of an entirely different and much darker design perspective, one in which a cheery Euro furniture mart like IKEA is a roiling Piranesian nightmare. What we witness in IKEA is a vast engine of planetary destruction, a gussied-up brothel for heedless consumerism, where raw materials are grubbed-up in whirlwinds of heedless greed, leaping from Swedish designers to Chinese engineers to Californian consumers in toxic spews of sky-scarring jet exhaust. They're plastered with seductive logos, and then sold to frantic, overweight Americans, who are sinking into debt in their mire of consumerist false-consciousness. And the upshot? Ugh... it's that landfill again.

The landfill is the system's ultimate endgame. Design aesthetics are profoundly beside the point; for everything that physically exists is a larval form of landfill. The clock is on junk's side. The junk piles higher and deeper. Is it any wonder that we shudder all over at a shelf full of gleeful consumer goods, or that we despair for ourselves and our great-grandchildren? We're like Banquo at the shopping mall's food court. When we open our mouths, out fly dispiriting jeremiads, guilt-inducing polemics, and pained remonstrances. We're never pleased with developments, for we can never become Green enough. To live is, in itself, to consume and therefore to do harm.

Although we tell the truth, very few flock to our banners. There is no one so entirely sustainable as the dead. Even Eileen Gray outdoes us in sustainability, because Miss Gray after an impressive 97-year lifespan had the good taste to die in 1976. So Eileen, to her credit, is being recycled into the biosphere, while we, who are still the living, must skulk around in this culturally dominant capitalist supermart, scowling at the wares and emitting carbon dioxide. Thank you very much for living lean and dying young; thank you, that was very sustainable.

Modernism is a mass design revolution waiting to turn into elite designer icons. Modernism is a scheme to make period tchotchkes, rendered charmingly retro by their timeless rationality. Sustainability is full of woe. Sustainability has no game plan and no clear victory condition. It sees every industry as a Ponzi scheme, a sour method for glutting ourselves now and exporting the havoc to the grandchildren. Neither philosophy works. They don't work because they treat time as an enemy, as a rude imposition.

While we dither and weary of philosophical ironies—modernist antiques, design to sustain the dead—the clock keeps ticking. Never mind saving the whales for our grandchildren; we already are the grandchildren. That's our own sky that breeds tropical storms in such profusion that they have Greek letters for names. Those are our snowy mountain peaks melting away, our scientists yelling at our politicians who blink and quote ancient scripture instead of practically rallying to save our future bacon.

We know pretty well what's necessary, but we can't find a way to arouse the passion needed to get on with it, or any commercial way to make that process pay. We know how to manufacture things, promote and distribute things in vast profusion, but we don't know how to come to realistic working terms with their inevitable entropy. We're still modern, or post-modern, or supermodern; we treat history as a nightmare from which we struggle to awake, instead of making the passage of time our ally, our friend.

The clock always ticks, and, if we approached the future as we should, we should find enormous comfort in this. The passage of time is an authentic, existential bedrock. We shouldn't struggle against the passage of time as if it were some alien imposition on our supposedly eternal philosophical verities. We human beings personify time. We are born and grow; we are made of time. It shouldn't be our line of work to aspire to so-called eternities. We are all historical figures in the making.

We needn't panic over the fact that the passage of time makes aging ideologies seem quaint. Ideologies don't merely seem quaint; they really are quaint. That is their nature. There is no shame in quaintness; quaintness is the measure by which we can recognize a genuine change in thinking. Even "sustainability" is cram-full of quaint and outdated ideas, like the idea that a "nature reserve" will stay "natural" if we leave it alone. That can't be true in a world of invasive species, tourism, and climate change. In our world, a "reserve" like Yellowstone is an entertainment destination, while the wildlife blooms and thrives in Chernobyl.

The best measure of a modern sustainable society is not that it freezes progress. The best measure would be to leave the next generation with as many options as we ourselves had. We will never freeze history into an icon of our period notions of futurity. Our best heritage to posterity is to give them the capacity to make some fresh mistakes.

There are three possible ways to be both sustainable and modern. First, make everything monumental. Permanent, long-lasting, perfect. Then there's no more consumer profusion or planned obsolescence; everything is scarce, rationed, sturdy, cherished, and built to last for many generations. This means deliberately trapping our descendants in a world with our own possessions, and our own chosen surroundings, for as long as possible. If any previous generation had chosen to do this to us, we would have passionately rebelled. This is a Thousand-Year-Reich notion. It's crazy and it will never work.

Second, make everything biodegradable. Our possessions still head straight for the landfill, but the landfill turns into harmless organic mulch. When we manage to do this to today's coal-burning, metal-bending industries, that feat is known as "biomimicry." Biomimicry yields a fabulous future world where weird bio-industrial analogs of bone and horn and spider-silk and ivory are grown at room temperature

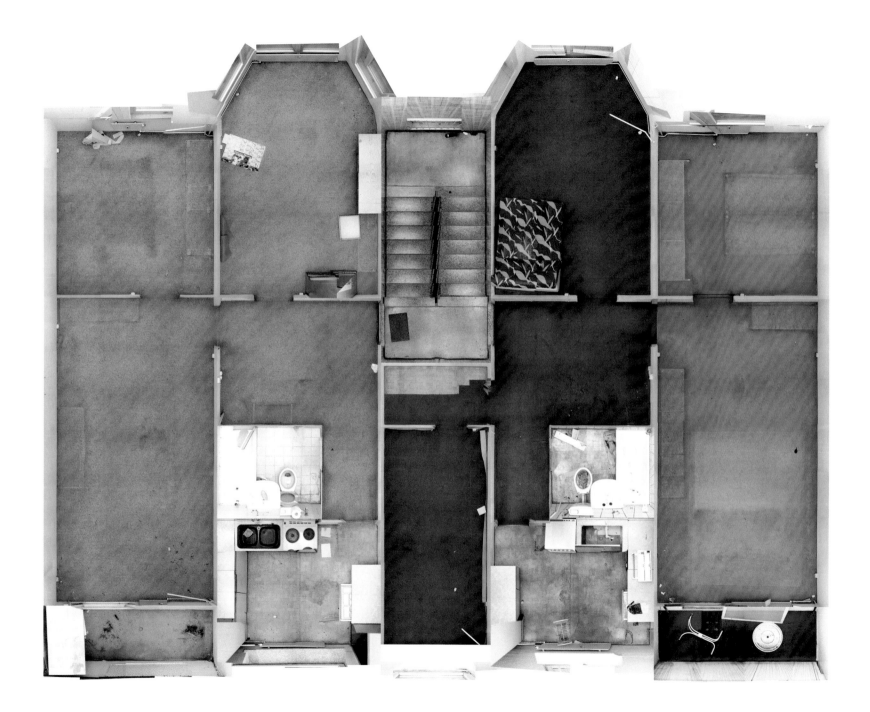

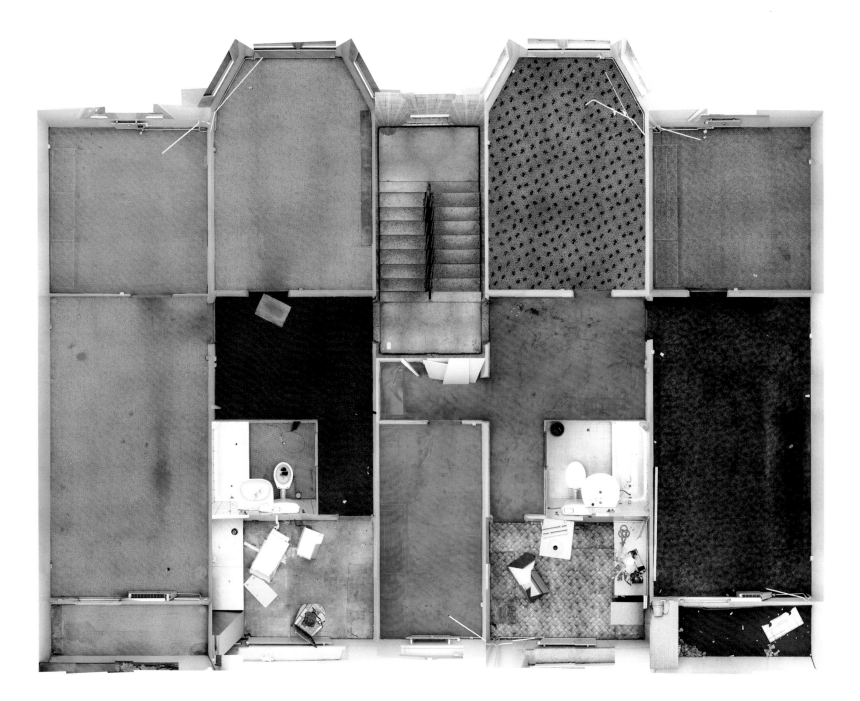

on massive industrial scales. This concept is superb. When it's possible, we should go for this prospect in a big way. Unfortunately, it's not very possible. If we make it to the end of this century in one piece, we'll likely be in sight of such marvels.

The last option is genuinely bizarre. It resolves the dialectic conflict of modernism and sustainability, by introducing a sneaky, disruptive innovation that was unimaginable in the twentieth century. Instead of making new objects, so often losing them in the muddle of history, and eventually consigning them one and all to the dump, we catalog the entire works, digitally. We create an unimaginably giant Internet archive of our possessions, a buzzy realm of electronic bar codes and hot-tags that forms a literal and ever- expanded Internet of Things. We industriously digitize materiality. It's a dot-com boom with real-life stuff. The actual becomes the new virtual. We label and tag every last Eileen Gray table, historicize it, from the blueprint sketches to the recycle truck. Then, if you buy one, it comes with a digital trigger that connects you, through various devious channels, to everything ever known about Eileen Gray and Eileen Gray's tables: who she was, why that table was, how it got there, who else has one, where you can get more of them, and, vitally, where to throw it away safely and profitably. Cybernization takes command.

We still lack words to describe a world like this. It is truly and radically different. But it offers advantages. For instance: even if every Eileen Gray table somehow physically vanishes, there's no tragedy there. The potential to recreate her work, and retrieve her heritage, is a search-engine's button-push away.

This interactive and ever-expanding history of own objects, and the digital systems that support them and dispose of them become much more important than mere materiality. We have resolved the past's debates about the future into a more advanced plane; we're unquestionably modern, while sustainability, once a matter of tortured mindfulness, is silently programmed into the design specs. Junk is always much easier to deal with if it comes prelabeled, and you know precisely what it is. We've got smart garbage. It can yell for a recycler on its own.

A world like this offers genuinely novel ideas about futurity. Time is on its side. The passage of time, instead of wearing away at our goods and demolishing our illusions, makes us more capable, more knowledgeable, more powerful, and more affluent. If we catalogue, archive, and data-mine the flows of objects and energies, then time becomes an industrial asset. The longer we wait, the more we learn about the physical world. We needn't gnaw our nails about the future, for we've transformed the passage of time into a genuine commercial resource.

Suddenly, we've got plenty of time. The prospect of ever-longer reaches of time doesn't drive us into panicked quests for utopia or oblivion. It's not that we've regained our lost optimism about "progress," for this situation is something deeper than mere doctrine. We've made futurity our production machine, in that painless, subtle way that Google and Amazon have turned their users into an unpaid but tireless labor force. The prospect of futurity gives us the warm, confident, glossy glow of people whose wealth is socked away at compound interest. To be modern and to think in the long term have become precisely the same thing.

The following statistics contain information on demographic and socio-economic developments relevant to the future of domestic living and residential architecture. These data also represent the empirical foundation of the visionary concepts proposed by the architects of Open House to meet future challenges. In order to emphasize the link to individual projects, statistics are cited from the specific countries for which Open House projects have been conceived.

EMPIRICAL DATA ON DOMESTIC LIVING

AVERAGE GLOBAL BIRTH RATE

The size of households is decreasing continuously...

The average number of people per household has been declining for decades. Fifty years ago, an average household had four members; in some countries today that number has decreased to less than two. In societies with declining birth rates, this trend is expected to continue.

The reduction in the size of Korean households is particularly significant.

1950–1955	5	children per woman
1995–2000	2.7	children per woman
2040–2050	1.54 – 2.0	children per woman (UN estimate)

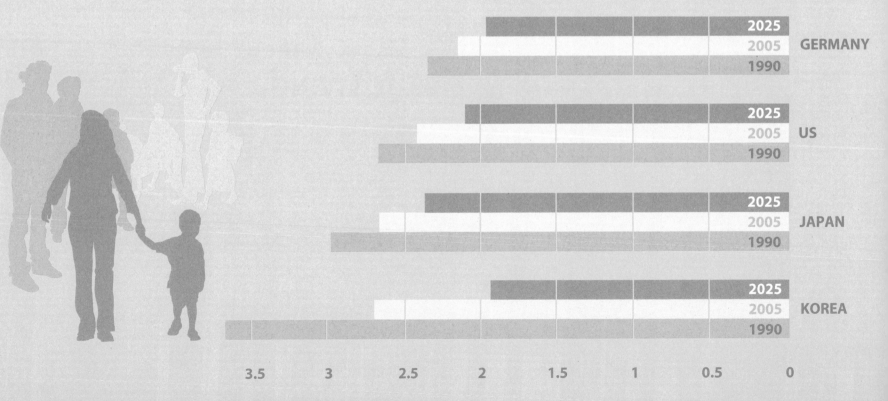

AVERAGE NUMBER OF PEOPLE PER HOUSEHOLD[1]

	GERMANY
2025	
2005	
1990	

	US
2025	
2005	
1990	

	JAPAN
2025	
2005	
1990	

	KOREA
2025	
2005	
1990	

3.5   3   2.5   2   1.5   1   0.5   0

AVERAGE LIVING SPACE PER PERSON IN GERMANY[2]

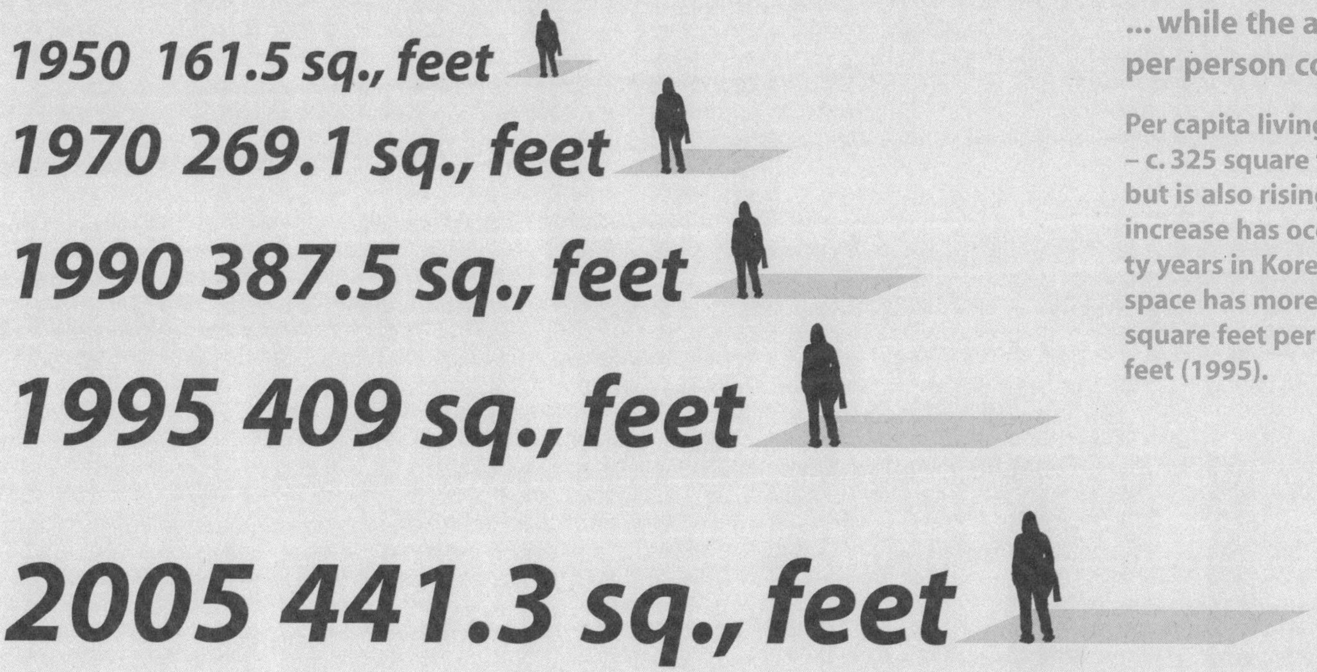

1950 161.5 sq., feet

1970 269.1 sq., feet

1990 387.5 sq., feet

1995 409 sq., feet

2005 441.3 sq., feet

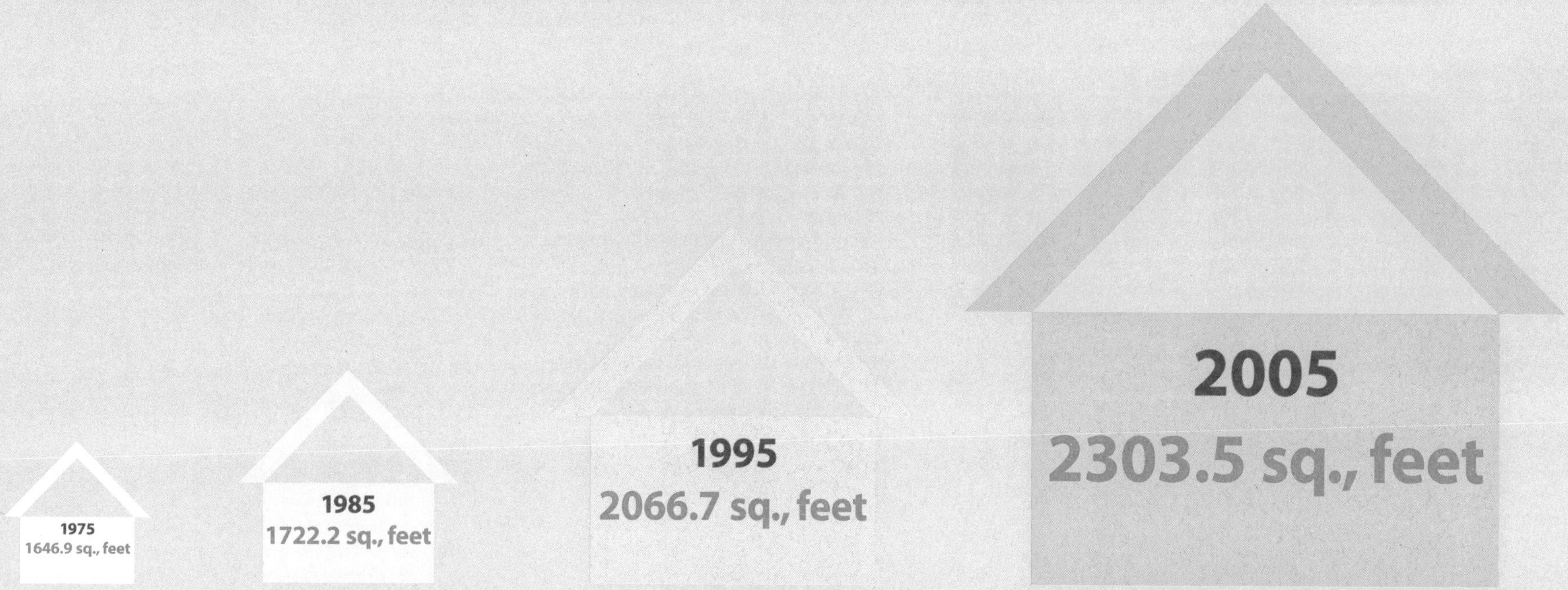

... while the amount of living space per person continues to increase.

Per capita living space in Asia is not as high – c. 325 square feet per person in Japan – but is also rising. An especially significant increase has occurred during the past twenty years in Korea, where the average living space has more than doubled from 86.1 square feet per person (1975) to 183 square feet (1995).

2005
2303.5 sq., feet

1995
2066.7 sq., feet

1985
1722.2 sq., feet

1975
1646.9 sq., feet

AVERAGE SIZE OF A SINGLE FAMILY HOME IN THE US[5]

PERCENTAGE OF POPULATION OVER AGE 65[6]

Between 1965 and 1970, the world population was growing at a rate of 2 percent—the highest ever in human history. A number of utopian concepts for urban development emerged within this context during the 1960s, which shared the aim of increasing the density of urban space.
Today the rate of world population growth is 1.2 percent.

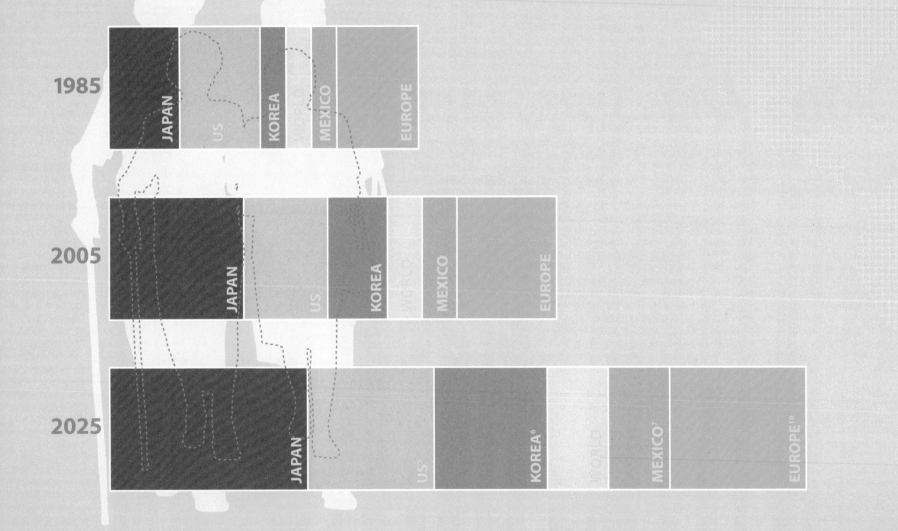

1985 — JAPAN — US — KOREA — WORLD — MEXICO — EUROPE

2005 — JAPAN — US — KOREA — WORLD — MEXICO — EUROPE

2025 — JAPAN — US[5] — KOREA[6] — WORLD[8] — MEXICO[7] — EUROPE[10]

1805 1
1927 2
1960 3
1974 4
1987 5
1999 6
2013 7
2027 8

BILLION

INCREASE IN LIFE EXPECTANCY[8]

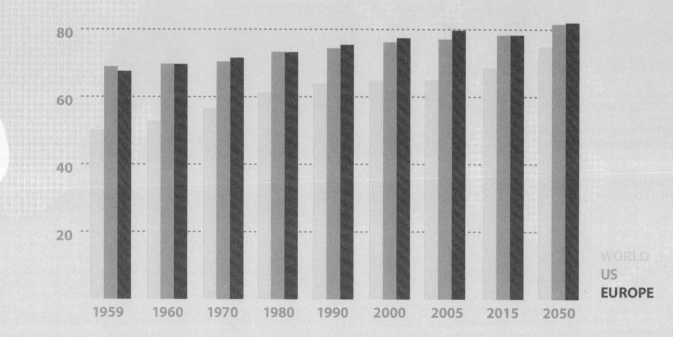

100

80

60

40

20

WORLD
US
EUROPE

1959 1960 1970 1980 1990 2000 2005 2015 2050

GLOBAL URBANIZATION: URBAN POPULATION (IN PERCENT)

... but more people than ever live in urban agglomerations.

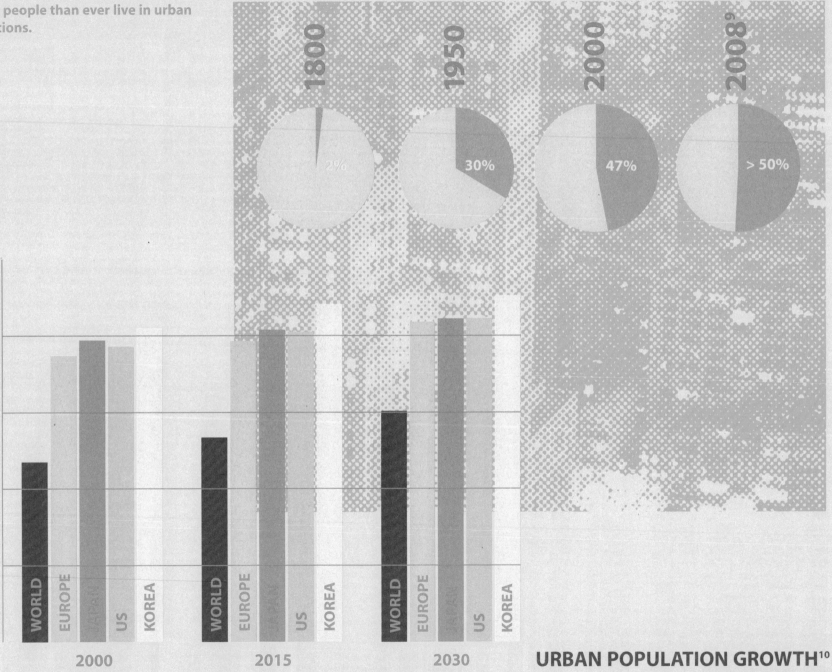

1800   2%

1950   30%

2000   47%

2008[9]   > 50%

100

80

60

40

20

WORLD   EUROPE   JAPAN   US   KOREA

WORLD   EUROPE   JAPAN   US   KOREA

WORLD   EUROPE   JAPAN   US   KOREA

2000   2015   2030

URBAN POPULATION GROWTH[10]

POPULATION DENSITY IN METROPOLITAN AREAS[11]

LOS ANGELES

7,876.8
persons/
square mile

LONDON

12,170
persons/
square mile

MEXICO CITY

14,947
persons/
square mile

NEW YORK

26,403
persons/
square mile

TOKYO

34.747
persons/
square mile

SEOUL

41,440
persons/
square mile

With 1,207 people per square mile, South Korea has one of the highest population densities in the world after Bangladesh, Taiwan, and city states like Singapore and Hong Kong.

MAIN TELEPHONE LINES PER 1,000 PEOPLE[12]

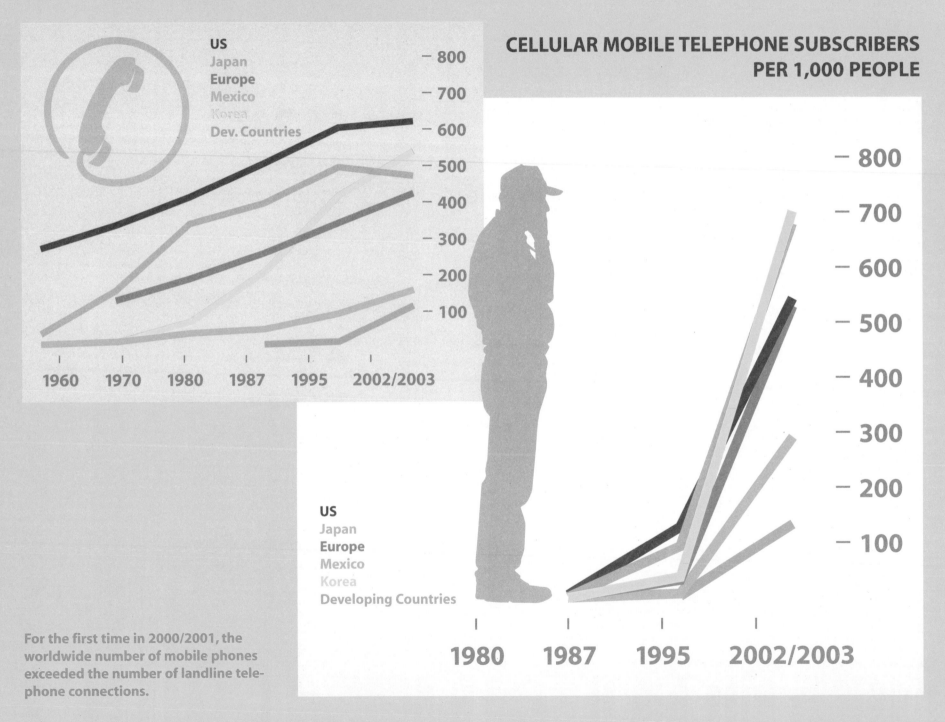

US
Japan
Europe
Mexico
Korea
Dev. Countries

— 800
— 700
— 600
— 500
— 400
— 300
— 200
— 100

1960 1970 1980 1987 1995 2002/2003

CELLULAR MOBILE TELEPHONE SUBSCRIBERS
PER 1,000 PEOPLE

— 800
— 700
— 600
— 500
— 400
— 300
— 200
— 100

US
Japan
Europe
Mexico
Korea
Developing Countries

1980 1987 1995 2002/2003

For the first time in 2000/2001, the worldwide number of mobile phones exceeded the number of landline telephone connections.

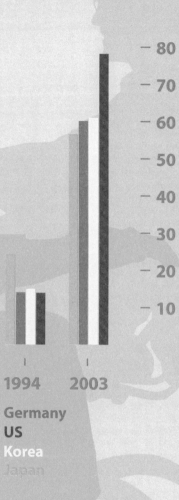

In many countries the number of Internet users increased more than a hundredfold within a decade. In the US, half of the population uses the Internet, compared to the European average of every fourth person, and only one in twenty-five people in developing countries.

PERCENTAGE OF HOMES WITH PCs[15]

— 80
— 70
— 60
— 50
— 40
— 30
— 20
— 10

1994   2003

Germany
US
Korea
Japan

INTERNET USERS PER 1,000 PEOPLE[14]

— 800
— 700
— 600
— 500
— 400
— 300
— 200
— 100

1994   2003

Germany
US
Korea
Japan

INCREASE IN COMPUTER STORAGE CAPACITY/ REDUCTION IN COSTS[16]

1951
UNIVAC I / 0,001 MB RAM
US$ 1,000,000

1966
IBM 3700/26 | 0,256 MB RAM
US$ 600,000

1981
IBM 4341 | 2 MB RAM
US$ 385,000

1986
HP 9000/840S | 8 MB RAM
US$ 385,000

1991
DELL 433P | 16 MB RAM
US$ 3,000

1996
PC Pentium II | 50 MB RAM
US$ 2,500

2001
PC Pentium IV | 256 MB RAM
US$ 1,600

2006
PC Pentium IV | 512 MB RAM
US$ 200

RESIDENTIAL ENERGY USE PER CAPITA / UNIT: KG OIL EQUIVALENT PER PERSON[17]

	1990	2000
World	204.9	312.0
US	822.0	927.8
Europe	392.1	660.1
Japan	321.5	380.7
Korea	290.4	311.1
Dev. Countries	91.9	216.1

Buildings are responsible for roughly half of the world's energy consumption. Almost one third of the world's energy consumption is attributed to residential buildings.

PERCENTAGE OF RESIDENTIAL ENERGY USE IN RELATION TO TOTAL ENERGY CONSUMPTION[18]

	1990	2001
World	19.3	27.5
US	16.1	16.6
Europe	23.8	27.5
Japan	13.5	13.6
Korea	19.5	12.4
Dev. Countries	22.9	35.7

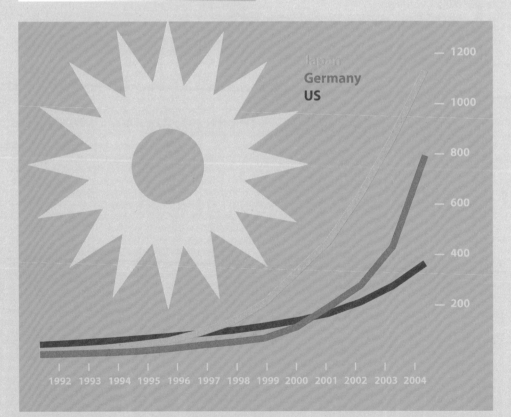

Japan
Germany
US

1992 1993 1994 1995 1996 1997 1998 1999 2000 2001 2002 2003 2004

Japan and Germany lead the world in the use of solar energy. Per capita installed capacity in 2004, measured in watts:[19]

Germany	9.62
Japan	8.87
US	1.24

Surface area of installed solar panels in Germany in 2004: 6 million square meters [20]

TOTAL PHOTOVOLTAIC ENERGY PRODUCTION[21]

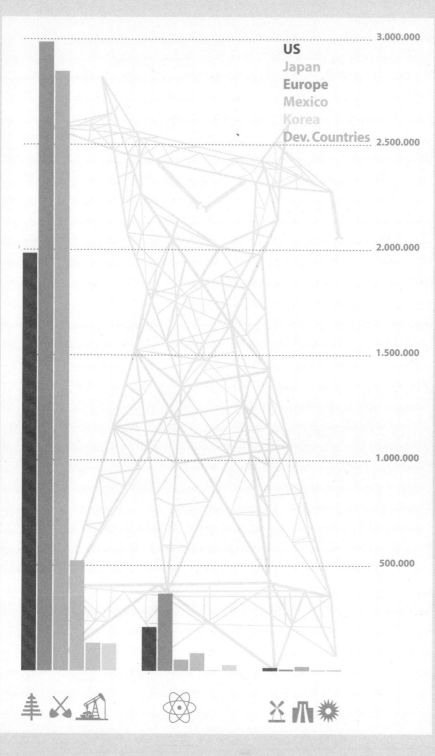

	2000
US	218,6
Korea	142,9
Mexico	134,5
Japan	129,2
Europe	87,2
World	63,3

US
Japan
Europe
Mexico
Korea
Dev. Countries

3.000.000
2.500.000
2.000.000
1.500.000
1.000.000
500.000

ENERGY PRODUCTION BY SOURCE IN 2000 / UNIT: 1,000 TONNES OF OIL EQUIVALENT[22]

US HOUSEHOLD ELECTRICITY CONSUMPTION BY END USE IN 2001 (%)[24]

other uses
miscellaneous
washing machines
electrical appliances
heating and air conditioning
lighting
hot water
kitchen appliances

[1] www.unhabitat.org

[2] Source: German Federal Statistical Office, 2002

[3] http://www.stat.go.jp

[4] http://www.willi-stengel.de

[5] http://www.census.gov

[6] http://hq.unhabitat.org; http://www.unhabitat.org; http://www.emergogroup.com

[7] http://www.census.gov

[8] http://globalis.gvu.unu.edu

[9] http://www.unhabitat.org

[10] Source: United Nations, World Urbanization Prospects: The 1999 Revision

[11] http://www.fedstats.gov; http://www.demographia.com; http://www.chijihon.metro.tokyo.jp

[12] http://earthtrends.wri.org

[13] http://earthtrends.wri.org

[14] http://earthtrends.wri.org

[15] http://earthtrends.wri.org

[16] Wolfgang Scheppe, Growing a Chair, Birsfelden 2004.

[17] http://www.earthtrends.wri.org

[18] http://earthtrends.wri.org

[19] http://www.oja-services.nl

[20] Bundesministerium für Umweltschutz-Pressedienst, No. 039/05, Berlin, Feb. 22, 2005.

[21] http://www.oja-services.nl

[22] http://www.earthtrends.wri.org

[23] http://earthtrends.wri.org

[24] http://www.eia.doe.gov

Changing Lives: The Return to Urban Living ¶

> HARTMUT HÄUSSERMANN

For centuries, how people lived was a by-product of how they worked. Farmers lived where they kept their animals, implements, and supplies; the private dwellings of craftsmen and tradesmen were connected directly with their workshops or storerooms; and the aristocracy lived in mansions or palaces that functioned primarily as administrative centers and as emblems of status. Private homes in the modern sense have not existed for very long, and buildings devoted exclusively to housing are therefore a fairly recent invention. They appeared *en masse* only in the wake of industrialization and the emergence of the modern city. The result of a long historical development, today's homes might be described as leftovers—what remained after certain clearly defined activities and functions, including waged labor, official representation, storage, education, and care of the sick and elderly, were transferred to outside institutions. Domestic life is not a clearly defined activity, and this makes it very difficult for architects and builders to design spaces or buildings that serve purely domestic purposes, and very difficult for them to say with reasonable certainty how such structures should change in order to meet future challenges.

This essay traces the development of living arrangements in modern societies, that is, the societies in which industrialization led to the form of civilization that came to dominate North America and Western Europe in the course of the twentieth century. The "modern age" standardized lifestyles and domestic arrangements, putting its stamp on them no less than on the development of our cities. By the end of the twentieth century, however, the Fordism implicit in the modernist ideal had passed its zenith and now new forms of living are again strengthening the city as a place of residence.

A Brief Cultural History of Domestic Life.
The notion of domestic life as a sphere free from outside obligations and from work is relatively recent. The concept developed in the course of the eighteenth century as a result of middle-class ways of life and gradually assumed the status of a generally valid model. Previous centuries had known a wide spectrum of domestic arrangements, where different groups of people lived in close proximity to one another and

various functions had to be fulfilled, from those aiding survival and to those in the interest of representation.

The palaces of the aristocracy were both living quarters and workplaces for members of the household or court. To a certain extent, spaces here were marked out as public or private, but the domestic realm consisted of individual rooms rather than separate, self-enclosed units. And even bedrooms and boudoirs were not private in the modern sense, but the scene of court politics until well into the eighteenth century.

On farms, work and domestic life were fully integrated. In fact, "domestic life" consisted of little more than taking meals together and sleeping: work was the chief occupation. Rooms in farmhouses were used temporarily for a variety of purposes. People slept on sacks or hay: beds had to be light and easily moveable, a characteristic that gave rise to the French word for "furniture", *meuble.* Economically, farms were largely self-sufficient, producing all their own food, clothing, and tools. There was no hard and fast distinction between spaces occupied by people and by animals. The homes of urban craftsmen resembled country farmhouses in that the household would contain distant relatives, servants, and apprentices and knew no strict separation of work from domestic life. Economic historians therefore refer to both ways of living as the "total household."[1]

A cultural countermodel to this kind of living arrangement emerged gradually in the course of the eighteenth century: the bourgeois household, which was marked by the *mise-en-scène* of the private sphere and from which wage-earning—generally a male preserve—was as much excluded as those who not belonging to the immediate family circle. The bourgeoisie cultivated the intimacy of the family sphere as a counterworld to bread-winning and to politics (in which they were starting to involve themselves). In deliberate contrast to the aristocracy, with their focus on property and power and codes of behavior, the middle classes placed love and affection at the center of family life. In this way, the private realm and the household became coded as feminine, while the world "outside," the world of public life, became the male arena.[2]

A mixture of bourgeois utilitarianism and domestic family idyll, these values acquired considerable normative force in the course of the nineteenth century. Friedrich Schiller praised them as natural givens in his 1797 "Song of the Bell": "The man must go out / In hostile life living, / Be working and striving / And planting and making, / Be scheming and taking, / Through hazard and daring, / His fortune ensnaring. / Then streams in the wealth in an unending measure, / The silo is filled thus with valuable treasure, / The rooms are growing, the house stretches out. / And indoors ruleth / The housewife so modest, / The mother of children, / And governs wisely / In matters of family, / And maidens she traineth / And boys she restraineth, / And goes without ending / Her diligent handling, / And gains increase hence / With ordering sense."[3]

In the mid-nineteenth century, as a result of increasing industrialization, ever larger numbers of people began moving to cities in search of work. They took with them the way of life they had been accustomed to in the country. Until 1810, for example, rural men had not been permitted to marry unless they cultivated their own land, and in the country there was no such thing as a woman who did nothing but tend hearth and home. The sentimentalized notion of the family bore no resem-

blance to the lives actually led by this new urban proletariat. When they arrived in town it was not unusual for such migrants to live in mass accommodation, sharing their homes, their rooms, and even their beds with strangers.

To bourgeois eyes, the lack of order in domestic arrangements of this kind must have appeared in urgent need of reform, not only for hygenic reasons, but also due to "moral" considerations. Hence, socially committed moves to improve proletarian housing conditions in the second half of the nineteenth century aimed at enforcing a standardized form of domestic life that accorded with middle-class notions of an ordered family existence. A prime goal was therefore to grant every household a self-contained dwelling and to have that dwelling divided up in functional terms. Such ideas were to be implemented in the 1920s and 1930s by the architects of "Neues Bauen" (New Architecture), who designed self-contained units of accommodation on a minimum floor space and with rooms given over to precisely defined functions. Examples are the housing estates built in Berlin while Martin Wagner was *Stadtbaurat* (Hufeisensiedlung and Onkel Toms Hütte, for instance) and those erected in Frankfurt am Main under the direction of Ernst May.[4]

What Is Domestic Living? The Functionalist View of Housing. Early in the previous century everyone seemed to know exactly what domestic life was and what kind of architecture suited it best, at least in the Western world of the 1920s. Housing reformers, those engaged in family politics, custodians of morality, doctors, hygiene specialists, business managers, economic experts, bourgeois critics of modern civilization, and pioneers of new lifestyles joined in promoting a clear idea of modern life and hence of modern housing.[5]

All of them deplored living conditions in working-class districts and sought political intervention in creating accommodation that enabled members of the proletariat to live together in small families and relieved them of the necessity to move continually as a result of unemployment or arbitrary increases in rent. How this could be achieved at a low cost and in a minimum of space was a major issue among architects and housing experts, the size of the units varying according to the public money available. In December 1929 new regulations concerning public loans brought about a trend toward small apartments. In 1930 the *Reichsgrundsätze für den Kleinwohnungsbau* (National Regulations for Apartment Building) limited living space to between 32–45 square meters (344–484 square feet), and those for families with children to 60 square meters (646 square feet).[6] In the Weimar Republic apartment building *en masse* was therefore a prime focus of avant-garde architects, as shown not only Wagner and May, but also Otto Bartning, Ferdinand Kramer, Max and Bruno Taut, Hans Scharoun, and Water Gropius.

Functionalism was seen as the solution to the problem. Functionalist theory adhered to the same principles as the "Taylorist" rationalization that was beginning to dominate industrial manufacture, permitting enormous increases in productivity. Functionalism became a central tenet of the modern age, in both the capitalist West and the communist East. In housing, it offered a quasi-scientific basis for establishing what domestic life should be like and which kinds of building best promoted it.

Functionalism entails the division of labor and specialization, that is, detaching individual functions from complex processes and optimizing their efficiency through rationalization. When it came to manufacturing cars and refrigerators at ever lower costs, the economic efficacy of this method was beyond doubt. But what did it mean when applied to housing? The attempt was made to apply functionalism to designing living spaces because the proven effectiveness of specialization and rationalization opened up the prospect of liberating millions of workers from wretched living conditions, raising them from an "uncivilized" state into modern life.

To specify exactly what constituted the ideal dwelling meant specifying exactly what function domestic life had. People worked in factories or offices, they shopped in department stores and specialist shops, and they took recreation in sports centers and outlying cafés. The home was thus left as the locus of the family, leisure, and sleep. This function was never defined very precisely, but it was clearly thought sufficient reason to use the same floorplans time and time again to tell millions of people how they should live—and, not least, how they should not live.

Gainful employment had no place in these apartments. Housework—which socialists, too, saw as the province of women—was to be minimized through mechanization until it virtually disappeared and took up next to no space. Apartment design seems to have taken this disappearance for granted, opting for tiny kitchens and a general lack of storage and working space. Kitchen and living room were separated because they fulfilled separate functions. This caused considerable inconvenience for mothers standing at their ovens because it forced them physically to split daily activities that real-ly belonged together. But from a theoretical and planning standpoint, this was the correct arrangement because it obeyed the functionalist imperative.

Along with development of the automotive city, the most disastrous development in urban planning in the modern age was undoubtedly the invention of the purely residential area as a distinct category. This justified—indeed, encouraged—the erection of the monotonous estates that extended the urban fabric on a vast scale in the post-World War II era. These urban "outposts," well-intentioned as a way of removing the population from industrial pollution, dust, and traffic noise, determined how people lived their daily lives in neighborhoods viewed primarily in terms of passive relaxation. Criticism came from social psychologists,[7] architects,[8] and sociologists alike.[9]

In a society that kept its children in educational institutions of one kind or another during the day while adults vacated the neighborhood to earn a living, just about the only thing left for people to do in residential areas of this type was to "reside." Hence, housing was principally used during the evening and on the weekend. This was especially noticeable in the large housing estates of socialist countries, where women enjoyed full employment, working hours were long, and children were looked after all day. The simplified, standardized floor plans and the lacking infrastructure seemed to do justice to the minimal needs of those who stayed at home during the day. But this situation, where most residents actually spent the day in town and had little time for "home life," only obtained in the relatively brief period of full employment. Subsequently, the unity and functional clarity of what "living" was or how

PETER PILLER,
PROJEKTIONSFLÄCHEN
[PROJECTION SURFACES],
2002–04

COURTESY FREHRKING
WIESEHÖFER GALLERY,
COLOGNE AND BARBARA
WIEN, BERLIN

IN THE 1970s AND 1980s,
NUMEROUS COMPANIES IN
GERMANY TOOK AERIAL
PHOTOGRAPHS OF SINGLE
FAMILY HOUSES, OFFERING
THEM TO HOMEOWNERS
FOR PURCHASE. IN 2002
THE ARTIST PETER PILLER
WAS ABLE TO PURCHASE
A COLLECTION OF
20,000 AERIAL HOUSE
PHOTOGRAPHS FROM A
DEFUNCT BUSINESS.
AFTER EXAMINING THE
PHOTOGRAPHS AND
INVENTORYING THEM, HE
ARRANGED THEM IN
SERIES ORGANIZED BY
SIMILAR MOTIFS.

domestic life was practiced began to dissolve and diversify.

Standardized Living. For official purposes, the term "dwelling" must be defined in order to avoid misunderstandings and to provide a basis for statistics. The German Federal Statistics Office established the following definition in connection with a microcensus carried out in 1995: "A dwelling is the sum of all rooms facilitating the running of a household and must include a kitchen or a room with cooking facilities. A dwelling must have a lockable entrance from outdoors, from a staircase, or from an antechamber, also a water supply, drainage, and a toilet, all of which may lie outside the lockable area of the dwelling." The most striking aspect of this definition is that a dwelling only qualifies as such when it has a lockable entrance not accessible through another dwelling. This characterizes the home as a private, intimate sphere. On the other hand, water, drainage, and toilet facilities—not exactly unimportant features of modern-day life—can be outside the dwelling proper. Thus, the definition is grounded less in practical matters of everyday comfort and convenience than in the culturally determined concept of privacy. From this basic premise, other widespread notions about the home can be deduced:

– In our culture, a home is equated with a certain body of occupants that forms a social unit, that is, the family, consisting of parents and their children. Housing since the early twentieth century has been oriented toward this idea, especially since World War II.

– A further cultural determinant of the home in our society is that it is a place from which work is excluded, a place of relaxation, leisure, and privacy.

– The home is an instrument both of social differentiation—it gives people an opportunity to express their individuality—and social cohesion—it enables them to articulate a sense of belonging to a certain group or milieu. To that extent, the home is closely bound up with constructions of the self.[10]

The definition of the home as a site of the family and privacy in which only a narrow core of directly related people live dominated architecture and urban planning for much of the twentieth century. Millions of small family housing units were built. This became the standard type because a certain way of life—families each living in their own home—was intended to become, or had already become, the norm. Housing policy favored home ownership, which was encouraged by means of financial incentives and promoted by savings banks and other purveyors of lifestyles. In the 1950s, family life in the single-family house became in a sense the epitome of the successful life. Millions realized this "dream," moving to the area surrounding the cities.

Suburbanization and Standardization. With the spread of the motor car and increases in purchasing power in Germany after World War II, vast numbers of young families with above-average incomes began to move out of the cities.[11] We are now quite familiar with the motivations behind this. In comparison to cities, outlying areas offered more property for the same money. For middle-income families, substantial savings and larger homes were for all intents only possible outside of town. Moreover, a detached house among trees became a symbol of a harmonious family life and evidence of a successful career ("produce a son, plant a tree, build a house"). The mobility between the city and its environs that this lifestyle entailed was not available to all: Those more affluent left the cities, leaving behind ever greater concentrations of the less privileged: the poor, the unemployed, and recent immigrants.

Living in the detached single-family home was unavoidably focused on the housewife.[12] Family life in the green belt presupposed a wife not engaged in gainful employment: The husband left this idyll every morning to go to work, and the wife was responsible for organizing a multi-functional household in an area with little infrastructure. Transporting food and other goods from the stores, looking after the garden, taking the children to school, sport, music lessons, friends, and the doctor—all this became much easier in the 1960s when above-average-income households rapidly began acquiring cars in Germany, but it did nothing to change women's responsibility for these and other household-related tasks.

Suburbanization perfected the form of home life that had been promoted as the only desirable one since the early twentieth century and had gradually come to dominate all others. But already in the 1980s, it became clear that there was a clear increase in "dissenters" from this ideal. The number of households without children rose sharply, and such households did not necessarily wish to live outside town. They preferred modernized older buildings in central city areas and rejected almost all aspects of the way of life outlined above, along with "petty-bourgeois" notions of life in general. A unit of accommodation need no longer be synonymous with a family: People chose either to live alone or to share their accommodation, with privacy occasionally breached sufficiently to prevent unwanted social isolation. Some even experimented with abolishing the separation of life and work, which was naturally both necessary and easier in the new service-sector jobs that emerged after the demise of industrial society.

The Urban Renaissance. Since the mid-1990s there has been a change in migration patterns between German cities and their surroundings, a development leading some observers to proclaim an "urban renaissance."[13] Indicators of this are an increase in the number of jobs in cities and a decrease in relocations to outlying areas. Have cities overcome the most critical structural change in their history? Are we experiencing the end of suburbanization and the start of renewed urban economic growth?

Economic trends and population movements suggest that we are. The long period during which cities decreased in relative economic importance, a development linked to the de-industrialization that began in the 1960s, seems to be drawing to a close. Economic factors have favored cities since the mid-1990s, and surrounding areas are becoming less attractive for young families.

The Urban Economy. The transition from an industrial to a service economy has been accompanied by fundamental changes in economic organization. The rise of large-scale industry caused cities to grow, but the functionalism of the industrial age, its rationalization and standardization, also destroyed them. "Cleaning up" or demolishing older urban areas with mixed functions was as much a prime aim of "modernist" urban planning as reducing the density of the urban fabric and standardizing housing design. The goal was to create order. Everyone and everything was to have their particular place in cities organized along Fordist lines, a way of facilitating centralized control to ensure maximum efficiency.

This concept was reflected in the masses of apartment blocks and in the suburban housing of the postwar era, both of them generally forming "purely" residential areas. And it was reflected in a proliferation of traffic areas and trading estates on city outskirts. Fordism meant the dissolution of the genuinely urban city. [14]

The significance of Fordist production methods has now declined drastically in industrialized countries, and in the postindustrial economy cities are taking on more importance. After low-skilled jobs have left for low-wage countries, the high skill service sector is showing high growth rates in our cities: in manufacturing research and development, planning, organization, and financing, as well as consulting, communication, and culture. The distinction between industry and culture is becoming increasingly blurred. Cultural creativity has become a crucial factor in economic growth, because economic growth in the "creative industries" [15] is based on innovations in products and technique resulting from creative combinations of theory and practice from various areas and the interaction of technical knowledge and cultural creativity.

The post-Fordist economy differs radically from the Fordist model in that small businesses cooperating with each other on a project basis have replaced large corporations as the dominant factor in the urban economy. Always the rule in artistic production, this model has now acquired general validity. An "economy of knowledge" is developing in our cities that is based not on manual skill, but on intellectual work, creativity, social interaction, and networking. The most important factor in economic growth has become what Richard Florida calls the "creative class," and they prefer living and working in urban surroundings.

The End of Suburbanization? Why are fewer families moving out of town? For private households, suburbanization, a famiy-centered lifestyle entailing investments in property, cars, and household technology, was a capital-intensive process. Long-term debts were incurred on the basis of secure jobs and rising income levels. Neither can be taken for granted by young families today. Increases in income are now more likely to be temporary and may be followed by a decrease. More flexible modes of work are making it more and more difficult to calculate future income, and low inflation is lacking as a financial aid to paying off debts.

In addition, demographic developments mean that typically "suburbanite" age groups are on the decline. The number of 26 to 40-year-olds has declined by approximately 25 percent since 1996, and the German Bundesamt für Bauwesen und Raumordnung (Federal Office for Building and Regional Planning) forecasts that this trend will continue.

It has also become increasingly standard for both partners to work, especially among those with academic training. This is a logical consequence of higher levels of education among young people, especially women, and the concomitant change in life plans. Increasing numbers of women are not attracted by the prospect of living in an own home on the edge of town and watching their qualifications go unused while they perform a shuttle service for their children and look after the house and garden. The "housewife model" is in decline not least because fewer and fewer women automatically withdraw into the private world of the family. Suburbanization, so to speak, is under-staffed.

Finally, there is a tendency to abolish the separation of work and life that was such a decisive factor in the development of the modernist city. In existing, multifunctional central urban areas it is easier to meet the challenges of flexible scheduling and rgw constant search for new contacts and opportunities for cooperation. It is also easier to balance the claims of job and family. Like the lifestyles they generate, mixed functions, varied infrastructures, and short distances suit the demands of the economy of knowledge. All these factors explain the growing attractiveness of the city center in the context of the new economy, which is an urban economy.

Diversification. A shift began in the 1970s in our ideas about domestic life, eventually leading to greater diversification. Small families are becoming rarer as the basic social unit occupying accommodation and alternative ways of life are becoming more widespread—living alone, unmarried cohabitation, roommate situations, and other freely chosen groupings. Whereas the social domestic unit is increasingly diversifying, the division of the functions of working and living is decreasing, as the two increasingly intend to combine. In the 1960s and 1970s, it was still a cultural provocation on the part of alternative lifestyle projects to abandon the separation of living and wage earning that had been cultivated for more than a century.

Homes are once again being used frequently for gainful employment, whether because telecommunications make it possible to work at home, or whether because longer periods of training and further training make it necessary to have a workplace in the home. The development of various lifestyles that can be grouped together has also encouraged diversification in domestic arrangements as a visible way of rejecting the small-family model. The different lifestyles manifesting themselves in different living arrangements can come into conflict in the confines of city neighborhoods, encouraging the segregation of different groups in different areas.

The number of singles in Germany has risen steadily over the past four decades. Living alone is no longer primarily the province of elderly people—notably women—for whom family life at home ceased with the death of their partner. Neither is it the preserve of those who have not (yet) founded a family. Rather, more and more people are deliberately opting to live alone in their "best years."

In Germany there are currently some five million cases of unmarried cohabitation. These may be temporary or experimental forms of cohabitation, or they may be more lasting arrangements along the lines of a traditional marriage. In addition, almost three million people, predominantly women, raise their children without a partner. The proportion of such single parents in all households containing children has increased steadily over the past two decades. Finally, the number of couples who "live apart together" (that is, occupy separate homes) or long-distance commuting families, where the children alternatively live at with the mother or father are also on the increase.

Greater diversification of domestic arrangements as a whole has been accompanied by greater diversification within individual biographies. This reflects not only increased life expectation, but also a considerable expansion of the available options. Today, it is not unusual for someone to live alone, then marry and have a family, then divorce and live either as a single parent or alone again, before entering into a new partnership on an unmarried basis. Choice of domestic arrangement is thus no longer a once-in-a-lifetime decision, as it still typically was in the mid-twentieth century. Instead, experimental, short-term lifestyles are becoming more widespread. This makes domestic life more various, more heterogeneous, and more flexible.

The history of living arrangements can be compared to a spindle or an hourglass. From a wide variety of household types in pre-industrial times there arose in the nineteenth and the twentieth century the idea of a "correct" form of domestic life that centered on the self-contained, small-family home, before issuing in increased diversification again in the final decades of the twentieth century. The property market has been slow to respond to this change, but at least less accommodation is being designed with the kind of functionally rigid floorplan that was built *en masse* in response to official regulations on social housing.

Changes in lifestyle and domestic arrangements affect urban development. The period ca. 1950–70 was dominated by a model that promoted living with a family in a self-owned home as the goal of every standard biography. After training in town, young people were to embark on a career that guaranteed them sufficient long-term income to found a family, a development crowned by relocation to a self-owned home on the outskirts of town. Living on the periphery was and is a "housewife model": It presupposes the participation of a non-wage-earner to organize the household. Since this model was available only to those with at least average incomes, it resulted in residential areas with relatively large social homogeneity.

By the end of the twentieth century this model had lost its general validity. Today, a good education no longer automatically leads to high-paid jobs over a long period of time. Furthermore, women's share in education has increased so much that they, too, are oriented more toward gainful employment than in the pre-1970 years. Since partners are usually chosen from within the same educational or vocational group, fewer women are now available to adopt the housewife's model by living with a family in a home on the edge of town.

Men and women decide individually whether they wish to remain single or live with a partner and whether they wish to have children or not. Greater job orientation and individualized ways of life have increased the attractiveness of the city center as a place of residence. Old neighborhoods offer a multiplicity of functions and a varied infrastructure that can be used easily and relatively quickly.

Ways of life and domestic arrangements alter constantly, whereas changes in available accommodation occur only slowly. This represents less of a problem in older buildings because their groundplans were conceived less hierarchically and less rigidly in terms of function than more recent housing. More adaptable in this way, older buildings are better capable of meeting the challenges posed by new living arrangements. Changes in lifestyles cause alterations in the social geography of towns. Historic central urban areas are thus currently experiencing a renaissance, the result of changes in the role of women brought about by higher qualification levels and of changes in the infrastructural needs of households without children.

HARTMUT HÄUSSERMANN

1   Otto Brunner, *Neue Wege der Verfassungs- und Sozialgeschichte*, Göttingen, 1956, especially the section entitled "Das 'ganze Haus' und die alteuropäische Ökonomik."

2   Karin Hausen, "Die Polarisierung der 'Geschlechtercharaktere': Eine Spiegelung der Dissoziation von Erwerbs- und Familienleben," *Sozialgeschichte der Familie in der Neuzeit Europas: Neue Forschungen*, ed. Werner Conze, Stuttgart, 1978.

3   "Der Mann muss hinaus / Ins feindliche Leben, / Muss wirken und streben / Und pflanzen und schaffen, / Erlisten, erraffen, / Muss wetten und wagen, / Das Glück zu erja gen. / Da strömet herbei die unendliche Gabe, / Es füllt sich der Speicher mit köstlicher Habe, / Die Räume wachsen, es dehnt sich das Haus. / Und drinnen waltet / Die züchtige Hausfrau, / Die Mutter der Kinder, / Und herrschet weise / Im häuslichen Kreise, / Und lehret die Mädchen / Und wehret den Knaben, / und reget ohn Ende / Die fleissigen Hände, / Und mehrt den Gewinn / Mit ordnendem Sinn." Friedrich Schiller, "Das Lied von der Glocke," *Sämtliche Werke*, vol. 1, Munich, 1960, pp. 432–33. English translation by Marianna Wertz, http://www.schillerinstitute.org/transl/trans_schil_1poems.html.

4   Ingeborg Beer, *Architektur für den Alltag: Vom sozialen und frauenorientierten Anspruch der Siedlungsarchitektur der zwanziger Jahre*, Berlin, 1994.

5   Christoph Mohr and Michael Müller, *Funktionalität und Moderne*, Cologne, 1984; Adelheid von Saldern, "Daheim an meinem Herd…," *Jahrhundertwende: Der Aufbruch in die Moderne*, vol. 2, ed. A. Nitschke, Reinbek, 1990.

6   Beer, *Architektur für den Alltag*, p. 93.

7   For example, Alexander Mitscherlich, *Die Unwirtlichkeit unserer Städte*, Frankfurt am Main, 1965.

8   For example, Jane Jacobs, *The Death and Life of Great Amercian Cities*, New York, 1961.

9   For example, Hans-Paul Bahrdt, *Die moderne Grossstadt: Soziologische Überlegungen zum Städtebau*, Opladen, 1998 (first published in 1961).

10 Hartmut Häussermann and Walter Siebel, *Soziologie des Wohnens*, Weinheim, 1996.

11 Hartmut Häussermann and Walter Siebel, *Stadtsoziologie: Eine Einführung*, Frankfurt am Main, 2004, pp. 72–73.

12 Susanne Frank, *Stadtplanung im Geschlechterkampf: Stadt und Geschlecht in der Großstadtentwicklung des 19. und 20. Jahrhunderts*, Wiesbaden, 2003.

13 Dieter Läpple, "Phoenix aus der Asche: Die Neuerfindung der Stadt," *Soziale Welt* 16 (2005).

14 *Zukunft aus Amerika: Fordismus in der Zwischenkriegszeit—Siedlung, Stadt, Raum*, ed. Stiftung Bauhaus Dessau and the Department of Planning Theory at the RWTH Aachen, Dessau, 1995; Siegfried Giedion, *Space, Time and Architecture: The Growth of a New Tradition*, Cambridge (Mass.), 1941.

15 Richard Florida, *Cities and the Creative Class*, New York, 2005.

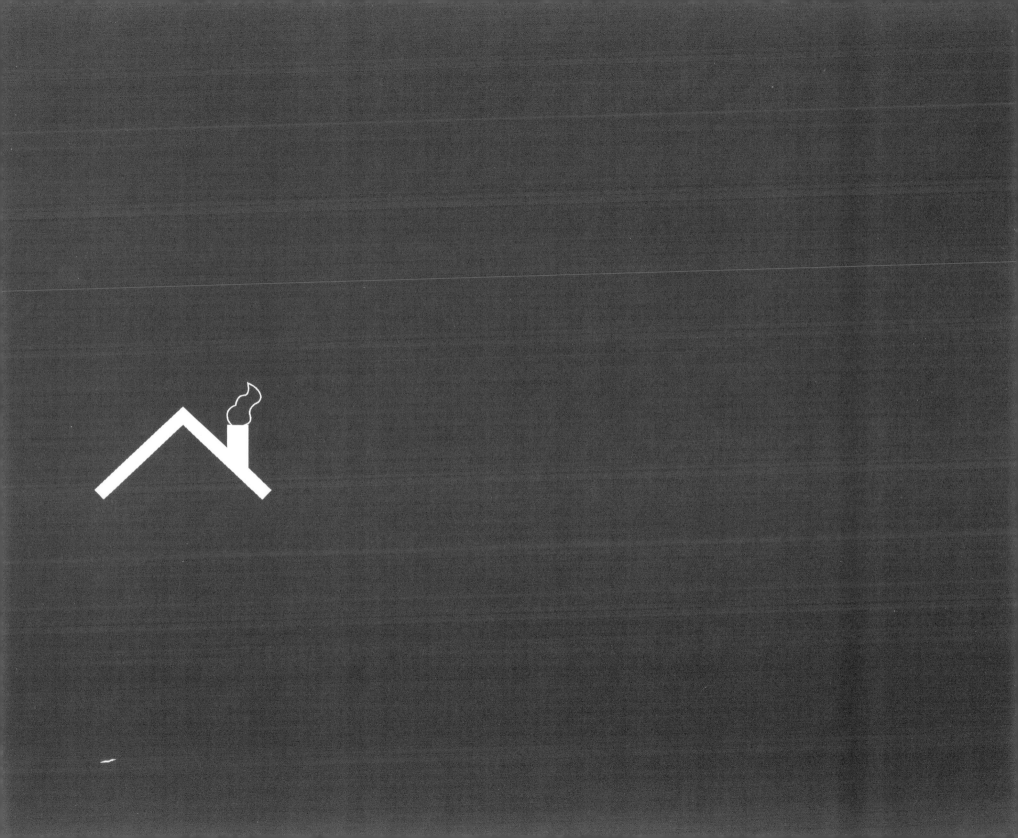

Escape from Today: Houses of the Future ¶

> BEATRIZ COLOMINA

The first men living comfortably in space will be watched on TV by billions on earth.

—Buckminster Fuller, in his 1968 *Playboy* article "City of the Future"

Science fiction meets architecture in the "house of the future." Fantasies of a distant world to come in novels and popular magazines since the mid to late nineteenth century turn into built visions of a more immediate future in the first decades of the twentieth century. As the imagination moves from the day after tomorrow to just tomorrow the vision becomes concrete, it can be touched, even physically occupied. Designers and manufacturers alike stretch the limits of the latest technologies and materials to construct a tangible experience of an idealized domestic space of the near future. It isn't simply an image of the future; it is a way of realizing that future by creating the desire for that image, that space.

Houses of the future, like industrial gadgets at a fair, are always tested by visitors, who inhabit them as if a 3-D advertisement in which they are taking part. But since the products they are advertising do not really exist yet, they create demand for those non-existent products. In this they differentiate themselves from another twentieth century tradition, model houses, which are also tested by visitors but are made with technologies and products that are already available. The model house is a house of today, no matter how innovative or radical its design, its technology, its fantasy. The house of the future is about escaping today. But it is not simply about escaping the present; it is about an idealized form of escape in the future. The visitor escapes into a fantasy future world where everybody can escape everything. The dream of the house of the future is the dream of the ultimate escape vehicle. Each house of the future is ultimately a spacecraft. To explore it is like inhabiting a science fiction movie set, seeing yourself as a protagonist in a sci-fi narrative. It is an escape not just from the house of today but from the city of today, and from the suburbs of today, into a different society, a different civilization, even a different world. To trace the tradition of houses of the future is to trace the evolution of the fantasy of escape. But escape from what?

Houses of the future are all about staying inside and keeping the outdoors out. There is no such a thing as the house and garden of the future. Elaborate kitchens present housewives with the illusion of a world at their command, full of push button, self-cleaning, self-monitoring, labor-saving, automated, technological wizardry. But they also presuppose that we are all eating in, not out—as a logical future with a clearly established division of labor might suggest. The inside, like the housewife herself, is immaculately put together: glamorous, irresistible, with appliances taking the shape of objects to admire, to watch even, as in the introduction of "windows" for ovens and washing machines in 1950s appliances. The interior becomes all-absorbing, fascinating, captivating. Why ever go out? Air conditioning ensures that the outside air is cleansed of all dust, impurities, and pathogens for the inside. New materials like steel, aluminum, glass, and plastic are presented as hygienic, dustproof and self-cleaning. Even visitors and delivery men are carefully screened or totally kept away, as in fantasies of fridges accessible from the outside of the house or hatches for dropping packages, mail, groceries, etc. Not even the inhabitants of the house cross the threshold. They never seem to leave. The majority of houses of the future presuppose a leisure time in which both partners are at home. It is no accident that many houses of the future are presented as vacation houses. They are based on the premise that leisure time will increase radically in the future and that office work could be carried out from home.

Houses of the future are all hyper-interiorized spaces. The house steadily excludes more and more of the outside world as the twentieth century proceeds, ultimately leading to no outside at all. The house is just an idealized inside. If the basic idea of a house is that it divides an inside from an outside, houses of the future radicalize that division, giving a primitive, even archaic, quality to their high tech fantasies.

At first sight it seems simple. Houses of the future are all about emergent technologies. They use the latest materials and technologies for both the fabrication of the house itself and the gadgets it contains. The idea of the house of the future goes back to the beginning of the twentieth century and its development is tied up with the emergence of new media and new technologies: electricity, telephone, radio, car, airplane, steel frame, concrete, glass, plastic, air conditioning, television, video, surveillance systems, computer, the Internet, broadband, wireless networks… The dream of the future is technological and the house its laboratory. But why the house, which is paradoxically avoided in most science fiction imagery of the future? In bringing the future closer to the present, designers and architects of the twentieth century filled the gap in science fiction writing.

"It is a curious and significant fact that the prophetic imagination of Mr. H.G. Wells has never been able to encompass the future house. Transportation, diet, and the rearing of illegitimate children in the year 2000—or even the year 802701—were easy enough. But when it came to shelter the Wellsian vision foundered," *Fortune* wrote in 1932 when evaluating Buckminster Fuller's Dymaxion House five years later.[1] While Wells did make some characteristically accurate predictions for the future house, including lighter walls, central heating, electric ranges, window washing mechanisms, round corners to avoid the accumulation of dust, etc., these were rather straightforward ideas. Only in a footnote did he speculate that it might some day be possible to build "sound, portable and habitable houses of felted wire-netting and weather-proofed paper upon a light framework."[2]

Fuller filled that void, imagining the house of the future in great detail. But while Wells had fantasized about a far away future, Fuller, who had trained at the U.S. Naval Academy and was experienced at forecasting in navigation, ballistics and logistics, was not so interested in imagining a distant future as in accurately forecasting a near future. He even elaborates on the temporal limits of predictions. He said he had come to the conclusion that it is only possible to make a "reasonable forecast" of about twenty-five years. In fact, when asked by the journal *Architectural Design* in 1967 to predict the year 2000, he declared himself "confident" that he was unable to do so, "I do not believe that any human being can foresee with any accuracy as far ahead as that 35 years."[3] Ultimately, 25 years would become the time measure for many architects' houses of the future. Alison and Peter Smithson's House of the Future, exhibited in the *Daily Mail* Jubilee Ideal Home Exhibition in London in 1956, was designed for the year 1980, and Archigram's Living 1990, commissioned by the *Weekend Telegraph*, was presented at Harrod's Knightsbridge in 1967, twenty-three years before the imagined future.

If the classic science fiction genre launched by Wells imagined an escape from urban life, Fuller's Dymaxion House provides the detailed architecture of the escape. The house was conceived as a mass produced, global, air deliverable unit, manufactured by a 'scientific dwelling industry" understood as "the preferred means of transferring high scientific capability from a weaponry to a living focus."[4] As if to reinforce the military connection, the first cartoonish drawings of the Dymaxion Tower project in 1927 show a zeppelin dropping a bomb to make a hole four meters deep for the 'service station" and to anchor the aluminum mast from which the house is suspended. The house, also carried by zeppelin, can be planted anywhere in the world, like a tree. Weight is the determining factor. If manufactured in large numbers, the house could be sold for 25 cents a pound, giving the small five-room unit, complete with furnishings and accessories, a price of $1500. Erectable in one day, it is complete in every detail, with all furniture and every existing—or imagined—appliance built in. The purpose of the house, Fuller claimed, was "to reduce the drudgery of cleaning, and cooking and washing."[5] In other words, the house itself is an appliance. Cooking is expedited by an arrangement of "vacuum mazda units." Dishwashing is replaced by a device that "washes, rinses and dries dishes as they are inserted" and the laundry room does the washing and drying in a few minutes.[6] Automatic vacuuming of the air at floor edges removes dust, smoke, and odors. The bathroom is made of one piece, a mold of translucent casein, "a sheeting made from vegetable refuse"[7] (the same "that my watch crystal is made of but, in this case, the casein is translucent rather than transparent"[8]). The housewife is finally liberated from the domestic slavery which, Fuller said, is much worse than that of Roman galley slaves because it is not only physical but also mental.[9]

Floating in the air, the inhabitants of the Dymaxion House are disconnected from the world around them. The house is enclosed in windowless double-layer transparent, translucent, or opaque "vacuum plates" made of casein. "Individual decks for each mature occupant above the dust, flood and marauder danger [offer] unimpeded views in all directions" of a world that remains distant. The entire house is self-sufficient, free from the "political nuisances of city water, and city sewage and city electricity and city light."[10] There are no infrastructural

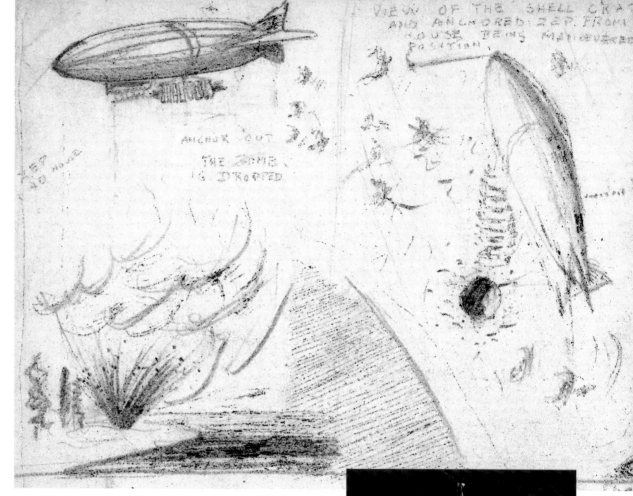

RICHARD BUCKMINSTER FULLER, SKETCH OF A 4D TOWER BEING DELIVERED BY ZEPPELIN, 1928.

MODEL, STREAMLINED DYMAXION SHELTER (RICHARD BUCKMINSTER FULLER, 1932).

RICHARD BUCKMINSTER
FULLER WITH A MODEL OF
DYMAXION HOUSE, 1928

BUCKMINSTER FULLER'S
DYMAXION HOUSE,
SECOND MODEL, FOLLOW-
ING THE 1928 STRUCTUR-
AL MODEL ILLUSTRATION
DEPICTS UNDERGROUND
BUILDING ELEMENTS
(FOUNDATION AND TANKS)
FULLER UTILIZED THIS
MODEL FOR THE LECTURES
HE GAVE IN 1929.

connections to the city. Any form of contact with urban culture is understood as a risk, a restraint on freedom, perhaps even a health threat. "Approximately one hundred thousand children were run over and killed in the cities of the United States last year," claimed Fuller in his lecture "Dymaxion House," held at a meeting of the Architectural League in New York in 1929.[11] The house should come and go freely, move around at will and be replaced every 5 or 10 years, like an automobile. Each disconnection from the city, and from civilization, is made possible by a new technological innovation. Water for example is delivered by truck or supplied by artesian well since the amount needed is minimal. "A ten-minute atomized bath, for example, requires a quart of water or less, and the toilets, constructed upon the present airplane system, require none."[12] The house produces its own light, heat and power—or "juice," as Fuller puts it—electricity use is extremely low due to a centralized lighting system in the mast that uses prisms, mirrors, and lenses. The lighting also acts as the heat source with the double pane vacuum windowless walls retaining all the heat generated by the illumination. Regulated temperatures without draft keep the house warm all year round. A famous photograph of Fuller with the model of the house shows a naked doll lying on top of the pneumatic bed, covered with just a fitted sheet to emphasize that the house was warm. Or should one say hot? A less well-known photograph of the same model removes any doubt by showing the figure of a man in a business suit arriving home to find three naked dolls lounging around looking up at him.

Meanwhile, a pocket-incinerator disposes of the garbage. The isolation from the outside extends to every detail. The air is filtered of all "dust and obnoxious gases," all the interior surfaces are automatically cleaned by a spray system and dusting is also automatic, "a combination of compressed air and vacuum."[13] The inhabitants are cocooned away from the world. Floors and surfaces are soft, pneumatic, covered in a "fabricoid," like that covering a "football."[14] "A child can fall on these floors and not hurt itself."[15] The doors are also pneumatic, silver balloon-silk inflated, and full of air, like the floors, "to kill sound." The house is "absolutely proof against earthquake, flood, fire, gas attack, dirt, pestilence and cyclone." The "transport unit," an amphibious wingless auto-airplane, was stored beneath the house. "This vehicle"—Fuller clarified—"is a theoretical design, like the house itself. We don't know that it works but it is dynamically correct."[16]

The disconnection with the city and governmental infrastructure is such that even schools are rendered obsolete. Fuller envisioned a system of education at a distance where through radio and television "children will no longer have to have compromise teachers. They will have Lowell in "government," or some other authority on another subject." Even socializing was envisioned through the medium of television: "With television, children will be able to see other children paint and draw in Tokyo…. There won't be any of this ridiculous crowd psychology."[17] The Dymaxion House was equipped with the latest media technology (telephone, radio, television, phonograph, dictaphone, loudspeakers, microphone, etc.), but some of these technologies barely existed in 1927.

Television, for example, was not widely introduced in the USA until after World War II. DuMont and RCA offered their first sets to the public in 1946, and between 1948 and 1955 nearly two thirds of American families bought a television set.[18] But in 1927, the year that

IN THE 1950S, TELEVISION BECAME A CORE ELEMENT OF THE AMERICAN PRIVATE HOME.

Fuller designed the house, there was the first public demonstration of television. Popular media speculated on the new machine through the 1930s and 40s. In the exhibition Land of Tomorrow of the 1939 New York World's Fair, for example, visitors marveled at the images transmitted on the new RCA television receiver. The opening of the pavilion at the fair was, in fact, the first news event ever covered by television in the USA. Ten days later, at the Fair's opening ceremonies, Franklin D. Roosevelt became the first American president to make a televised speech. And in 1950, the most famous of mass produced suburbs, Levittown in Long Island, offered a "built-in" television set embedded in the wall of its prefabricated Cape-Cod houses. Television had become part of the architecture of the American house. What Fuller pointed to 25 years in the future had arrived two years ahead of time. Other predictions, like the flying amphibious transport unit, still have yet to come.

It is again important to distinguish here between a model house, such as the Levittown house, which was also visited by hundreds of thousands and used to sell itself as a product, and houses of the future, which are typically set up as a lure to sell something entirely different. The first public presentation of the Dymaxion House project took place in 1929 in the Marshall Field and Company department store in Chicago. The store had imported a large collection of modern furniture from France. To attract attention to the furniture, they asked Fuller to set up and demonstrate a model of the house he had designed for mass production in 1927 (During the exhibition, the tireless Fuller gave a continuous series of lectures (at the rate of six a day for two weeks) about the house, stressing its technical merits. But what the management had in mind was not selling the house or even promoting its mass production. The objective was "to contrast the furniture with the openly radical design of the house, in order to make the public less nervous about the more modest modernity of the furniture." Fuller, in turn, benefited from Marshall Field's PR department. They found the original name of his house "4D" (for fourth dimension) banal ("it sounds like an apartment number"), and commissioned a couple of "high powered word sculptors," one of them the inventor of the word "radio," to come up with a new one. [19] After listening to Fuller for hours they came up with "dymaxion" (from "dynamic," "maximum" and "ion"), a name that Fuller exploited all his life to capture the sense of the immediate future.

In the US, modern architecture is inextricably linked to commerce and the department store. Even the International Style exhibition toured the country's department stores—Sears Roebuck in Chicago and Bullock's in Los Angeles—after closing at MoMA in 1932. But the stores were not trying to sell architecture; they were pushing furniture and industrial design, consumer objects that could modernize space. The alliance in the US between modern architecture and commerce by way of the department store or the Museum of Modern Art attests to the publicity value of architecture—or more precisely, the house. The model house is an American institution. From the Frank Lloyd Wright's Houses of the Prairie, first published in the *Ladies Home Journal*, to the prefabricated houses for the war worker, to the post-war houses built in full scale in the garden of MoMA, and the Case Study Houses in California, Americans have always been fascinated with the house. Model houses throughout the century have stolen the show at every exhibition or fair and have played a crucial role in promoting and realizing modern architecture in the US.

Houses of the future are necessarily more radical. The audience is typically smaller. The exact product is less clear. And yet the houses also play a key role in the realization of the future. They operate something like the concept cars displayed by automobile manufactures each year. Cars filled with new materials and technologies that are not quite operational yet have a real effect. An image of the near future triggers a desire for the latest model in the present.

Buckminster Fuller's Dymaxion House is arguably the definitive house of the future. It was the blueprint for many new dreams and contains in itself many houses of the future. At the same time, the house is part of the consistent twentieth century dream of transparency, and its ultimate realization.

The Dymaxion House is a glass house with a crystal like structure. The core of the house contains all the services, allowing the inhabitants 360-degree views of the outside world thought the continuous transparent surface of the outer wall. The house represents a stage of the dream of a transparent house. From the science-fiction quality of Paul Scheerbart's images of glass buildings in an ideal future in his novels and in his collection of aphorisms *Glasarchitektur*, dedicated to Bruno Taut, to Taut's own Glashaus (the glass industry pavilion at Cologne's Werkbund Exhibition in 1914), to Mies van der Rohe and Lily Reich's Glass Room in Stuttgart (1927), the German Pavilion at the 1929 International Exposition in Barcelona and the project of a glass house on a Hillside (1934), to George Fred Keck's House of Tomorrow and the Crystal House (shown with Fuller's Dymaxion Car parked in the garage), both built at the Century of Progress International Exhibition in Chicago in 1933–34, and so on.

By 1949 the dream of the all-glass house was fully realized in Mies's Farnsworth House

DYMAXION HOUSE ON THE OCEAN SIDE WITH DYMAXION CAR (ANNE FULLER, 1934)

HOUSE OF TOMORROW (GEORGE FRED KECK, 1933–34), EXHIBITED AT THE CENTURY OF PROGRESS INTERNATIONAL EXPOSITION IN CHICAGO

CRYSTAL HOUSE (GEORGE FRED KECK, 1933–34), EXHIBITED AT THE CHICAGO CENTURY OF PROGRESS INTERNATIONAL EXPOSITION, A DYMAXION CAR BY R. BUCKMINSTER FULLER IS PARKED IN THE GARAGE.

LUDWIG MIES VAN DER ROHE, *SKETCH ELEVATION FOR GLASS HOUSE ON A HILLSIDE*, INK ON PAPER, 10.7 X 20.3 CM., 1934 (NEW YORK, MUSEUM OF MODERN ART, THE MIES VAN DER ROHE ARCHIVE, GIFT OF THE ARCHITECT)

EXTERIOR REAR VIEW OF FARNSWORTH HOUSE, PLANO, ILLINOIS (LUDWIG MIES VAN DER ROHE, 1951).

in Piano, Illinois, floating just above the ground like a craft coming in to land, and Philip Johnson's Glass House in Connecticut, finally resting on the ground, down on its solid pad, anchored in place and yet somewhat a "raft," in Johnson's words, or perhaps a flying carpet. What had been experimented in drawings, models, writings, or pavilions in fairs became useful. As Louis Kahn put it, "The glass house is a marvelous building because it stated very elegantly what was in the secret recesses of everybody's mind at the time of its conception. It brought out the picture of what modern architecture wanted to be." [20] The house as an image then, a photograph of what everybody had in mind, a dream in physical form. The dream of transparency finally inhabited.

It doesn't mean that the inhabitants of glass houses are exposed. They are usually much more protected than in an opaque house since their settings are so isolated. Or as Johnson said about his house in a 1965 CBS TV program: it was an "opportunity to live in the woods." [21] "A wall is only an idea on your mind," he insisted. "If you have a sense of enclosure you are in a room." And to the repeated question of whether his house is a fishbowl that exposes his body to the eyes of others, he answers that he has lived sixteen years in the house and nobody has come up to look in: "I think it is because people are afraid that you are looking at them." [22] The glass house operates both ways, something that artists like Dan Graham have been exploiting since the 1970s. But Johnson doesn't experience the glass as transparent but as wallpaper. In a different TV program he said, "[The Glass House] works very well for the simple reason that the wallpaper is so handsome. It is perhaps a very expensive wall paper but you have wall paper that changes every five minutes throughout the day and

GLASS HOUSE, NEW CANAAN, CONNECTICUT (PHILIP JOHNSON, 1949; PHOTOGRAPH BY EZRA STOLLER)

surrounds you with the beautiful nature that sometimes—not this year—Connecticut gives us."[23] The glass provides enclosure rather than openness, containment: "This house I built it after Mies gave us all the model in his famous glass house near Chicago. But "I wanted to be contained. I don' believe in indoor-outdoor architecture…. What you want is a contained house to cuddle you, to hold you, to hold you near the hearth…. This house is contained… the black band that runs around the house keeps the landscape away. It turns the landscape into kind of wall paper"[24]. It is this sense of complete envelopment that makes the minimalist statement architecture: "If you are in a good piece of architecture you have the feeling that you are surrounded."[25] The glass reinforces the traditional role of architecture rather than dematerializes it. "Architecture is how you enclose space. That's why I hate photographs, TV, and motion pictures," Johnson says during one of his multiple TV interviews.[26] If Fuller's Dymaxion house floats in the air among the trees and Mies and Johnson's Glass houses float down to the ground among the trees, Alison and Peter Smithson's 1956 House of the Future goes one step further by inverting the glass house, putting the landscape and trees in the middle of the house and all the services around it[27]. Unable to see out, the occupants look through glass walls at the inner landscape or up to the sky. Once again, the future is envisioned as an increasing sense of enclosure and disconnection. The more the technologies of communication establish non-physical links to the outside world, the more the physical links become redundant, if not an antiquated embarrassment. The intensity of the interior increases dramatically; it becomes a landscape that can be toured. Life on the inside becomes a kind of miniaturized version of life on the outside. The outside is swallowed by the house and fastidiously cleaned of all threats.

The Smithson's House of the Future was commissioned by the *Daily Mail* for their Jubilee Ideal Home Exhibition in London in March 1956. Surrounded by traditional model houses, it imagined that the house of 1980 would be molded out of smoothly curving plastic and assembled in a factory like an automobile with all interior fittings built in (an idea also employed in the Monsanto House of the Future built In Disneyland also in 1956). The house is entirely closed to the outside except for one highly sexualized orifice, an opening sealed off by a panel that can be momentarily raised, like the entrance to a medieval castle, at the push of a button. The house is impregnable. The inhabitants are protected by an array of technologies. Even during the few seconds that the door opens, a special filtration system acts as an air barrier, removing all foreign particles. Several hatches by the door for mail or food mean that the door doesn't need to be opened for deliveries. Those few that cross the threshold are subjected to a decontamination procedure that keeps the outside air out: "To admit the visitor the occupant operates the shutter control and automatically the anti-draught blast of warm air from the grille under the door comes into operation."[28] From the front door, the visitor then passes through a curtain of warm air to remove dust. The house is air-conditioned throughout and all smells are mechanically extracted. At the time, the US was introducing the concept of air conditioners for widespread domestic use. Advertisements for window units used X-rays of lungs. Air conditioning stood for health as much as comfort. It is no accident that the H.O.F. depicted in perspective resembles a lung inside a box, becoming, in its community form, a "mat cluster" (to use Smithson's terminology) [mat cluster is Smithson's terminology] of boxed lungs. The city of the future is a city of artificial lungs.

Not only is the air continuously controlled and purified, but every surface is obsessively cleansed of any trace of dirt, dust or germs. The house's continuous surface with round corners, they insist, is easily maintained with a damp cloth. The sunken bathtub fills from the bottom and has an automatic rinsing system that swills down the bath with a foamless detergent. The lavatory is "a room in its own right . . . and its continuously spinning self-digesting unit needs no flushing mechanism and makes no noise." The "glass" wall to the garden is "self-washing externally." A "portable electro-static dust collector works on its own replacing the traditional vacuum cleaner to remove the little dust that may creep in." Towels are considered a health hazard. The shower in the bathroom is also a drier, with nozzles for water and warm air. Disposable paper towel dispensers are installed near all water sources. There is a sun lamp built into the lavatory wall. The bed has only one fitted nylon sheet, since the controlled temperature of the house eliminates the need for bedclothes.[29] And so on. Even posture was carefully attended to in the H.O.F. as another form of hygiene.[30]

In this search for a completely controlled environment, the obsession with dust, hygiene and cleanliness, the Smithson's House of the Future echoes Buckminster Fuller's Dymaxion House in every detail but takes the exclusion of the outside to the next level. The structure smoothly seals itself off from the dangerous outside with a series of prophylactic layers. Everything that enters has to sanitized whether it be people, air, or food. "All the food is bombarded with gamma rays—an atomic by-product to kill all bacteria,"[31] stored in airtight plastic and preserved for a long stay. As with

MONSANTO HOUSE OF THE FUTURE, DISNEYLAND, ANAHEIM, CALIFORNIA (MARVIN GOODY AND RICHARD HAMILTON, 1957)

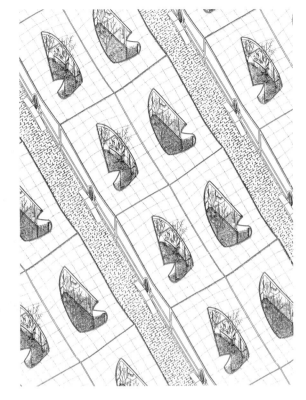

VOLUMETRIC DRAWING OF MAT CLUSTER OF HOUSES OF THE FUTURE (ALISON AND PETER SMITHSON, 1957)

HOUSE OF THE FUTURE, DAILY MAIL IDEAL HOME EXHIBITION, LONDON (ALISON AND PETER SMITHSON, 1955–56) VIEW FROM THE PATIO INTO THE KITCHEN

HOUSE OF THE FUTURE, DAILY MAIL IDEAL HOME EXHIBITION, LONDON (ALISON AND PETER SMITHSON, 1955–56) ENTRANCE DOOR WITH EXTRACT GRILLE TO REMOVE DIRT FROM SHOES BEFORE ENTERING

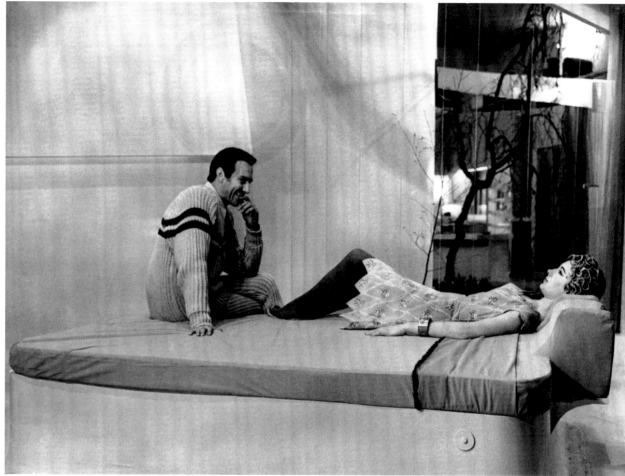

"INHABITANT" OF THE HOUSE OF THE FUTURE OPERATING THE SELF-CLEANING BATHTUB

BEDROOM WITH "INHABITANTS," HOUSE OF THE FUTURE THE ISLAND BED HAS ITS BASE MOLDED INTO THE FLOOR. THE MATTRESS AND HEADRESTS ARE LATEX-FOAM COVERED WITH NYLON, AND THE BEDCLOTHES CONSIST OF ONE EASILY WASHABLE NYLON SHEET.

VERTICAL TUBE OF UNBREATHED PRIVATE AIR

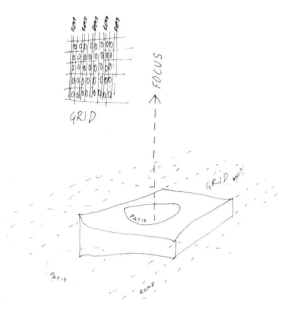

ALISON AND PETER SMITHSON, *VERTICAL TUBE OF UNBREATHED PRIVATE AIR* (DIAGRAM OF HOUSE OF THE FUTURE), 1956

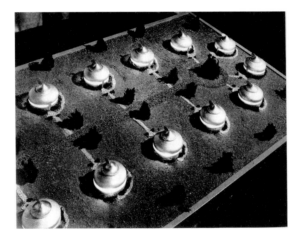

MOCK-UP OF A VILLAGE OF DYMAXION DWELLING MACHINES (RICHARD BUCKMINSTER FULLER, 1956)

Fuller, there is a polemical insistence on self-sufficiency. Rainwater is collected from the roof allowing inhabitants to eventually cut themselves off from the outside world. Even if the Smithsons imagined that such houses could be lined up back to back to form a dense urban array, a "mat cluster," the perfection of their seal would mean that the inhabitants will be completely isolated from their next door neighbors. Each house is its own world, a complete world. In the same way, when Fuller presents a later model of the Dymaxion House, the Wichita house of 1946, in a suburban array, it does not imply an intimate link between the houses. Each house can see the houses around it but remain self-contained. It is as if a squadron of super-sealed spacecrafts has landed in an empty field.

The extremely controlled interior environment involves a new concept of privacy. The Smithsons' house doesn't even look around at the local environment—it looks up. The heart of the house is an opening to the sky above. The house, Alison wrote, "speaks to a portion of the sky, for this was also the period in which we had created our 'Private Sky' diagram that would allow dwellings their right to address a portion of the sky with its, as yet unbreathed air"[32]. The essence of private space is air that has yet to be breathed, anticipating the current obsession with unbreathed air in airplanes, restaurants and public buildings. Air that has not been breathed is space that has not been occupied. You sit on the minimum footprint of land in order to access an infinite vertical tube of unoccupied territory: an architecture of air rights, unbreathed air as the ultimate measure of privacy in an ever more congested world.

Fuller had already spoken of "your private sky." By the late 1940s, he had disconnected his domestic spaces from the local environment in order to make connection with the macro environment, the planetary system. As his research on geodesic domes evolved, his houses increasingly asked the occupant to look up at the sky—a departure from Dymaxion House and Wichita House, which framed a horizontal, all around view of the world immediately outside. From the first plastic Garden of Eden dome constructed at Black Mountain College in 1948 to the "Skybreak" houses of the early 1950s, the primary purpose of the building was simply to create a controlled environment, an idyllic garden in which the occupants can claim the sky above as their own territory, "your private sky." The Smithsons were following and radicalizing his thought. Their House of the Future focuses exclusively on the vertical view. In 1956, with the Sputnik about to be launched, the spatial order had changed. Site was no longer global, as it had become with the previous generation of modern architects, but planetary. The house itself was in orbit.

The Smithson's House of the Future was a space house—both in the sense of Kiesler's 1933 project Space House, where the curved skin already acted as the structure, and in the look and logic of the recently launched space program—a spaceship. A significant part of the *Daily Mail* exhibition of 1956 was dedicated to the space program and filled with imaginary rockets and spaceships. The House of the Future was commissioned to tie in with this display and was full of allusions to space travel: from the airtight seal of its seams, to the food packaging and even the clothing to be worn inside the house (designed to counter the severity of a space suit).

"The answer to the housing problem lies on the way to the moon," wrote Fuller in 1966.[33] A new international generation of experimental architects, for whom Fuller was a guru, committed themselves to the project. Architectural groups such as Archigram, the Japanese Metabolists, Haus-Rucker-Co, Coop Himmelb(l)au , and Ugo la Pietra produced an array of interrelated capsules, mobile and plug-in units, which constitute the house of the future of the 1960s.

Warren Chalk gave meaning to the historical moment when he declared in manifesto-like form, "In this second half of the twentieth, the old idols are crumbling, the old precepts strangely irrelevant, the old dogmas no longer valid. We are in pursuit of an idea, a new vernacular, something to stand alongside the space capsules, computers, and throw-away packages of an atomic and electronic age."[34] Chalk was the first to apply the word capsule to architecture in 1964, when the Archigram group was still part of the Taylor Woodrow Design Group under Theo Crosby.[35] "The statement was capsule dwelling with the ergonomy and the sophistication of the space capsule."[36]

The capsule dwelling is a house and a vehicle capable of existing in a hostile environment. Archigram member David Greene's 1965 Living Pod reconfigures the private house as a space ship resting on the earth as if on the moon. Its molded shape was openly inspired by the Smithson's house of the future and supplemented by gadgetry from the space program. The house is held off the ground by hydraulic legs adjustable to any terrain and fed conditioned air through a technical package attached to the outside. The house is capable of surviving in any hostile environment by reproducing a terrestrial atmosphere. The interior is defined by molded inflatable furniture and clusters of mobile technical equipment, including an educational machine that echoes the Dymaxion media center. The floor is inflatable. Bathing

SPACE HOUSE, NEW YORK (FRIEDRICH KIESLER, 1933)

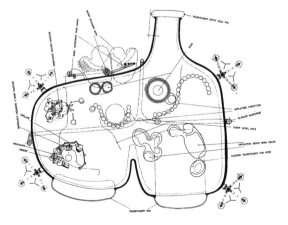

WARREN CHALK
(ARCHIGRAM),
UNDERWATER HARDWARE,
COLLAGE FROM
ARCHIGRAM 5, 1964

DAVID GREENE
(ARCHIGRAM), *LIVINGPOD,*
COLLAGE FROM
ARCHIGRAM 7, 1966–67

LIVINGPOD, MODEL
(DAVID GREENE,
ARCHIGRAM, 1967)
© ARCHIGRAM ARCHIVES
2006

LIVINGPOD, FLOOR PLAN
AT CAPSULE LEVEL (DAVID
GREENE, ARCHIGRAM,
1965)

and cooking is clearly inspired by the Smithsons' interior. Once again, great attention is paid to sealing out the outside world. The "access aperture" has vacuum fixing seals. For Archigram it is likely that "the need for a house (in the form of permanent static container) as part of man's psychological make-up will disappear." Archigram thinned down the house to its most minimal mobile condition. And yet, Greene's Living Pod is in their minds still a house. "Although this capsule can be hung within a plug-in urban structure or can sit in the open landscape it is still a house." [37]

The Environmental Bubble of 1965, a project by Reyner Banham and Francois Dallegret, was a key model for the new generation of radical architects of the 1960s and 1970s. The project presents the section of an inflatable house with a group of naked people (in fact, multiple images of Banham and Dallegret) sitting around a dense technical unit. This portable "standard-of-living-package" (again a Fuller concept) provides for all the physical and psychological needs of the occupant: heating, music, information. Based on the idea of the car, the Environment Bubble is a transparent Mylar 30-foot dome, inflated by the air conditioning output, with membrane flaps for entry at any point. Banham called this minimalist reduction of the traditional house an "unhouse." A lightweight version of Johnson's too "monumental" un-house: the Glass House in New Canaan. [38]

A year later, Mike Webb, another Archigram member, came up with the Cushicle (1966–67), an even more compact piece of equipment that can be carried on your body and opened up when necessary to provide an instant house, a "complete environment" for one person. In its fully inflated state it offers a small tent-like house complete with food, water, radio, TV and heating, Like an astronaut, the occupant sits in an ergonomically molded and wired chaise lounge, with a helmet providing media connections to the outside world. The portable package is "autonomous," but can be plugged in to service nods and additional equipment to constitute "part of more widespread system of personalized enclosures." With the Suitaloon of 1968, Webb developed the concept further to allow two people to occupy the same space. The tightly fitting "clothing for living in" works like a space suit with internal air, heating and communication, but can open up to form a transparent bag that can be plugged into someone else's bag so that both people occupy the same space. Two portable houses temporarily become one, in a highly sexualized scenario. In the 1968 Milan Triennale, David Greene demonstrated a prototype of the Inflatable Suit-Home. Again a person's suit is inflated out to form a bubble, a "suit as home."

Coop Himmelb(l)au, founded in Vienna by Wolf Prix, Helmut Swiczinsky and Michael Holzer (who would leave the group in 1971), continued the assault on walls. Their objective is "to do an architecture as floating and changeable as the clouds," they declared in 1968. Their 1968 project Villa Rosa explores technology as a "natural" extension of the body: mobile, change able and aerial. It was a prototype of an inflatable habitat, with purified space, relaxation room and stage for performances. Color projections, sounds and smells intensified the experience. "Our architecture does not have a physical plane, but a psychic plane. There are no walls. Our spaces are palpitating balloons. Our pulse becomes the space, and our face, the building's façade." [39] The Cloud (1968–72), another prototype for future living designed for Documenta 5, was a mobile, inflatable sphere containing a

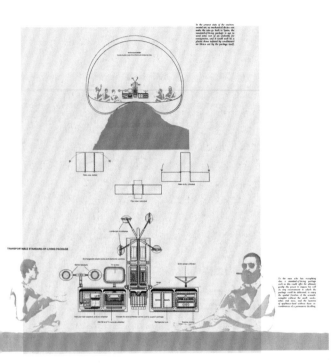

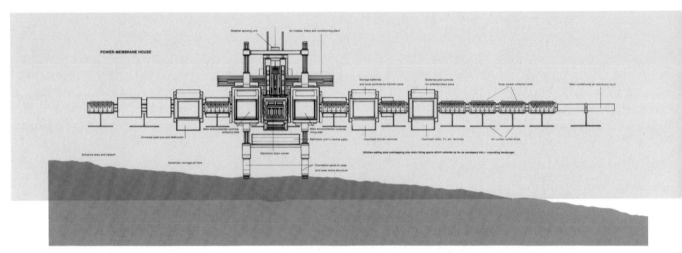

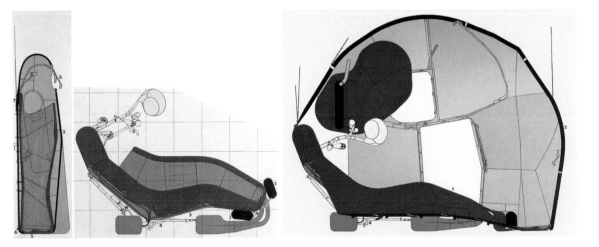

TRANSPORTABLE STANDARD-OF-LIVING PACKAGE/THE ENVIRONMENT BUBBLE (ILLUSTRATION FOR REYNER BANHAM'S ARTICLE "A HOME IS NOT A HOUSE," PUBLISHED IN *ART IN AMERICA*, APRIL 1965), FRANÇOIS DALLEGRET, 1965

POWER-MEMBRANE HOUSE, FRANÇOIS DALLEGRET, 1965

CUSHICLE (MIKE WEBB, ARCHIGRAM, 1966) SCHEMATIC DRAWING SHOWING HOW THE STRUCTURE UNFOLDS IN THREE STEPS

MOCK-UP OF INFLATABLE SUIT HOME FOR THE ARCHIGRAM EXHIBITION AT THE 14TH MILAN TRIENNIAL MADE BY DAVID GREENE AND STUDENTS IN NOTTINGHAM, MAY 1968

core of technical elements providing for physical and psychological pleasure. The pneumatic house could be stored in a container, transported on a truck, and assembled in 97 minutes.

Haus-Rucker-Co, a group of architects founded 1967 in Vienna, were carrying out similar experiences with lightweight pneumatic structures, "non-physical" environments and "provisional architecture" enhanced with an array of technologies, sensory effects, and performances. A whole series of occupiable bubbles—Pneumacosm (1967), Balloon for Two (1967), Connection Skin, Yellow Heart, and Air Unit (all 1971)—explored the effect of isolation from the impurities of the outside world. Haus-Rucker were particularly committed to excluding pollution, protecting the body, a farmhouse, and a whole village with translucent bubbles[40].

While these Austrian experiments resembled those of Archigram, there was a new simultaneous concentration on the quality of the outside air and the inside of the mind, an intensely psychological component. The more minimal the dwelling unit, the more intense the psychological effect, as became polemical with Haus-Rucker-Co's Mind Expander series from 1967–71.

After a succession of such full-size plastic mockups and performances, happenings, by radical architects around the world, these bubble experiments became more and more speculative, unbuildable fantasies of future houses and lifestyles. The houses of the future that were built in the meantime exposed a different, more heavyweight trajectory.

When Archigram, for example, was commissioned in 1967 by the *Weekend Telegraph* to build a prototype of "a house for the year 1990" to be exhibited in Harrods department store in London, the spaces suits and Mylar

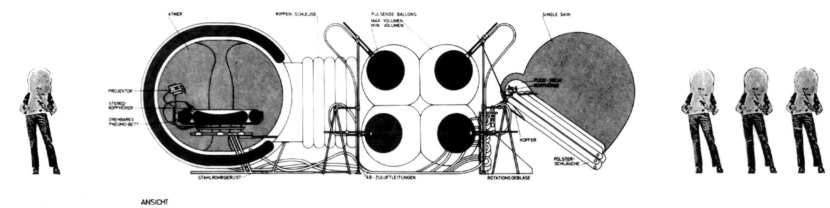

ANSICHT

GRUNDRISS

VILLA ROSA (COOP HIMMELB(L)AU [WOLF D. PRIX, HELMUT SWICZINSKY], 1968) PLAN AND SECTION OF PNEUMATIC LIVING UNIT

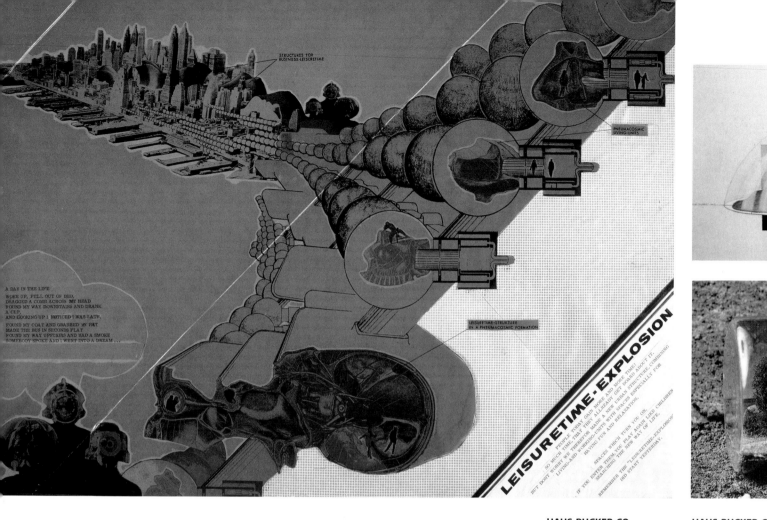

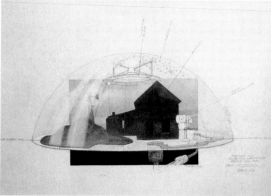

HAUS-RUCKER-CO,
LEISURETIME EXPLOSION,
COLLAGE, 48 X 68 CM
(COLLECTION FRAC
CENTRE, ORLÉANS)

HAUS-RUCKER-CO,
PNEUMATIC SKIN
PROTECTING A FARM-
HOUSE AGAINST
POLLUTION, COLLAGE,
1970

HAUS-RUCKER-CO,
EINWECKGLAS
[PRESERVING JAR], 1970

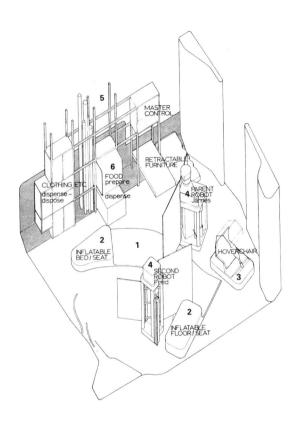

ARCHIGRAM, *LIVING 1990*
(COMMISSIONED BY THE
***WEEKEND TELEGRAPH*),**
AXONOMETRIC DRAWING
SHOWING COMPONENTS,
1967

bags gave way to walls, ceilings and floor treated as adjustable movable elements. Even the softness of the surfaces could be controlled. The house is no longer defined by an outside envelope but by a set of mobile elements containing furniture, information and services. In the grand tradition of houses of the future, a big point is made of the fact that dust is automatically extracted by 2 robots named Fred and James who also provide the media enveloping the inhabitants in sounds, images and smells. The robots are movable and, in Archigram's words, "can shoot out screens" to make a private space and serve refreshments. The bed-capsule can turn into a hovercraft and operate outside, but the house itself remains on earth.[41]

In 1968 the Finnish architect Matti Suuronen responded to a commission for a ski cabin "quick to heat and easy to construct in rough terrain"[42] with the design of Futuro, an elliptical fiberglass capsule on little legs that soon took off in the public imagination. "A Man's Home Is His Saucer" and "Spaceship Homes of the Near Future," as the newspaper headlines announced. It was, like so many houses of the future, exhibited in department stores and successfully promoted as a leisure house, and constructed all over the earth. On the same day that Apollo 11 landed on the moon, the *New York Times* announced that Futuro had arrived in Philadelphia with the headline "Saucer-Shaped House Arrives on Earth." The interior of Futuro was always presented as pleasure pad inhabited by women models acting like stewardesses, and the house became such a cult object that it was presented in *Playboy* as a "portable playhouse," one of its series of ideal designs for a bachelor's "lair" and in *Private*, which used it as the setting for *The Goddess of Galaxy*, a sadomasochist sci-fi porn fantasy.

It is hard to separate the idea of the capsule from the Japanese Metabolists, whose founding member Kurokawa published the "Capsule Declaration" in 1969:
The capsule is cyborg* architecture. Man, machine and space build a new organic body which transcends confrontation. As a human being equipped with a man-made internal organ becomes a new species which is neither machine nor human, so the capsule transcends man and equipment…. The word "capsule" usually conjures up either a capsule containing medicine or the living quarters of an astronaut…
* "cyborg": a cybernetic organism, hence an organism which is partly automated, based on feedback and information processes; usually appears in science fiction as half man, half machine.[43]
But when Kurokawa builds his famous capsule tower, the Nakagin Capsule Tower of 1972, all traces of the delicate membranes of pneumatic skins have disappeared. The tower is assembled of 144 independent and removable capsules. Each compact self-contained unit contains a bed, bathroom, storage, a desk, and media equipment. The 4 x 2.5 meter "container" is made of solid reinforced steel panels and punctured by only one round window. The compact seamless capsule defends the single occupant (typically a commuting businessman) rather than launch him into space.

This combination of space age architecture and defense was already established in the Smithson's House of the Future of 1956 with its soft interior protected by a hardened outer shell. In the space age, the house can land anywhere but it keeps its wary eye on the sky. The freedom to go up into the air is indistinguishable from the threat of being exposed or attacked from the air. If the origin of the traditional window is defensive, both an opening to

MATTI SUURONEN'S
FUTURO HOUSE BEING
AIRLIFTED IN SWEDEN ON
OCTOBER 22, 1969

EXTERIOR VIEW, FUTURO
HOUSE (MATTI SUURONEN,
1969)

FUTURO HOUSE (MATTI
SUURONEN, 1969)
VIEW OF THE INTERIOR,
1970s

**NAKAGIN CAPSULE
TOWER, TOKYO (KISHO
KUROKAWA, 1970–72)
INTERIOR VIEW**

keep an eye for intruders and a launching site for your weapons, before it turned into a contented view (with the increase in leisure time and the sophistication of security system), a new kind of defensive opening is needed when the major threat is above you. With Sputnik in orbit, the spatial system had changed. Up and down matters more than the horizontal view. The house can float, hover, or fly up in the air, but the Smithson's house bunkers down, acting a safe cave. The image of a playful domestic life cannot be separated from a fear of the outside. The Smithsons' House of the Future cannot be separated from the thought of war. The house was an escape from both the threats of the present and from the fresh memories of the war. The house is itself a mechanism of escape, an all-interior space the overly happy inhabitants will never need to leave: a bunker.

Bomb shelters, submarines, and spaceships defend themselves against the ultimate hostile environment outside. The latest technologies are used to establish a sense of security. Yet the Smithsons claimed their inspiration for their House of the Future was an archaic form of architecture, the Caves Les Baux de Provence, near Remy, in the south of France, which they had visited in 1953. They speak of the space of the House of the Future as rooms of different sizes, shapes and heights that flow into one another like the compartments of a cave, and as in a cave "the skewed passage that joins one compartment to another effectively maintains privacy."[44] Cave dwellings, like bomb shelters, submarines and spaceships, correspond to a time of extreme danger outside. Caves are all interiorized spaces, the first bunkers.

The elaborate plans, in the end unrealized, for an artificial sun (built as a light open metalwork sphere, seven feet in diameter, with orange tungsten lamps projected radially over the

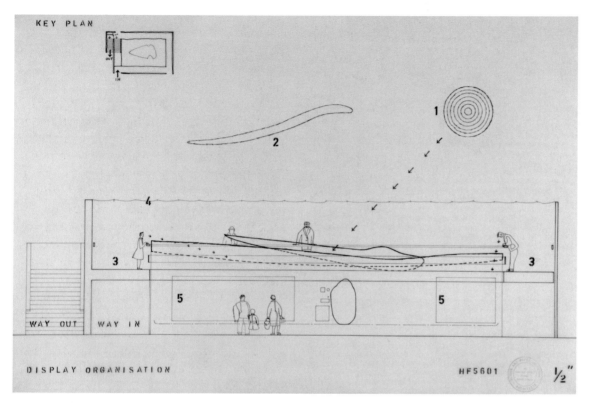

KEY PLAN

1

2

4

3   3

WAY OUT   WAY IN

5   5

DISPLAY ORGANISATION

HF5601   ½"

HOUSE OF THE FUTURE, DAILY MAIL IDEAL HOME EXHIBITION, LONDON (ALISON AND PETER SMITHSON, 1955–56) SECTION THROUGH THE OUTER CASE SHOWING PROPOSED ARTIFICIAL SUN AND FLOATING CLOUD, 1956 (1) SUN, (2) CLOUD, (3) UPPER VIEWING GALLERY, (4) VELARIUM, (5) VIEWING WINDOWS

PREFABRICATED FALLOUT SHELTER FULLY EQUIPPED, 1961

SECTION OF THE UNDERGROUND HOME PAVILION, NEW YORK WORLD'S FAIR (JAY SWAYZE, 1964)

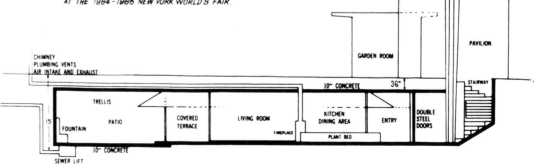

CUTAWAY VIEW OF UNDERGROUND WORLD HOME EXHIBIT AT THE 1964-1965 NEW YORK WORLD'S FAIR.

CHIMNEY
PLUMBING VENTS
AIR INTAKE AND EXHAUST

GARDEN ROOM   PAVILION

10" CONCRETE   36"   STAIRWAY

TRELLIS   KITCHEN DINING AREA   ENTRY

PATIO   COVERED TERRACE   LIVING ROOM   DOUBLE STEEL DOORS

FOUNTAIN   FIREPLACE   PLANT BED

10" CONCRETE

SEWER LIFT

UNDERGROUND GARDENING, UNDERGROUND HOME PAVILION, NEW YORK WORLD'S FAIR (JAY SWAYZE, 1964)

THE LIVING ROOM IN AN UNDERGROUND HOUSE, UNDERGROUND HOME PAVILION, NEW YORK WORLD'S FAIR (JAY SWAYZE, 1964)

whole surface and suspended from the Exhibition Hall roof) and a floating cloud (made of pale blue nylon stretched over a metal frame suspended from the roof and spot lit from above)[45] suggest the bunker-houses of the postwar years, in particular, the Underground House presented at the New York World's Fair of 1964 where visitors descended into a kind of cave, an underground walled artificial garden, a safe space containing a house.

The Underground Home was a traditional suburban ranch-style house buried as protection from the new threat of nuclear fallout.[46] It was the project of Jay Swayze, a Texas military instructor-turned-building-contractor of luxury houses who in 1962, during the Cuban Missile Crisis, had been commissioned to build a demonstration fallout shelter to specifications by the Department of Civil Defense. Swayze turned the military project of a shelter into a project for a family house: "It seemed more logical to make the home and its surroundings a safe harbor where the family would be protected in comfortable, familiar surroundings"[47]. The house offered a controlled environment where one could create one's own climate by "dialing" temperature and humidity settings. "The breeze of a mountain top, the exhilarating high pressure feeling of a spring day can be created at will."[48] Traditional windows are superimposed on "dial-a-view" murals. Every room in the house looked out on a panoramic landscape that can be changed at will. The time of the day or night can be " dialed" to fit any mood or occasion. The sponsor of this house was General Electric, which also commissioned Walt Disney to produce the Carousel of Progress, a series of theatrical sets that exhibit the history of the domestic interior from 1880 to 1964 by tracing the progressive transformation of the house with electricity

**UNDERWATER MOTEL,
GENERAL MOTOR'S
FUTURAMA PAVILION,
NEW YORK WORLD'S FAIR,
1964**

(and is still on display at Epcot Center in Disney World). In the General Electric Pavilion there was a demonstration of thermonuclear fusion every fifteen minutes. Nuclear power, a by-product of military technology, was offered simultaneously as mass spectacle and as a transformation of the house.

The Underground House is consistent with the idea of the city presented by the 1964 Fair in its Futurama exhibit. Whereas Futurama 1, in the 1939 World Fair, could still present the viewer with a coherent, unified image of the city—a modernist proposal of steel and glass towers, an object, over which the visitor, a detached, amazed, viewer—had no control, Futurama 2 in the 1964 Fair could no longer present a unified urban idea. Instead, it offered a collection of "improbable" places where people will live in the future: the moon, the jungle, under ice, under the sea, and in the dessert. A wide range of spacecrafts: Science fiction about to be inhabited.
Starting with the Fullers' paradigmatic Dymaxion project, the evolution of the twentieth-century house of the future relentlessly exhibits two trajectories (both represented at the 1964 Fair). On the one hand, the house gets lighter and lighter, as if preparing for flight. On the other hand, it never takes off, gains strength, fortifying itself and bunkering further down into the ground. In fact, these two trajectories are inseparable. The ever-increasing dematerialization of the house and the displacement of its traditional functions by new technologies of information are exactly matched by an increasing rematerialization at its borders and the emergence of ever more enclosing security systems. The house of the future is a stationary escape vehicle. The inhabitant of the future can escape without leaving.

IN THE DESERT: ELECTRONIC AND COMPUTERIZED FARMING OF RECLAIMED DESERT WASTELAND IRRIGATED WITH DESALTED SEA WATER, GENERAL MOTOR'S FUTURAMA PAVILION, NEW YORK WORLD'S FAIR, 1964

1   "After Five Years of Dymaxion History: Five Questions… and a Striking Answer," *Fortune* (July 1932).
2   H.G. Wells, *Anticipation of the Reactions of Mechanical and Scientific Progress Upon Human Life and Thought*, London, Harper Brothers, 1901, p. 100.
3   R. Buckminster Fuller, "The Year 2000," *Architectural Design* (February 1967).
4   R. Buckminster Fuller, 50 *Years of the Design Science Revolution and the World Game*, Carbondale, Southern University, 1969, p. vi.
5   Buckminster Fuller, "Dymaxion House Invented," *Fortune* (July 1932).
6   Ibid.
7   "Harvard Society of Contemporary Art Catalog-4D," *50 Years of the Design Science Revolution and the World Game*, ed. R. Buckminster Fuller, Carbondale, Southern University, 1969, p. 6.
8   Buckminster Fuller, "Dymaxion House," Architectural League, New York, (July 9, 1929). Reprinted in *Your Private Sky: R. Buckminster Fuller Discourse*, eds. Joachim Krausse and Claude Lichtenstein, Zurich, Lars Müller, 2001, p. 93.
9   Ibid., p. 92.
10   Buckminster Fuller, "Dymaxion House Invented," *Fortune* (July 1932).
11   Buckminster Fuller, "Dymaxion House," *Your Private Sky*, p. 86.
12   Buckminster Fuller, "Dymaxion House Invented."
13   "Modern Living," *Time* (January 1964). Reprinted in Buckminster Fuller, *50 Years of the Design Science Revolution and the World Game*, p. 122.
14   Buckminster Fuller, "Tree-Like Style of Dwelling is Planned," *The Chicago Evening Post Magazine of the Art World* (December 18, 1928), p. 5. Reprinted in Buckminster Fuller, ed., *50 Years of the Design Science Revolution and the World Game*, pp. 2–3
15   Buckminster Fuller, "Dymaxion House," *Your Private Sky*, p. 90.
16   Ibid., p. 98.
17   Ibid., p. 96.
18   Lynn Spigel, *Make Room for TV: Television and the Family Ideal in Postwar America*, Chicago, The University of Chicago Press, 1992.
19   "Modern Living," reprinted in *50 Years of the Design Science Revolution and the World Game*, p. 122. See also, Michael John Gorman, *Buckminster Fuller: Designing for Mobility*, Milan: Skira, 2005, p. 41.
20   Louis Kahn in TV program *Accent*, "The Architect (Philip Johnson and Louis Kahn")", CBS May 14, 1961.
21   *This Is Philip Johnson* (CBS television documentary, 1965).
22   Ibid.
23   Johnson in TV program *Accent*: "The Architect (Philip Johnson and Louis Kahn")", CBS May 14, 1961.
24   "Philip Johnson Interviewed by Rosamond Bernier," 1976. In *Museum of Television & Radio Seminar Series. The Artist at Work: Philip Johnson*," Sept. 26, 1991.
25   Ibid.
26   Ibid.
27   About the Smithson's House of the Future, see Beatriz Colomina, "Unbreathed Air: 1956," *Alison and Peter Smithson: From the House of the Future to a House of Today*, eds. Dirk van Heuvel and Max Risselada, Rotterdam, 010 Publishers, 2004, pp. 32–49.
28   Alison and Peter Smithson, "The Ideal Home Exhibition 'House of the Future' 1956: General statement," manuscript, 1956; ed. Peter Smithson, 2000. In A&P Smithson Archives.
29   Fitted sheets were then unknown in England and the clothes designer had to mock them up.
30   In the kitchen, all fittings are above waist level, even storage cupboards. This was often pointed out by the popular press. For some years after World War I, the Ideal Home Exhibition was replaced by the Efficiency Exhibition, focusing on the disabled (war veterans). Labor-saving devices in the workplace proposed in the Efficiency Exhibition had much in common with those proposed in the domestic sphere by the Ideal Home Exhibition. Deborah S. Ryan, *Daily Mail-Ideal Home Exhibition: The Ideal Home through the 20th Century*, London, Hazar Publishing, 1997, p. 40
31   Alison and Peter Smithson, "The House of the Future," *Daily Mail Ideal Home Exhibition, Olympia, 1956*, catalogue of exhibition, p. 99.
32   Alison Smithson, "Patio and Pavilion, 1956", *Places: A Quarterly Journal of Environmental Design*, Vol. 7, no. 3, 1991, p. 10.

33   Wolf von Eckhardt, "That Bucky Fuller Sure is a High Flyer", *The Washington Post*, October 2, 1966. Reprinted in Buckminster Fuller, *50 Years of the Design Science Revolution and the World Game*, p. 90.
34   Warren Chalk, *The Living City*, London, 1963. From: *Amazing Archigram 4 Zoom* issue, 1964.
35   Peter Cook, *Archigram*, London, Studio Vista, 1972, p. 44
36   Amazing Archigram 4 Zoom Issue, and Peter Cook, *Archigram*, p. 44.
37   David Greene, "Living-pod", Archigram, ed. Peter Cook, London, Studio Vista, 1972, reprinted by Birkhauser, 1991, p. 52.
38   Reyner Banham, "A Home Is Not a House," *Art in America* (April 1965). Reprinted in *Design by Choice*, London, Academy Editions, 1981.
39   Coop Himmelb(l)au, "Cities that beat like a heart," 1967, quoted in Frédéric Migayrou, *Arquitectura radical*, Las Palmas de Gran Canaria, 2002, p. 353.
40   Dieter Bogner, *Haus-Rucker-Co*, Vienna, 1992.
41   "Living 1990," in P. Cook, *Archigram*, p. 62.
42   *Futuro, Tomorrow's House from Yesterday*, ed. by Marko Home & Mika Taanila, Jyvaskyla, Gummerus Kirjapaino Oy, 2003, p. 12
43   "Capsule Declaration" Space Design, March 1, 1969. Reprinted in Kisho Kurokawa, *Metabolism in Architecture* (London: Studio Vista, 1977), p. 75.
44   Alison and Peter Smithson, *The House of the Future*, catalogue of exhibition, p. 97.
45   "Ideal Homes. House of the Future. Suggestions for Outer Case and Viewing Platforms," Manuscript in A&P Smithson Archives. See also drawing 5526.
46   About the Underground House see, Rosemarie Haag Bletter, "The 'Laissez-Fair', Good Taste, and Money Trees: Architecture at the Fair," *Remembering the Future: The New York World's Fair from 1939 to 1964* (New York: Queens Museum and Rizzoli International, 1989), pp. 105–35. And Beatriz Colomina, "Domesticity at War," *Discourse* 14.1 (Winter 1991–92), pp. 3-22.
47   Jay Swayze, *Underground Gardens and Homes: The Best of Two Worlds-Above and Below*, Hereford, Texas, Geobuilding Systems, 1980, p. 20.
48   *The Underground Home: New York World's Fair 1964-1965*. Underground World Home Corp. publicity brochure.

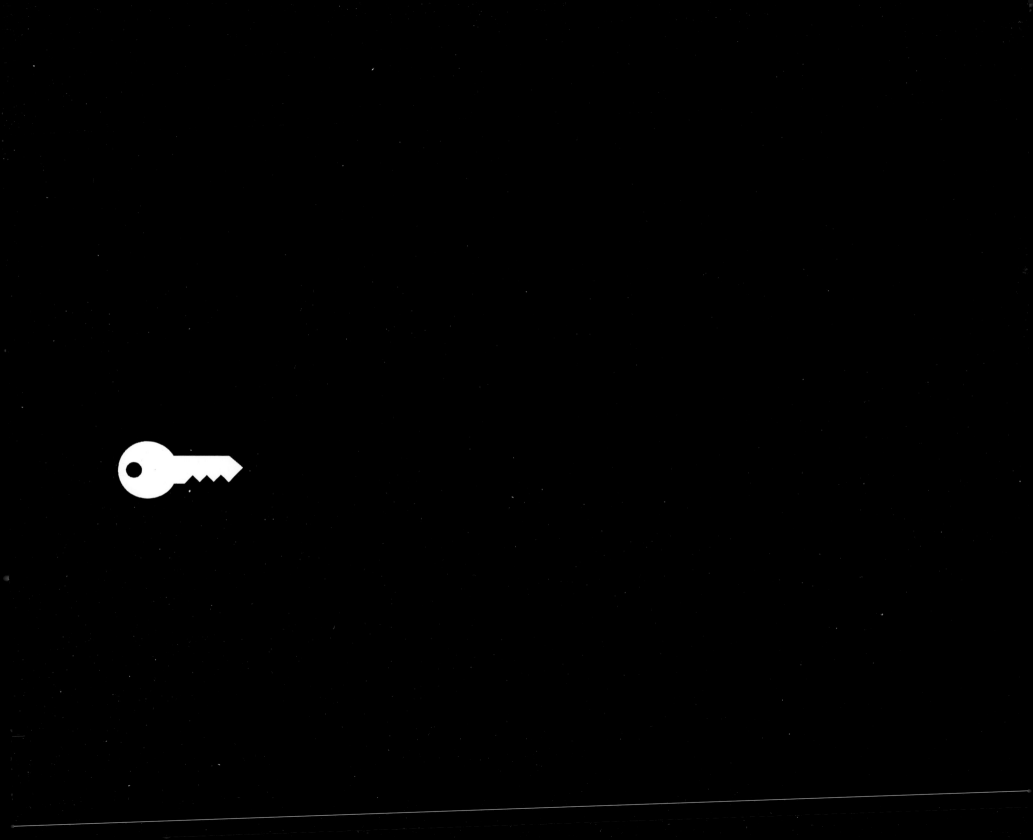

Future Terms: A Glossary

Throughout this catalogue, there are terms used in the essays and project descriptions worth annotating, as they refer to emerging technologies or are technical terms used in a sense specific to designers. These entries should then be read more as descriptions than definitions, and are provided to give some sense of the technology and why this technology is of interest or use to designers.—Linda Taalman

Aerogel
An ultra-lightweight material, 90 to 99.8 percent air, that is the result of the liquid molecules present in silicone jelly being replaced with air or gas. Also known as frozen smoke, due to its cloudy transparency, the material feels like hard foam. Its microporosity makes it an excellent insulating and dense substance; and while transparent, it is many times stronger and efficient than conventional materials like glass or fiberglass. Aerogel can be used for applications such as windows, building cladding systems, and clothing.

Ambient intelligence
The vision of networked technology invisibly and seamlessly embedded into our surroundings. Imagined to replace present day PC-based computing with multiple micro-devices that are easily accessed through intelligent interfaces and networked together to form a naturalistic yet responsive environment. Developed by ISTAG (Information Society Technologies Advisory Group) to the European Commission.
See also *ubiquitous computing,* and *nanotechnology.*

Ambient technology
Technology less present in terms of itself than the effects or moods that it creates. As part of the dwelling environment, like air, sound, and light, the technology allows the inhabitant to interact with the environment in a more ephemeral, temporary, and responsive manner. Also known as calm technology.
See also *ubiquitous technology.*

Biodegradability
The ability to safely and relatively quickly break down by way of biological means, converting organic material back into base matter, such as carbon dioxide and water, through microbial action. Various standards bodies, such as the European Norm EN 13432, the Japanese Greenpla standard, and the American Society for Testing and Materials, define biodegradable materials as those materials able to break down within six months.
See also *disposable design, zero footprint.*

Bioluminescence
Light emitted by a chemical reaction within an organism, such as the firefly or jellyfish. Bioluminescence can be engineered through the genetic modification of organic material, potentially creating materials that illuminate without the requirement of electricity, or the production of radiant heat, and react to environmental or internal chemical shifts.
See also *electroluminescence.*

Biometric recognition
Recognition of a person based on his or her biological or chemical make up (fingerprints, DNA, or iris recognition), typically to allow entrance to a limited access system.

Biomimicry
The science of studying and imitating natural methods and systems to solve human problems. For example, designers are looking to nature as a model for producing more efficient and less wasteful solutions to meet the sustainability problems at hand.

Biomorphic
Resembling organic shapes and structures. In the pursuit of an architecture that takes on forms similar to those commonly found in nature, designs using complex computer-generated forms and smooth shapes have emerged.

Biotechnology
Any technological application that uses biological systems, living organisms, or derivatives thereof to make or modify products or processes for a specific use.

Composite
A material made by combining elemental or base materials, usually with the intention of increasing strength or adding another level of performance without losing the original properties of the individual materials. Primitive composites, such as reinforced concrete, are more visibly the combination of two distinct materials, while advanced composites, such as carbon fiber, are engineered to form a seamless new material.
See also *recombinant.*

Disposable design
Designed for disposal after use. Disposable design anticipates the lifespan of use and the ultimate final destination once the use has been fulfilled. Many disposable products are intended for a specific number of uses. Disposable design should also include the method of disposal, ideally by way of biodegradability, recycling, or some other ecological process.
See also *biodegradable, zero footprint.*

Dynamic growth
Pertaining to cities, structures and systems, a design strategy for growth responding to contextual activities and forces, adaptive rather than prescriptive.
See also *emergent systems.*

Electroluminescence
A phenomenon causing a material to emit light when electrical current is passed through it, making electrons release energy as photons. Electroluminescent materials are used to produce an even-illumination over a surface with minimal infrastructure for producing power and minimal depth of surface, such as backlit displays.

Emergent systems
Activities that combine to form a collective transformation to allow for organic or irregular growth, anticipating and responding to input. Designers are looking towards emergent systems as a strategy for understanding for how larger structures, planning strategies, and urban environments can form without an imposed overall master plan or superstructure.
See *dynamic growth.*

Generative architecture
An architecture based on the process either of allowing an outside order (such as music, traffic flows, or independent algorithms) to generate patterns that are translated into design or of producing a form from a scripted set of rules that compute a resulting shape. Generative architecture privileges complexity and unpredictability over regularity.
See also *parametric modeling.*

Geotextiles
Engineered fabrics woven into the earth and used as a reinforcement mesh in soil and vegetation to minimize erosion. The mesh can then be planted with grass or other vegetation. With geotextiles, designers can rethink earth retainment at landscape sites, substituting organic material for artificial surfaces.

Graywater
Wastewater resulting from household processes, such as washing dishes, laundry and bathing that can be reclaimed and treated for reuse. Where water is limited, the reuse of graywater aids in the conservation of resources.

Hydrogen fuel cell
A source of energy where hydrogen and oxygen atoms are joined, producing water and electricity. Unlike batteries, fuel cells never run out, since the by-product (water) contains the elements (hydrogen and oxygen) required to replenish the process. Because hydrogen fuel cells rely on chemistry and not combustion, their emissions are virtually zero, making them far superior in terms of emissions than even the cleanest fuel combustion engines. Once the method of extracting hydrogen becomes more efficient, hydrogen fuel cells will be a more sustainable alternative to fossil fuels.

Hydroponics
The method of growing plants in water instead of soil by introducing nutrients artificially. By providing a more controlled environment, hydroponics enables plants to grow both faster and larger and avoids soil-borne diseases. Since hydroponic planting does not require large tracks of land, food production can occur locally, minimizing land use and the amount of energy exhausted in transporting produce.

Interaction design
Design that centers on the visual interface between technology and users, with the primary goal of enhancing and enabling user understanding and experience and improving the dialogue between people and interactive devices. Interaction design is increasingly important as more technology is embedded in the environment and interaction is required with electronics and computerized products on a daily level

Interactive surface
A spatial divider or interior treatment that allows a user to engage with and transform the architectural quality of the space. Systems such as servos, touch screens, and sensors (e.g. motion sensors, temperature sensors) are capable of influencing the shape, look, or feel of a surface, facilitating privacy, tactility, mood, and functionality.
See also *media façade*.

Light emitting diode (LED)
A semiconductor device that emits light when an electric current passes through it. The light is not particularly bright and in most LEDs is monochromatic, for example, silicon carbide produces blue light. An organic light emitting diode (OLED) uses a thin-film in which the emissive layer is an organic compound. As a lightweight, low power, high output light source, LEDs have the potential to alter the way designers conceive illumination.
See also *electroluminescence*.

Media façade
An exterior skin that communicates with its surrounding environment via technological devices such as screens, LEDs, or other mechanisms programmed to react to prerecorded or live input. The media façade transforms the visual appearance of the building without altering its physical form.

Micro electron sensors (MOTES)
Tiny, self-contained, battery-powered computers with radio links that communicate and exchange data with one another and self-organize into ad hoc networks. MOTES form the building blocks of wireless sensor networks and allow designers to create interactive environments that respond to changing conditions over time, regardless whether climate or inhabitant induced.

Microclimate
A localized climate within a larger one, different from its surroundings. Microclimates can be created by a change of vegetation, elevation or artificial man-made environmental changes. Designers are looking to create microclimates within built environments that respond to users,

even customized to each individual, minimizing energy usage and radically altering our experience of space.

Nanotechnology
The art of manipulating materials at the scale of a single atom or small molecule. Through nanotechnology designers are able to build new materials or alter existing ones for improved performance.

Nomads, nomadic
Migratory or mobile people, detached from the land and free to move about in response to climactic or socio-economic forces. Designers are currently looking into nomadic solutions to problems that cannot be solved by static, site-specific architecture; and are developing nomadic solutions that can flexibly respond to needs that have arisen as people and information continue to commute and evolve over time.

Open source
The principal of product development that allows users to access to the sources of the end product. While most prominently used in relation to software, the principal is generally applied to other fields of research where a system open to all enables advancement. Open source underscores collaborative development, expansive growth, and full transparency in efforts to promote progress.

Parametric modeling
A design process accomplished by identifying and creating key design features with the aid of computer

software, which then allows these features to be varied at any time. Through the use of parametric modeling, designers are able to create extremely complex three-dimensional forms.

Phase change materials (PCM)
Materials that release energy when changing state (solid to liquid, liquid to solid) to balance the change in environmental temperature in a predictable manner. As solid-liquid changes occur due to melting or solidifying, phase changing materials respond with the opposite temperature release, maintaining a nearly constant temperature. These materials can be useful for the thermal stabilization of spaces, objects and clothing. Certain PCMs, such as inorganic hydrated salts, can undergo an unlimited number of phase changes without degradation.

Photovoltaic cells
In photovoltaic cells, sunlight photons free electrons from silicon, allowing sunlight to be converted into electricity, bypassing thermodynamic cycles and mechanical generators. Research is currently being conducted on new micro-solar and organic photovoltaic technologies that can be integrated into clothing, fabrics, paint, and other more versatile forms.

Phytoremediation
The use of plants in the clean-up of contaminated soils and toxic waste sites. Certain plants hyper-accumulate particular metals in their leaves, thereby absorbing the environmental pollution. Genetic modification of existing plants could enhance their ability to remediate other pollutants.

Phytoremediation is currently available for certain metal pollution problems, such as arsenic.

Radio Frequency Identification (RFID)
An automatic identification method, relying on storing and remotely retrieving data using devices called RFID tags. An RFID tag is a small object that can be attached to or incorporated into a product, animal, or person; the tag performs as communication hardware enabling it to receive and respond to radio-frequency queries from a remote device. Through the use of RFID tags designers can track the origins of materials and components used in larger assemblies, seek and find contents of spatial or storage systems, and embed pertinent information.

Recombinant
Hybrid combination of two or more materials to create a new material. The hybridization of materials makes an enormous number of material options available, allowing for more specific and responsive design.
See also *composite*.

Responsive architecture
An architecture that creates spaces where elements such as shape, color, light can respond to conditions. Intelligent responsive architecture would allow the space to create its own system of rules based on repetitive actions.

Seamlessness
Digital and information technologies have recently allowed the boundaries of daily life, work, and play to merge into a continuous and ubiquitous ex-

perience of twenty-four hour access, multifunctionality, and connectivity. This lack of separation between types of activities allows designers to rethink the traditional division of activities by rooms and walls, increasing the potential for the reinterpretation of the role of shelters.

Servomechanism (Servo)
A small automatic device used to provide mechanical control at a distance using electrical input. Servos, commonly used in robotic technology, can control a large power output by means of a small power input. Designers are now using servos for interactive surfaces and responsive architecture.

Shape memory alloy
A metal alloy that has a particular stored shape that it can revert to after deformation. The memory shape is restored by a change in temperature, as in the case of memory metals, or through the release of stress, as in superelastic alloys.
Memory metals allow for long-term deformation at normal low temperatures, while superelastic alloys are capable of extreme manipulation and yet bounce back to their preset shape. Attracted to this play of long-term and temporary effects, designers are currently using these materials to create flexible environments.

Sustainability
A concept intending the continuity and preservation of environmental, social, and economic wellbeing. The original term "sustainable development" was adopted by the Agenda 21 program of the United Nations as a guideline for global and local com-

munities to minimize and control human impact on the environment. Official standards, such as the LEED (Leadership in Energy and Environmental Design) System, have been established to measure the level of sustainable design in a building based on a variety of factors regarding the building's construction, materials, systems, and operation.

Thermochromics
The ability for a material to change color due to a change in temperature; for example, the material used to make "mood rings" is thermochromic. Crystals, dyes, papers, paints, and inks that are able to transform in response to heat and cold and are currently commonly used in thermometers, thermal printers, and batteries can also enable designers to incorporate temperature and climactic changes into the visual experience of the environment.
See also *phase change materials*.

Ubiquitous computing
Computation that ubiquitously integrates into the environment rather than having computers as distinct objects. Ubiquitous computing forces the computer to live in the world with people as opposed to virtual reality, which puts people inside a computer-generated world. Ubiquitous computing enables devices to sense changes in their environment and to automatically adapt and react to these changes based on user needs and preferences. Designers see this advancement as having the potential to shatter standard conceptions of perception as well as context specificity, supplanting or augmenting architecture in its ability to frame space

and experience.
See also *seamlessness, ambient technology*.

Variable repetition
The process of implementing change incrementally over a series of modules. Computer controlled fabrication methods allow a series of element to be produced so that each is unique while together the elements create a complex effect. Fabrication based on variable repetition allows designers to create multidimensional spaces and surfaces.

Zero footprint
A product, system, or built environment whose energy consumption in terms of assembly, construction, and maintenance is minimized to the point where there is no ecological impact. A zero footprint design would have no impact on its surroundings.
See also *biodegradable, disposable design*.

Page numbers in italics
refer to illustrations.

Atelier Hitoshi Abe: 101, 102, 103, 104, 131 bottom
Archigram Archives: 132 center, 244, 246 bottom right, 247, 250
Art + Com AG: 151

BASF AG: 153 left,
V. Bennett: 183/2
Courtesy The Estate of R. Buckminster Fuller: 28 top, 231, 232, 235, 242 right

Collection Canadian Centre for Architecture, Montréal: 253 top left
Chicago History Museum: 236 top left, 236 bottom right (HB-14490-U)
Coop Himmelblau: 248
Livia Corona: 1, 4/5

François Dallegret: 29, 246 top left, 246 top right
Wilfried Dechau: 183/15
Deutsches Zentrum für Luft- und Raumfahrt (DLR): 164 left
Thomas Dix/Vitra Design Museum: 11, 144

Escher GuneWardena Architecture: 107, 108, 109, 131 top
Ezra Stoller © Esto: 31, 32 top, 237

© FLC / VG Bild-Kunst, Bonn 2006: 34
Formorf: 158 right, 159
Foster and Partners: 42, 43 left
FRAC Centre/François Lauginie: 249 left
Fraunhofer Institut für Fertigungs-technik und Materialforschung – IFAM: 161 top
Galerie Frehrking Wiesehöfer, Köln, and Barbara Wien, Berlin: 214, 215, 216, 217, 218, 219

Collection of the Gemeentemuseum Den Haag: 136
Dennis Gilbert/VIEW Pictures Ltd: 42 top
GM Corporation/Used with permis-sion/ GM Media Archive: 255, 256

Sean Godsell Architects: 77, 78, 79, 139

Roland Halbe Fotografie: 50, 51
Mark Hanauer: 182/12
Simon Heijdens: 150
Steven A. Heller: 183/16, 183/11
Steven A. Heller/Art Center College of Design: 13
HookerKitchen: 95, 97, 98, 135 bot-tom
Haus-Rucker Co: 249 r. o., 249 bottom right

Institut d'arquitectura avancada de Catalunya: 49
Toyo Ito & Associates: 140, 183/10
IwamotoScott: 65, 67, 68, 135 left

William Katavolos: 129
Kennedy & Violich Architecture: 156
Dmitri Kessel/Getty Images: 253 top right
Kharbine-Tapabor: 26
KieranTimberlake Associates: 160
Österreichische Friedrich und Lillian Kiesler-Privatstiftung: 243
Kisho Kurokawa Architect & Associates: 132 bottom, 252
Krets: 157, 158 left

Kent Larson, MIT House_n Research Consortium: 52
Patricia Layman Bazelon: 41
Marielle Leenders: 153 right
Les Films de Mon Oncle, Paris: 30
LiTraCon Bt, 2006: 148
Frances Loeb Library, Harvard University Graduate School of Design: 240 top right, 240 bottom left, 241
Stefan Wolf Lucks, Berlin: 154 bottom right

Mass Studies: 57, 58, 59, 60, 61, 62, 63, 132 top

Thomas D. McAvoy/Getty Images: 234
Thomas Mayer Archive: 15
Microsoft Corporation: 45 bottom
Craig Ming: 183/8
Architecture and Design Collections, MIT Museum: 37
MIT Museum: 239
Museum of Finnish Architecture/Foto: Lasse Nio: 251 top right
Museum of Finnish Architecture/Foto: John Zimmerman: 251 l. u.
DIGITAL IMAGE © 2006, MvdR Archive/The Museum of Modern Art, NY/Scala, Florence: 236 top right

NASA/JPL: 144
NMDA: 183/7
Nio Architekten, Rotterdam: 147

Tomio Ohashi: 140
OMA, Rotterdam: 152

Personal Media Corporation: 44
Philips: 46 top center and bottom center
PVACCEPT Berlin: 154 left, 154 top

R&Sie (n): 117, 119, 120, 129
Marc Räder: 2, 3
Realities:united, berlin: 111, 113, 114, 138 top
Thomas Rehbein Galerie, Köln: 190, 191, 194, 195
Ralph Richter/architekturphoto: 146
RMN/Collection du Musée national d'art moderne Centre Pompidou/©bpk, Berlin, 2006: 137
Rojkind Arquitectos: 81, 82, 83, 85, 133
Arthur Rüegg Archive: 35 right

Ken Sakamura (Toyota Dream House PAPI designed by Ken Sakamura): 46 right

Joel Sanders, Ben Rubin, Karen van Lengen: 87, 88, 89, 90, 91, 135 right
Christiane Sauer: 155, 161 bottom, 164 center, 164 right
©Julius Shulman archive/The Getty Research Institute: 35 left,
Smithson Family Collection: 240 top left, 242 left
Werner Sobek Ingenieure, Stuttgart: 149
Solar Oriented Architecture, Arizona State University: 36
Stabilight: 162
su11 architecture+design: 71, 73, 74, 75, 138 bottom
Jay Swayze, Underground Gardens & Homes (Hereford, Texas: Geobuilding Systems, Inc, 1980): 254

T-com: 46 left
Testa: 163

„The Underground Home, Publicity brochure from the New York World's Fair 1964-1965": 253 bottom right
Urban Salon: 45 top

Michael van Oosten, www.michaelva-noosten.nl: 48
©VG Bild-Kunst, Bonn 2006: 29, 136, 246 top left, 246 top right
Vitra Design Museum Archive: 27, 28 bottom, 32 bottom, 38, 39

Nana Watanabe: 183/14
Jens Willebrand: 42 bottom

Manuscripts & Archives, Yale University Library/Avery Architectural and Fine Arts Library, Columbia University: 33
Nigel Young/Foster and Partners: 43 right